D1715177

WOODROW WILSON'S WARS

The U.S. President as Commander in Chief

Meena Bose and Margaret Tseng, editors

This series examines the role of the U.S. president as commander in chief (CinC) of the nation's armed forces. Specific topics will include how presidents led in wartime (if they did), how they formulated strategy, how they engaged with senior military leadership, how their policy planning influenced their leadership and actions, how previous military experience (if any) informed their work as CinC, how they shaped the armed forces, and how they conducted military actions. Of particular importance for each volume in the series will be a president's civil-military relations, approach to military organization and training, and interactions with senior military leaders. Historians, political scientists, policy professionals, and politically informed audiences will find these volumes instructive and engaging.

WOODROW WILSON'S

The Making of America's First Modern Commander in Chief

MARK E. BENBOW

Naval Institute Press
Annapolis, Maryland

Naval Institute Press
291 Wood Road
Annapolis, MD 21402

Note: All photographs are from the Library of Congress Prints and Photographs Division with
the exception of the postmortem image of Haitian nationalist leader Charlemagne Péralte,
which was sourced from Wikimedia Commons.

ISBN: 978-1-68247-830-1 (hardcover)
ISBN: 978-1-68247-831-8 (eBook)

Library of Congress Cataloging-in-Publication data is available.

♾ Print editions meet the requirements of ANSI/NISO z39.48-1992 (Permanence of Paper).
Printed in the United States of America.

30 29 28 27 26 25 24 23 22   9 8 7 6 5 4 3 2 1
First printing

For Annette

CONTENTS

ACKNOWLEDGMENTS

Projects like this always require the help of multiple people to whom the author is in debt. I'd like to thank them for their support and assistance. First, my colleagues at Marymount were all supportive. It's a strong academic community where we back each other's ongoing projects, and their support was invaluable. Special thanks go to Dr. Margaret Tseng, who as my department chair first mentioned this project to me some years back. She and fellow project editor Dr. Meena Bose have been nothing but supportive and helpful in their advice and guidance.

My program's library consultant at Marymount's Emerson G. Reinsch Library, Hall Baldwin, was great about finding obscure articles and sources for me throughout my research, making sure I had what I requested quickly.

At the Woodrow Wilson House in Washington, DC, then-curator Asantewa Boakyewa deserves thanks for allowing me to view and study Wilson's codebook.

Lloyd Ambrosius was gracious enough to meet me during the SHAFR conference to talk about this work when I first began. Thank you, sir!

The retired CIA historian Gerald K. Haines reviewed the section on Wilson and intelligence gathering. Thank you, Dr. Haines.

Much of the material in the chapters on Mexico in 1913–14 came from my dissertation and in publishing my first book through Kent State University Press. Kent State's Dr. Ann Heiss and the others at the press still have my profound thanks for their help, as do the staff and librarians at the Library of Congress and the National Archives and Records Administration for their help during my research. My advisor, Dr. Alonso Hamby, especially has my thanks and gratitude.

The two reviewers, John Milton Cooper and John Hamilton, deserve thanks for their patience in reading my draft and for their helpful comments and corrections. The book is much better for their efforts. Of course, any remaining errors are my own.

Finally, the biggest thanks go to my wife, Annette, whose constant love and support made this work possible. To her I dedicate this book.

Introduction

At 2:30 a.m. on April 21, 1914, President Woodrow Wilson, Secretary of State William Jennings Bryan, and Secretary of the Navy Josephus Daniels held an emergency telephone conference. American consul William W. Canada, based in Veracruz, Mexico, had learned that the German freighter *Ypiranga* was due to land that morning with arms for Mexican dictator General Victoriano Huerta. Wilson supported the anti-Huerta Constitutionalist revolutionaries and had ordered an embargo to prevent the Mexican government from buying arms. To stop the *Ypiranga*'s cargo from reaching Huerta, Wilson told Daniels to "send this message[:] 'Take Veracruz at once.' "[1] U.S. Marines and sailors began landing shortly before noon. It took three days of fighting to secure the city and cost the lives of seventeen American servicemen, more than three hundred Mexican soldiers and militia, and an unknown number of civilians.[2]

Wilson's authority to launch the assault came from Article II, Section 2, and Clause I of the Constitution, which established the president as "Commander in Chief of the Army and Navy of the United States, and of the Militia of the several States, when called into the actual Service of the United States." Ordering the occupation of Veracruz was not an isolated incident for Wilson. During his administration (1913–21), he ordered American armed forces into action multiple times. Of course, joining World War I against Imperial Germany is the most prominent example. However, he also sent troops into Mexico twice, into Russia during its revolution and civil war, into Haiti and the Dominican Republic, and into ports from the Caribbean to China to protect Americans during unrest. In eight years, Wilson sent troops into harm's way more than most of his fellow chief executives. Only Abraham Lincoln and Franklin Roosevelt had to deal with the weight of being responsible for the loss of more American lives in war than Wilson. This book focuses on how Wilson viewed this responsibility, how he carried it out, how he used military force to meet specific diplomatic policy goals, how he decided when to send American armed forces into the field, and when he refused to do so. Throughout these challenges Wilson had a distinct tendency to delegate authority to his military advisers and to the commanders in the field. He kept watch to make sure they did not cross over into making decisions that would affect Wilson's diplomacy, but for military matters Wilson generally kept a loose hand on the reins.

THE FEDERALIST PAPERS

While there are countless books on the American military during wartime and many on how presidents decided to go to war, comparatively few specifically focus on the presidents fulfilling their role as commander in chief (CinC). Samuel Huntington's classic, *The Soldier and the State*,[3] while more than sixty years old, remains a standard work. Unfortunately, Huntington's interpretation of history is an example of the badly outdated consensus school of the 1950s.[4] Other more recent works, such as Sarah Burns' *The Politics of War Powers* (2019), have examined how presidents have used their war-making authority over the past two centuries.[5] This volume attempts to fill at least a small portion of this historiographic gap.

The title and responsibility of being commander in chief derives from Article II of the U.S. Constitution. However, the relevant passage is somewhat vague and does not specify any duties or conditions. Alexander Hamilton discussed the president's role in three of the Federalist Papers: Nos. 69, 70, and 74.[6] Hamilton's arguments centered not on the commander in chief role, but on the need for a strong, single executive, with his role as commander in chief being one example. In Federalist No. 70, Hamilton discusses why a single executive is preferable to distributing the office's powers among multiple men. He begins by arguing that "energy in the Executive is a leading character in the definition of good government. It is essential to the protection of the community against foreign attacks." The executive had to be centered on one person for efficiency, and "decision, activity, secrecy, and dispatch will generally characterize the proceedings of one man in a much more eminent degree than the proceedings of any greater number." It also allowed the community to better judge and hold the executive responsible for their actions because distributing responsibility among multiple executives could hide faults and misconduct. Without the ability to determine who was responsible for particular actions or decisions, "the restraints of public opinion" would "lose their efficacy." Moreover, distributed responsibility diminished the "opportunity of discovering with facility and clearness the misconduct of the persons they trust."[7]

In Federalist No. 74, Hamilton again revisited the efficiency argument. He noted making the president the commander in chief was so evidently proper that "little need be said to explain or enforce it." Hamilton continued, "Of all the cares or concerns of government, the direction of war most peculiarly demands qualities that distinguish the exercise of power by a single hand. The direction of war implies the direction of the collective strength. The power of directing and employing the collective strength forms a usual and essential part in the definition of the executive authority."[8]

Reminding his readers that the various state constitutions vested the same authority in their governors, Hamilton then spent most of the rest of the article discussing the pardoning power vested in the executive by the proposed new U.S. Constitution.[9]

Federalist Papers authors Hamilton, John Jay, and James Madison were wary of executive power, even as Hamilton vigorously defended its occasional necessity. As a result, many of their arguments were devoted to explaining why their proposed single executive was different from the European monarchs. In Federalist No. 4, Jay argued that the thirteen states should form a stronger union to protect against more powerful foreign nations and noted the danger of powerful kings to make war, not for the good of the community, but for their own reasons:

> Absolute monarchs will often make war when their nations are to get nothing by it, but for the purposes and objects merely personal, such as thirst for military glory, revenge for personal affronts, ambition, or private compacts to aggrandize or support their particular families or partisans. These and a variety of other motives, which affect only the mind of the sovereign, often lead him to engage in wars not sanctified by justice or the voice and interests of his people.[10]

Just as Hamilton would later argue that a single executive was more able to take effective action, John Jay said that in case of war, a single government would be more able to marshal the entire nation's resources than would multiple officials scattered among multiple states or smaller groupings of states. He elaborated,

> It can apply the resources and power of the whole to the defense of any particular part. That more easily and expeditiously than State governments or separate confederacies can possibly do, for want of concert and unity of system. It can place the militia under one plan of discipline, and, by putting their officers in a proper line of subordination to the Chief Magistrate, will, as it were, consolidate them into one corps, and thereby render them more efficient than if divided into thirteen or into three or four distinct independent companies.[11]

Note Jay's use of "Chief Magistrate." While he emphasizes the efficiency of a single government, he nonetheless is placing the command under the single executive. Indeed, Hamilton uses the phrase "Chief Magistrate" to describe the president on multiple occasions, such as in Federalist Nos. 69 and 70.[12]

In their discussions of the single proposed executive, Hamilton and Jay each discuss the critical role of the various state militias. As commander in chief, the president could command the militias, but only when called up for national duty. They emphasized the use of militias, anticipating the existence only of a relatively small professional army and navy. In Federalist No. 60 Hamilton discusses the president's limitations as commander in chief compared to kings or even the governor of New York. For instance, he writes, "First. The President will have only the occasional command of such part of the militia of the nation as by legislative provision may be called into the actual service of the Union. The king of Great Britain and the governor of New York have at all times the entire command of all the militia within their several jurisdictions. In this article, therefore, the power of the President would be inferior to that of either the monarch or the governor."[13]

As for the regular army and navy, his power would still be limited because, unlike kings, the president could command the military, but could not declare war. That power was centered upon the legislature. Moreover, Congress also held the power to allocate the money needed to fight a war. The authors did not answer the contradiction between the need for a single executive to efficiently prosecute a war with placing the power to provide the resources the president needed to fulfill that role.[14]

With little specificity delineating the president's role as commander in chief, the specific duties, powers, and responsibilities of that role evolved as the United States fought multiple wars. Starting with John Adams and the naval Quasi-War with France, Congress had passed both declarations of war and authorization to use force in more limited circumstances. As president, Wilson would ask Congress for both, but he always had to contend with a Congress that was still accustomed to asserting its role in war matters. It should be remembered that Wilson's administration occurred when the presidency was regaining power after the post–Civil War period of congressional ascendency. The executive had not yet reached the dominance in military matters the United States has seen since World War II and the beginning of the Cold War in the late 1940s.

As a student, Wilson read the Federalist Papers and made marginal notes. As a professor at Wesleyan and Princeton, he gave *The Federalist* to his classes as assigned reading. This is not to suggest that he agreed with every detail in them, but that they helped shape his view of how the Constitution was constructed, although in his own writings he wrote about the U.S. government as it actually operated, as opposed to how the contributors to *The Federalist* thought it should operate in the late eighteenth century.[15] In his marginalia in his copy of *The Federalist* and in his own writings Wilson did not pay any attention to what the essays said about the commander in chief. However, he did make a note about the need for a strong executive. In a margin comment to Federalist No. 70 in which the author wrote, "Energy in the executive is a leading character in the definition of good government," Wilson jotted, "! As if a weak executive is not inconsistent with government of any kind." Most of what Wilson otherwise noted about *The Federalist* had to do with the need for a strong separation of powers between the different branches of government, and his wish for a strong cabinet government. He called for a clear division of powers, but with each section "coordinated with and assisted by the others."[16] Wilson also noted the importance of force as a legitimate governmental power; specifically, he wrote in 1898, "Force, lodged in a force drawn from the people *to keep out foreign interference, —maintain a secure national independence.*" While not mentioning the commander in chief specifically, this would fit within its natural—or as Wilson would write, its "organic"—role.[17]

CHAPTER ORGANIZATION

This work is divided into eight chapters, and also includes an introduction and a conclusion. This introduction discusses some of the constitutional roots of the powers of commander in chief using Hamilton's writings in *The Federalist Papers*. Chapter 1 summarizes Wilson's attitudes toward war and the military examining Wilson's writings as a scholar before he entered politics to set the groundwork for gauging his actions as president. The chapter also discusses Wilson's leadership style, and his cabinet picks for the secretaries of state, war, and the navy. Chapter 2 surveys the world situation as it existed in 1912 when Wilson was elected. Chapters 3 through 5 focus on particular examples of Wilson's use of the military in Mexico and the Caribbean. Chapter 6 covers World War I, while chapter 7 discusses the related topics of American intervention into the Russian Revolution. Chapter 8 briefly discusses other, smaller interventions where the United States used force to protect American citizens or interests. Finally, the conclusion assesses Wilson's overall record.

The domestic side of World War I is beyond the scope of this study, which focuses on Wilson and the U.S. military. This should not be taken as meaning that Wilson's wartime record is without problems and controversies. The Wilson administration's management of war production and coordination was overall quite poor, leading to shortages of material both civilian and military. The Council of National Defense, established in 1916, was never as effective as it could have been, and it was replaced by the War Industries Board, which Bernard Baruch ran effectively. The major exception to production troubles were the efforts of Secretary of the Treasury William G. McAdoo. For example, when sales of the first Liberty Bonds were slow, the problems were fixed and sales vastly improved. McAdoo's taking over responsibility for coal production and the railroads eliminated bottlenecks and improved both coal production and shipment across the United States. Likewise, the Wilson administration's wartime record on civil rights was dismal. Censorship of the press reached new heights as multiple publications were barred from the U.S. postal system. German language newspapers, which for the main part were self-consciously supportive of the war effort, were closed, and in some places there were even attempts to ban use of the German language. The Espionage and Sedition Acts stifled free speech and resulted in the jailing of many Americans for opposing the draft. As a result of the Wilson administration's zeal in rooting out "disloyal" Americans and Wilson's refusal to rein in the abuses of his administration, the nation suffered through a period of anti-German hysteria that turned into the Red Scare of 1919 and its accompanying abuses. Works detailing Wilson's domestic war record are cited in the bibliography.

CHAPTER I

Wilson Views the Presidency

Writings and Advisers

orn in Staunton, Virginia, in 1856, Thomas Woodrow Wilson spent his childhood in Augusta, Georgia; Columbia, South Carolina; and then Wilmington, North Carolina, as his father, a Presbyterian minister, moved from congregation to congregation. Although a native southerner, Wilson spent most of his adult years in the North. He graduated from Princeton University (then the College of New Jersey) in 1879 and received his PhD in politics from Johns Hopkins University in 1886.[1] The new professor taught at Bryn Mawr College for three years, then at Wesleyan University for two more. In 1890, he returned to Princeton as professor of jurisprudence and political economy, teaching what would later be named political science and public administration.

WILSON'S WRITINGS

As a university instructor, Wilson built a national reputation as a writer and speaker, producing books and articles and giving numerous speeches as an after-dinner speaker. Wilson was most prolific from 1885 until 1902 when he became president of Princeton, and found he no longer had as much time to write. Given the plethora of his available writings, it is tempting to pull out Wilson's books and significant articles, dive into them, and emerge with a fully formed Wilsonian theory about politics, the Constitution, and America's role in the world. Of course, it is not that simple. His ideas evolved as time passed. Moreover, his focus as a scholar was the idea of representation, leadership, and the legislature; he spent little time writing about or thinking about civilian leadership of the military. As a result, in discussing Wilson's actions as commander in chief and his expectations of acting in that role, there is little to cite from Wilson's works directly. Instead, we must look for more subtle suggestions in Wilson's discussions about executive leadership and how he wrote about previous wars fought by the United States.

Wilson's books written before his career in politics roughly fall into two categories: political theory (including *Congressional Government: A Study in American Politics* [1885], *The State: Elements of Historical and Practical Politics* [1889], and *Constitutional Government in the United States* [1908]) and history (including *Division and Reunion: 1829–1889* [1901], *George Washington* [1896], and *A History of the American People* [1902]). They vary wildly in quality and readability.

POLITICAL THEORY

Wilson first wrote his most important theoretical works, *Congressional Government* (which was essentially his dissertation) and *The State*, then turned to his historical works. In his last book, *Constitutional Government in the United States*, he reverted to his use of theory to illustrate how the American government worked.

Congressional Government received favorable reviews and remained in print for the next fifteen years.[2] In it, Wilson attempted to describe how the U.S. government actually worked, as opposed to the theories of how it was supposed to work. Wilson spent most of his chapters on the House of Representatives, where he despaired, since most work is done in committees. Committee work eliminated the chance for stirring debates, like those of Webster and Clay. Moreover, it hid the making of legislation from the public. Wilson preferred the British model, in which a party was elected to carry out a specific program and was then turned out if it failed or if its program lost public support. He spent less time on the Senate, but in a foreshadowing of troubles to come, he commented how the Senate had no substantive role in making treaties, despite the constitutional provision that it was to be consulted on such matters. As for his future office, Wilson saw the presidency as subordinate in power to the Congress, not an unreasonable judgment in the 1880s. He noted that the president could stir up trouble in diplomacy, but he had no real "presence" in the Senate and little influence in making legislation other than the use of his veto.[3]

Wilson's criticisms of how the U.S. government worked centered on leadership and representation. No one leader was accountable. Power and therefore responsibility were too diffuse. "The only fruit," Wilson wrote, "of dividing power has been to make it irresponsible."[4] It is crucial that Wilson divided this responsibility from the actual administration. A leader accountable to the electorate was supposed to define policy, reflect public opinion, and lead it. Ideally, the actual administration of said policy was left to the permanent government structure that remained even as elections turned out leaders and replaced them with new men and new policies.[5] This distinction between the leader and the administrator is key in understanding how Wilson would approach his role as commander in chief. Policy flowed downward. This left those below to carry out the leader's program, but it also meant that those below were expected to faithfully do so. This could in turn mean that the policy-maker would interpret faithfully, carrying out the leader's policies as a form of personal loyalty. Failure to follow through on official policy could be construed as disloyalty. Likewise, a lack of personal loyalty could be interpreted as leading to a failure to follow policy faithfully. Indeed, when it came to choosing his subordinates, Wilson looked for both personal loyalty and the willingness to carry out the policies he defined. Wilson especially valued personal loyalty in picking most of his civilian aides. In his military leaders, he also primarily looked for a willingness to follow his policies. Accordingly, he shied away from those commanders who showed too much independence.

Wilson's next book was much drier than *Congressional Government.* In the textbook *The State,* Wilson spent very little time on the role of the president in either foreign policy or as commander in chief. For the latter, he simply wrote, "He is the commander-in-chief of the army and navy of the United States, and of the militia of the several states when called into the actual service of the United States." He briefly mentions that the secretary of war controls the Army and West Point and that the secretary of the navy "has charge of the naval forces of the general government," as well as of the Naval Academy and the Naval War College. Wilson spent more space discussing the Post Office Department than he did describing the secretaries of war and the navy combined.[6] When he did discuss wars and leadership, he did so to provide historical context. For example, Wilson used the ancient Greek city-states and Rome as illustrations of how governments formed and operated.[7]

It was in *The State* that Wilson developed his idea of the organic development of government. Each community's form of government evolved from its own unique conditions. The "body politic" evolved as an organic whole.[8] In *The State,* he focused on the evolution of the different cabinet positions in the British government. The cabinet, he noted, acts as an executive, "in a sense the ministers have inherited the ancient prerogatives of the Crown." The cabinet can carry out its duties, including placing "troops and naval forces at pleasure." Wilson wrote, "without any *previous* consultation with Parliament, whom they serve" (emphasis in the original). "The House of Commons," he concluded, "can punish but cannot prevent."[9] This last point is particularly important when it comes to Wilson's understanding of the president's role as chief executive in his dealings with Congress. Of course, Wilson knew the restrictions placed on the president's action by the Constitution and Congress' role. However, he was also aware of a different model, the British one, which gave the executive the freedom of action Wilson would have wanted for himself.

HISTORICAL WORKS

Division and Reunion was a serious scholarly work and an early attempt to write an unbiased history of the Civil War. Wilson wrote the tome from 1889 to 1892 after being approached by noted historian Albert Bushnell Hart, editor of the series "Epochs in American History." When it was released, it was generally well received. As historian Henry Bragdon noted in his study of Wilson's academic career, it was "comforting" to read that "the great struggle had been the result of inexorable processes and that both sides were in a measure right!"[10]

Wilson was too young to have served in the Civil War. However, as a boy he witnessed the effects of the war from his father's church in Augusta, Georgia, and the Reconstruction era in Columbia, South Carolina. Augusta was a manufacturing center for the Confederacy with large munitions works. In the fall of 1863, Reverend Wilson's church was transformed into a Confederate hospital, its pews removed to make room for the wounded. Later it became a makeshift holding pen for Union prisoners, some of whom talked with the young Wilson. When Gen. William Tecumseh Sherman and his army moved through the state destroying Georgia's ability to aid the Confederate war effort, Augusta citizens piled their bales of cotton out in the streets in hopes that Sherman's troops would burn the cotton and leave their homes intact. They no doubt felt an enormous sense of relief when the avenging Union force bypassed the city.[11]

Young Wilson spent his teenage years in Columbia, South Carolina, before the family moved to Wilmington, North Carolina. Columbia was severely damaged by Union forces in early 1865, while Wilmington was mostly spared destruction. As a result, Wilson saw the war's destruction and surely heard numerous war stories from his father's friends and parishioners as well as from one of his teachers, a Confederate veteran. Unsurprisingly, although he spent almost all of his adult life in the North, Wilson always sympathized with the South and once noted that his home region had "nothing to apologize for." This did not mean that Wilson uncritically accepted everything about the South, including its arguments about the Civil War's justice. Instead, as Arthur Link noted, "For Wilson personally, this meant an ability to accept southern history without quarreling with it or feeling any shame about it."[12] Wilson did not mourn for the Confederacy and noted more than once that he was glad the Union had been preserved.

The worst of Wilson's historical works is his biography of George Washington, which he wrote mainly for the extra income; Wilson supported not only his wife and three children on his professor's salary, but also two of his wife's younger siblings and his elderly father. First published as a series of articles in *Harper's New Monthly Magazine*, it was well received at the time, but is now generally seen as Wilson's weakest work. Based on secondary sources and showing no original thinking or research, its prose sometimes dips embarrassingly into a pseudo-colonial form and sometimes flirts with being twee.[13]

The third and final of Wilson's historical works was *History of the American People*, which was, like *Washington*, written in part for the extra income it would provide. He produced the manuscript under a contract with Harper & Brothers as a book designed for a national audience. In it, Wilson borrowed heavily from his previous writings, especially *Division and Reunion*, some sections of which were cribbed wholesale. A popular volume rather than a scholarly study, *History of the American People* was padded with numerous, sometimes extraneous, illustrations. It was immediately successful despite its faults and went through numerous printings over the next several decades. However, as a history, it is uneven at best and reflects Wilson's poor grounding in American history outside of its political development.[14]

How did Wilson cover the presidential role as commander in chief in his historical works? None of them have a long, detailed, sophisticated discussion of that responsibility. However, taken together, they do provide some clues toward understanding Wilson's views as a scholar. The reader must keep in mind that Wilson's historical works were based mostly upon secondary sources and were intended for a popular audience. With the possible exception of *Division and Reunion*, they do not reflect any particularly deep thought or research on Wilson's part. They reveal basic assumptions from the period when he was a professor, but the reader should not draw too rigid a judgment from what Wilson wrote in these particular works.

In his *History of the United States* Wilson barely touches on the first two foreign wars fought by the new United States: the Quasi-War with France (1798–1801) during the John Adams administration and the Tripolitan War (aka the First Barbary War, 1801–5) during Thomas Jefferson's tenure as president. Wilson wrote that the Quasi-War was "brief and of no significant consequence." He also noted that "no formal declaration of hostilities was made," but cites the July 7, 1798, Congressional resolution allowing Adams to use military force to respond to French naval attacks on American shipping.[15] Wilson then goes on to praise the performance of the American Navy against France and observes that France came to terms with the United States. His focus was on the use of military force as a tool by John Adams to gain a diplomatic advantage. Congress' role was briefly mentioned and then ignored in favor of the action by the executive branch.

In his brief coverage of the Tripolitan War, Wilson was critical of Jefferson over the war with the Barbary states. In a discussion of the third president's plan to use small gunboats rather than oceangoing vessels to defend American shores, Wilson wrote, Jefferson had been obliged to send a squadron against the pirates of Tripoli, who openly made war on the commerce of the United States. The six frigates then kept in commission proved unsuitable for the service, and he was forced to consent to the construction of a few vessels more suitable, which brought Tripoli to terms. But he did not allow even the Tripolitan War to bring a real navy into existence.[16]

Here Congress was not even given a walk-on role, approving military action, in Wilson's account. As with the Quasi-War, Wilson notes how military force was used to win a favorable diplomatic settlement ("Tripoli was brought to terms"), but then sniffs at Jefferson's inability to see the utility of a real navy.

Wilson's discussion of the War of 1812 is brief and unsurprising. He focuses on the United States being caught between the British and French. "It was a tragical but natural accident that the war should be against England, not against France." In their attempt to defeat "the Corsican,"

Britain impressed American sailors and interfered with American trade. Wilson blames Congress, not President James Madison, for declaring war in June 1812, however. New leaders such as Henry Clay and John C. Calhoun had "made up their minds that the country should fight." As for Madison, "the President could not but take their purpose, having no alternative to suggest."[17] Wilson briefly discusses the conduct of the war but focuses on naval victories. He does discuss the defeats on land and spends a few paltry sentences on the burning of Washington in the summer of 1814. He ignores Madison's role. Instead, Wilson focuses on a few notable American commanders who succeeded, notably Oliver Hazard Perry and Gen. Andrew Jackson.[18] Wilson's treatment of later wars would follow this same type of "great man" history.

The Mexican-American War discussion reflects Wilson's opinion that the war was unjust, even if he does temper his judgment somewhat. While he does not use the term "commander in chief," he does place the responsibility for action on President James K. Polk. Wilson notes that Polk, "without consultation with Congress, which was then in session, took the responsibility of ordering General Taylor to advance to the Rio Grande. . . . Of course, Taylor obeyed."[19] Once Polk had acted, and Mexico predictably reacted, there was little for Congress to do but to officially declare war and then pass the necessary spending bills to support it. As for the military, their task was to carry out the president's orders. Wilson's description of the Mexican-American War followed a theme that he would repeat: the president sets policy and is responsible for the greater strategic vision. Subordinates are delegated the authority to carry out the commander in chief's strategy and are given enough leeway to make not just tactical decisions, but strategic ones as well so long as they do not conflict with the president's overall goals.

In both these cases, the War of 1812 and the Mexican-American War, Wilson emphasizes leadership by a few strong-willed individuals such as Clay and Polk. In both cases, however, he places credit for American military victories with the commanders in the field, not the political leadership in Washington. Strong political leaders set the policy and the military made the decisions needed to carry it out. Civilian leaders' role was to allow the military to do their jobs and not to get in their way, and to support the war by marshaling resources, such as taxes. Once the fighting finished, civilian leadership reasserted its prerogatives, setting the diplomatic terms for peace.

Wilson discusses the Civil War more than any other war in his historical writings. This is understandable not just because of the sheer scale of the conflict, but because Wilson places an unusually large emphasis on it as shaping the modern American understanding of the Constitution. Wilson's account of the war is a relatively straightforward narrative description. Generals moving troops, winners and losers of battles, and some discussion of the politics within the U.S. and Confederate governments. For the purposes of this study, what is telling about Wilson's treatment of the Civil War is his discussion of Lincoln and the war.

The discussion of Lincoln is brief, but favorable. Indeed, Wilson admired Lincoln. Wilson's Lincoln is a strong executive, but one that allows his subordinates a great deal of leeway. Lincoln uses his powers as commander in chief to call up troops after Fort Sumter, issue the Emancipation Proclamation, and suspend the writ of habeas corpus. Wilson makes only a brief mention of Lincoln's firing and hiring of generals to command the Army of the Potomac. Nor does he discuss Lincoln's leadership of his cabinet. There is no trace of a "team of rivals" in Wilson's account. Lincoln is responsible for commanding the military, but leaves the details to his subordinates. He oversees the broader strategy. For example, Wilson notes that Lincoln issued the Emancipation Proclamation to increase and reinforce northern support for the war: "By September 1862 he [Lincoln] had made up his mind that it would stimulate the forces of the North if the war were made a war against slavery, as well as a war for the Union."[20] Wilson did not discuss Lincoln's greater involvement in strategy, or his pressing his generals to be more aggressive. This omission is odd, given that during World War I, Wilson said he did not want to repeat Lincoln's mistakes in over-managing his generals, he would pick one commanding general and stick with him.[21]

Wilson paid little attention to the Indian Wars after the colonial period. However, he did spend an entire chapter on the Spanish-American War and even discussed the Philippine War that followed. Wilson's account differed little from the general interpretation of its era in the causes of the war. He emphasized the destruction of the battleship *Maine* in Havana Harbor on February 14, 1898. He cited the official U.S. Navy report, which stated that "an examination of the twisted wreck made it plain that it had come from no accident within the ship itself. The explosives which had destroyed her had lain beneath her at the bottom of the harbor where she had her anchorage."[22] However, Wilson did not lay the blame on the Spanish government: "There was no evidence whatever that anyone connected with the exercise of Spanish authority had so much as guilty knowledge of the plans made to destroy the *Maine*." The blame for the United States entering the war, according to Wilson, was how the ship's destruction heated American public opinion. McKinley was too weak a leader to control the forces for war—sensationalistic newspapers, men eager to profit from the war, those who wished to expand American power in the West Indies. McKinley, in Wilson's view, was a weaker leader than Grover Cleveland had been. He "did not act as an independent, originative force in the determination of policy." "Congress," Wilson wrote, "was the war-making power."[23]

Wilson praised his late predecessor's character as a person, but his disapproval of McKinley's deferring to Congress the initiative in making diplomatic policy leading to war shines through. In quick succession, McKinley asked Congress to declare war, and Congress agreed and voted for the necessary funds. McKinley called for volunteers to reinforce the small regular Army. Recruits came from every region of the country. Then McKinley took a back seat to the commanders in the field.

The descriptions of the battles are unexceptional, except that Wilson mentioned the Army's "blundering and mismanagement" at Tampa, which was the main U.S. port of embarkation for Cuba. He praised the individual officers and soldiers but showed his disdain for the supply issues that plagued the American military during the Cuban campaign:

At Tampa, the blundering and mismanagement had been stupid, irritating; here they were deeply tragical. It was pitiful what rank and file alike had to endure, with stores unpacked, untouched at the rear, and medicines left where they could be of no service. Nevertheless, pluck and intelligence carried the regiments forward to the over-coming of difficulties and the winning of battles there as they had carried the men like them who went with Major General Scott to the conquest of Mexico fifty years before. Division commanders proved more efficient and resourceful than their superiors in command; privates knew their duty without orders, shifted for themselves in camp, at mess, and on the march like men who did not need to be cared for, endured what came to them without murmur or discouragement, and moved like those who act confidently without command, carried forward by their own wits and courage and habits of concerted action.[24]

WILSON'S ADVISERS

From these bits and pieces, there is enough to construct a basic framework of Wilson's views. His interpretation of the president's leadership role, at least as he saw it at a distance as a Princeton professor, was to choose capable leaders to run individual departments while overseeing the overall direction of policy. The president would step in when his department heads or congressional leaders failed to push in the direction that the president felt the people wanted them to go. Wilson especially emphasized that he was the sole representative of the entire people because he was selected by the nation as a whole, in contrast to the representatives and senators.

Of course, there remained outside influences on Wilson's policies after he took office. Wilson's belief in a "Common Council" required a capable staff and good advisers with access to a reliable source of information. How capable and how reliable were Wilson's staff and their flow of information? Particularly, how capable were those that advised him on foreign policy and military matters? These aspects of being commander in chief that neither Wilson nor those who wrote the Federalist Papers considered.

It should be noted that Wilson's worst appointments tended to be within the diplomatic corps—where he typically appointed amateurs—rather than those who oversaw the U.S. military.[25] Ambassadors and ministers were political appointees being rewarded for their service to whichever party was in power. Most consuls were Americans who were living as expatriates in the county where they represented U.S. interests. The Republicans had controlled the White House since March 1897, so the pool of experienced amateur diplomats for the Democrats to choose from was somewhat limited. Nonetheless, Wilson's use of what Secretary of State William Jennings Bryan, a committed spoilsman, called "deserving Democrats" often limited the effectiveness of his administration's diplomacy.

Wilson's appointments were often made for political reasons rather than related to expertise. This was still common practice, so his appointments were not a deviation. However, the timing was, at best, unfortunate, as the challenges presented to American national security from 1914–19 were of far greater severity than faced by Wilson's immediate predecessors, and a group of advisers selected more for their expertise than for their political connections would have served the president, and the country, better. Nonetheless, Wilson's choices were, mostly, capable men, and generally attempted to carry out Wilson's policies as best as they could.

Leadership theories aside, some of Wilson's reliance on his staff was simple practicality. For example, Wilson knew little about agricultural policy, so Secretary of Agriculture David F. Houston had a free hand. Likewise, departments such as Labor, Interior, and Commerce were left to continue operations with little interference from Wilson, unless national issues involving broader questions arose. Besides, Wilson had, for the most part, picked capable men for his cabinet. There were a few exceptions. Franklin Lane at Interior was, at best, mediocre. In contrast, Secretary of the Treasury William Gibbs McAdoo was exceptionally skilled and was by far the most capable man among Wilson's chief advisers. Wilson's cabinet appointments were based more upon political calculations than experience in the relevant department.

The Secretary of the Navy for his entire administration was Josephus Daniels. A North Carolina native and newspaper publisher, Daniels was most remembered for his role in overthrowing the legitimately elected mixed-race government in Wilmington, North Carolina in 1898.[26] Despite this, Daniels was on many issues a progressive reformer. He supported child labor laws and women's suffrage. He opened the Naval Academy at Annapolis to the average seaman. He also forbade alcohol on Navy installations and ships and ordered all brothels within five miles of any U.S. naval base to be closed. The Navy did not respond to Daniels with enthusiasm or affection, although they remained, in his presence, polite and professional, respecting his position. Daniels' assistant secretary of the Navy was the young Franklin Roosevelt, who was carefully following his elder cousin Teddy Roosevelt's path to the White House. Daniels delegated a great deal of authority to Roosevelt, especially during World War I.[27]

Lindley M. Garrison of New Jersey was Wilson's first secretary of war. A lawyer with no military experience, from 1904 to 1913, he was a vice-chancellor of New Jersey, which meant he served as a circuit court judge for the state's Chancery Court, which heard cases on contracts, wills and trusts, and land ownership. He came to Wilson's attention when Wilson served as New Jersey governor (1911–13). The two men never had a close relationship, and Garrison often pushed Wilson toward a more interventionist foreign policy in the Caribbean and Latin America than Wilson wanted. Garrison was succeeded by Newton Baker, mayor of Cleveland, Ohio. Baker was a West Virginia native who studied at Johns Hopkins in Baltimore, where he took classes from Wilson and even ate at the same boarding house, where he could listen to Wilson discuss the news of the day. His father was a Confederate cavalryman who served under J. E. B. Stuart, and Baker grew up listening to his father's war stories. Of particular importance was his father's telling the young Newton ("Newt") how important it was that Confederate president Jefferson Davis had left Lee to make military decisions without interference from the administration in Richmond.[28]

When the Spanish-American War began in April 1898, Baker tried to enlist but was rejected due to poor eyesight. His career took off in 1899 when he moved to Cleveland and began working with the city's Democratic Party. In 1911, he was elected mayor and earned a national reputation as a reformer. In 1913, Wilson tried to recruit Baker as secretary of the interior, but the mayor refused. When Garrison resigned in 1916 over differences in the Preparedness Campaign with Wilson, Baker accepted the offer to become secretary of war. As Wilson's new head of the War Department, Baker seemed out of place. As one historian noted, "A civilian's civilian, Baker saw the military as a necessity, but he had no awe of people in uniform, no romantic feelings toward them, and no dreams of glory. . . . On the day President Woodrow Wilson announced Baker's appointment as Secretary of War, he admitted his ignorance of military matters. 'I am an innocent,' he told reporters, 'I do not know anything about this job.' Nevertheless, he had a sharp, analytical mind and considerable skill at administration."[29]

Baker's principal military adviser was the Army chief of staff. Created in 1903, the chief of staff was usually chosen from the most senior generals then on active duty. There were five that served during Wilson's time in office. First was Maj. Gen. Leonard Wood (1910–14). A close friend of Teddy Roosevelt, Wood was ambitious and aggressive. Wilson distrusted him, although Wood was influential because of his many powerful friends among the Republicans in the Senate. He was replaced by Maj. Gen. William W. Wotherspoon, who served for a few months in 1914. He retired and was replaced by Maj. Gen. Hugh L. Scott (1914–17). Scott was influential, first as commander of the U.S. Army Southern Division, where he often acted as the U.S. representative to Mexican revolutionary Pancho Villa. Scott acted as a mentor to Newton Baker and was trusted by both Baker and Wilson. When he retired, he was replaced by Maj. Gen. Tasker H. Bliss (1917–18). Bliss was influential with both Baker and Wilson and became one of the American representatives to the Supreme War Council in 1918. He was also part of the U.S. delegation to the Paris Peace Conference. The fifth was Gen. Peyton C. March (1918–21). March was hindered somewhat in his duties by the refusal of Baker and Wilson to make clear the chain of command, particularly on the question whether Gen. John J. Pershing, commander of the American Expeditionary Forces (AEF), reported directly to Baker through March. Pershing was not chief of staff until after Wilson's term in office, but as commander of the AEF, was perhaps the most influential military adviser to both the president and the secretary of war from 1917–18.

Wilson had three men serve as secretary of state, William Jennings Bryan (1913–15), Robert Lansing (1915–20), and Bainbridge Colby

(1920–21). The first two were poor choices. Bryan was a purely political appointment. A former congressional representative from Nebraska, Bryan was the leader of the Democratic Party from his nomination as the youngest candidate for president at the age of thirty-six in 1896, until Wilson supplanted him as the party's nominee in 1912. The Democratic candidate in 1896, 1900, and 1908, Bryan lost each time, but he remained an influential power broker in the party until he died in 1924. His backing Wilson at the 1912 Democratic convention in Baltimore was an essential factor in Wilson's winning the nomination. He was, arguably, the second most powerful man in the party after Wilson. Cabinet positions were an essential means to reward supporters and solidify support among different party factions and regions of the county.

Wilson's biographer Arthur Link noted that the president-elect had "little respect for Bryan's judgement." Nonetheless, his advisers agreed that Wilson had little choice. Bryan "had to have the premier post." To leave Bryan out of the cabinet would have weakened Wilson's ability to lobby Bryan's supporters in Congress for the bills he wanted passed. To give him a minor cabinet post would have been insulting. Secretary of state was one of the most important cabinet slots, along with the secretaries of Treasury, the War Department, and the Navy Department, as well as the attorney general. None of these seemed to Wilson to be a good fit for Bryan. He did not trust Bryan's economic instincts. The military positions were inappropriate for a pacifist such as Bryan, and he did not have the legal experience needed for the Justice Department.[30]

Wilson met with Bryan and offered him the position. Bryan accepted. First, however, Wilson assured his prohibitionist appointee that the decision on whether to serve alcohol at official State Department functions was Bryan's decision. Bryan's main interest was to begin negotiating a series of bilateral "cooling off" treaties, in which the parties agreed to defer armed conflict for six months to a year without resorting to armed conflict or building up their militaries. Both parties were free to reject the decisions made by arbiters if they wished. Eventually, he succeeded in negotiating thirty such treaties, twenty of which were ratified. They were mostly with nations with which the United States was unlikely to go to war. The first was with El Salvador.[31] Bryan resigned in 1915 over differences with Wilson over the President's messages to Germany over the sinking of the *Lusitania*. Bryan thought Wilson was pushing too far, risking a war. With Bryan gone, Wilson dominated the making of his administration's foreign policy even more.

Robert Lansing was an associate counsel for the United States in the State Department and was promoted to counsel by Wilson in 1914. The career diplomat was appointed as secretary of state in 1915 when Bryan resigned. Unlike Bryan, Lansing was very pro-British during World War I and did his best to steer American policy in that direction. While he supported Wilson in his statements, behind the scenes he opposed some of the president's policies, particularly those he felt were not pro-British enough, and Lansing was dubious of Wilson's emphasis on national self-determination. Lansing was also far more pro-business than Wilson and much more willing to intervene to protect American business interests overseas than was the president. Wilson finally fired him in early 1920 after the Paris Peace Conference, but Lansing may have been a worse appointment than Bryan to the position as he had come to resent the president (who treated him at times like a lowly clerk) and sometimes undermined Wilson's policies from behind the scenes.[32]

Bainbridge Colby was a lawyer with no diplomatic experience. A former Republican and a founder of the Progressive Party, Colby's sole qualification for the position was his loyalty to Wilson. The president was incapacitated by his stroke his last year in office, and so Colby had little contact with him, nor much influence on policy. A placeholder in the slot, Colby supported Wilson's policies but had little time to make his mark during his tenure.

Wilson's principal foreign policy adviser for most of his time in office was Edward M. House. Known as "Colonel" (the title was an honorific, not a military rank), House became Wilson's primary adviser during the 1912 presidential campaign. He played on Wilson's weakness for praise and providing a sympathetic sounding board and soon became the president's main adviser on most domestic and foreign issues. House was intelligent and a good adviser on domestic politics, although he was neither as smart nor as farseeing as he thought he was. He overshadowed both Bryan and Lansing as Wilson's diplomatic adviser, but that is more of a reflection of their weaknesses than it is of House's strengths. Wilson considered House capable enough to provide sound advice during World War I and reliable enough to be a go-between for Wilson in dealing with the belligerents. However, Wilson was not as fooled by House as his adviser assumed he was, and House never realized that Wilson depended upon him more for friendship and emotional support than for the subtly of his advice.[33]

WILSON AND THE MILITARY

Wilson's childhood in the South during the Civil War and Reconstruction made Wilson deeply aware of the effects of war. His secretary, Joseph Tumulty, remembered that the president once told him, "I come from the South and I know what war is, for I have seen its wreckage and terrible ruin."[34] His earliest memory was hearing that Lincoln was elected and there would be a war. That was shortly before his fourth birthday. When he was only eight, his father's church in Augusta was used as a Confederate field hospital and as a prison yard to hold Union prisoners on their way to Andersonville. Historians disagree on what effect this may have had on Wilson. Arthur Link argued that they "made an indelible impression on him and left him with an abhorrence of bloodshed."[35] In contrast, John Milton Cooper notes that Wilson "almost certainly saw and heard wounded and dying soldiers in the town, and in his father's church." "Yet," Cooper argues, "those sights and sounds do not seem to have affected him deeply." Cooper quotes Wilson as saying, "To me the Civil War and its terrible scenes are but a memory of a short day."[36] Unfortunately, Edwin Weinstein barely mentions the war in his *Woodrow Wilson: A Medical and Psychological Biography* (1981). Wilson's official biographer, Ray Stannard Baker, discusses the things young Wilson may well have experienced during the war, but he only hints at the possible effects they may have had on the adult Woodrow Wilson. These memories did not make Wilson bitter, judging from how he later wrote about the war in *Division and Reunion*.[37]

Whatever its effect, the experiences of the Civil War and its aftermath did not make Wilson a pacifist. Wilson accepted the reality of military force in international affairs. States would use war as an instrument of policy, whether justly or no. In a 1911 speech on the Bible, Wilson stated that he would "not cry 'peace' so long as there is sin and wrong in the world." The Bible "does not teach any doctrine of peace," Wilson noted, "so long as there is sin to be combated and overcome in one's heart and in the great moving force of human society."[38] Examining the motivation behind the action could determine if it were justified. During Wilson's 1912 presidential campaign, he distinguished between wars for noble causes and those prompted by an opponent's "ugly ambitions." Force wielded to preserve liberty or righteousness was permissible. "If I cannot retain my moral influence over a man except by occasionally knocking him down . . . then for the sake of his soul, I have got to occasionally knock him down."[39] In his 1916 preparedness speeches, Wilson commonly referred to a rusty sword or old musket hanging over a fireplace in a home as a sign of respect for an ancestor's sacrifice for a greater good. Moreover, in his *History of the American People*, Wilson judged the American use of force in wars by an aggressor-defender standard. For example, he criticized the Mexican-American War as clearly unjust, "an inexcusable aggression" by the United States. On the other hand, Wilson accepted the Spanish-American War as just because it liberated Cuba from Spain. The U.S. seizure of the Philippines as a colony during the same war, however, was unjust.[40]

As noted earlier, Wilson did not discuss the role of commander in chief in his writings. His discussions of American wars tended to be brief and focused more on significant battles than the use of war as part of a broader view of national security. Indeed, his primary concern was if the use of force was justified morally. Was the United States right to use force? In his judgments, Wilson used a variation of the doctrine of "just war" as well as an "aggressor-defender" model. The use of military force was "just"—that is, morally defensible—if it met specific criteria:

- It was a last resort, including defense against aggression.
- It was in proportion that the evil that force was used against had to be greater than the evil of the force used.

- It had to be declared (or otherwise legally approved) by a sovereign authority.
- Moreover, Wilson used a form of an aggressor-defender standard: war is not only evil, but it is also often unnecessary. Initiating a war is a deliberate evil act, thus absolving the victim of wrong-doing for using force in self-defense.[41]

WILSON AND INTELLIGENCE

Part of both the military and diplomatic bureaucracies were their still-developing capabilities as intelligence organizations. Wilson was not the first commander in chief to deal with the problem of gathering foreign intelligence. George Washington understood the role of intelligence gathering in making military decisions. The CIA describes him as the "First DCI (director of Central Intelligence)," noting that he was "a key practitioner of military intelligence during the Revolutionary War."[42] While all presidents used intelligence gathering when necessary, generally via the military during wartime, there was very little formal structure created. Even when there was a more active intelligence-gathering operation, such as during the Civil War, it was abandoned once the immediate need passed. Still, some bare beginnings to a formal intelligence capacity did begin to emerge in the late nineteenth century.

In 1913 the existing official intelligence organizations were in the military, although they tended to be small, often with limited resources and narrow focus. The two main organizations were the Office of Naval Intelligence (ONI, founded in 1881) and the Military Information Division (MID), founded in 1885. Note that the latter used the term "information" rather than "intelligence," which was more associated with newspaper names at the time. Both organizations gathered reports and intelligence, such as maps for the Navy Department and the War Department. Not unexpectedly, the information they gathered tended toward the technical and scientific. Often gathered by American officers on short assignments, they were supplemented starting in 1888 by military attachés. The information still tended toward the general, such as basic studies of foreign military and its capacities, or the technical and scientific. MID's limited areas of interest demonstrate just where the Army expected threats to the United States to manifest themselves and where American interests lay, not only in the western hemisphere but the northern half of the western hemisphere. The limited value the Army placed on its intelligence organization was demonstrated during the Spanish-American War when their officers were not allowed to operate in Cuba. The American officer in command feared that they would be reporting on his actions rather than on the Spanish.

In 1903 the General Staff was created with three general sections: administration, intelligence, and plans. MID was placed under the second section, but not every part was equal. In 1908, the intelligence and operations sections were merged due to internal political battles over control of resources. The new combined division was named the War College Division. The former intelligence division was renamed the Military Information Committee. Even worse, its members were not assigned to it full time, but as an addition to their regular duties. In essence, military intelligence, as far as much of the Army was concerned, was a part-time duty, and still focused on tactical information.

The Navy's General Board was created in 1900 in reaction to the Spanish-American War which revealed the weakness of the Navy's planning ability. Its members were senior admirals, those nearing retirement, and it had a purely advisory function. It was eclipsed by the creation of the chief of naval operations in 1915. It was, like the Army's General Staff, kept on a tight leash by Wilson who distrusted war planning. In 1913 during a war scare with Japan the Joint Board (with representatives of both the Army and Navy) suggested moving portions of the Navy to reinforce Manila, Honolulu, and the Panama Canal. Unfortunately, Wilson learned of this through the press. The cabinet discussed this on May 16. Wilson was worried that the leak to the press had been made to force his hand. Secretary of War Garrison wanted the Joint Board's opinion to weigh more than that of the civilians in the cabinet. Secretary of State Bryan was furious. The problem he noted was not how to wage a war but how to keep out of war. The discussion continued after the cabinet meeting between Wilson, Bryan, and Garrison. Garrison noted that the United States was free to move its ships where it wished between its own territories. Wilson was worried it would make it appear to Japan that the United States was preparing for war, thus making it more likely. He ordered the fleet to stay where it was, noting that he "feared the Joint Board has made a mistake." The next day Rear Adm. Bradley A. Fiske (then aide for operations) asked Daniels to request that Wilson move ships from California to Hawaii. Wilson was "greatly put out." The cabinet, and Wilson, had made their decision. It was up to the military to obey it, not to question. "I wish you would say to them," Wilson told Daniels, "that if this should occur again, there will be no General or Joints Boards. They will be abolished." They were not to meet again unless Wilson gave them permission.[43] The Joint Board members had overstepped into what Wilson considered his area of responsibility, that of diplomacy. It was clear which would take precedence for Wilson, the needs of diplomacy would come before the needs for military preparedness.

There were a few small, bright spots to this rather grim intelligence picture. There were more attaché spots available, but they were still not given guidance on what to investigate. The idea of issuing intelligence requirements had not yet formed. Moreover, their reports tended to get filed and lost in a bureaucratic maze. A somewhat better intelligence posture could be found in the Philippines, the only spot where Army intelligence resembled a modern structure. American officers gathered tactical and even strategic military intelligence, but also political. They ran spy rings among the Filipinos to watch for possible uprisings and attacks on American forces and installations. The Philippines also acted as a base from which to send officers to China, often under civilian cover, to survey Chinese railroads as well as into Japan to report on their fortifications and harbor facilities. The most notable section may have been the Army Signal Corps. Founded in 1860, it is remembered mostly for using balloons as aerial observation platforms. Indeed, this caught the public imagination in both the United States and the Confederacy: a young Wilson drew such balloons in a schoolbook as a child. They also organized spy rings and created codes and ciphers. By the 1890s the

Signal Corps referred to itself as a "service of information" and managed to gain control over at least part of the MID.

The ONI was founded in 1882. It was created as a reaction to the realization that the American Navy had been not just surpassed in technology by the European naval powers, but by other countries within the western hemisphere that the United States considered minor powers, including Chile and Peru. The ONI's original task was to gather as much technical information as possible "as to the progress of naval science, and the condition and resources of foreign navies." Tasked with both intelligence gathering and technology transfer, the ONI sent naval attachés to Europe to gather books, blueprints, and any information that would allow the United States to close what had become an alarmingly wide technical gap with the European powers. By the end of the nineteenth century and the Spanish-American War, however, while the ONI still looked to technological matters, it had begun to practice more traditional spy craft against Spain.[44]

STATE DEPARTMENT

The State Department is also part of this grouping of organizations with intelligence functions. During Theodore Roosevelt's administration (1901–9), the State Department reorganized into several sections divided along geographic lines. Secretary of State Elihu Root also standardized how information was disseminated, copying the British system of issuing regular reports on diplomatic developments so American diplomatic officers would understand the broader context of their nation's foreign affairs. Root also had the State Department redo its filing system into "cases" or subjects. While this system had its problems, such as where to file a cable relevant to multiple issues, it was far better than its predecessor which filed cables chronologically, sometimes not even divided by country. By the time Wilson took office in March 1913, the State Department was far more effectively organized than it had even been before, staffed by professionals. Secretary of State Bryan's desire to appoint "deserving Democrats" to State Department posts seemed ominous initially as he replaced experienced men with political novices. However, Bryan was not given enough leeway by Wilson to seriously impede the department's work. Politically appointed ambassadors were replaced with supporters of the new administration, and some officials left, but the overall turnover in personnel was light.[45]

In the State Department, Wilson made his changes to the organization for efficacy rather than political patronage. In 1915, the State Department added a new department known informally as U-1. The "U" stood for "undersecretary." Various subunits within the State Department (the number varied depending on the secretary of state) collected intelligence reports and sent them to U-1, which acted as a clearinghouse for information for the secretary. Wilson created this basic structure in 1915. Not too surprisingly, this came after Bryan had left. Despite this innovation, Wilson was never comfortable with the more clandestine aspects of intelligence gathering. To Bryan, it would have been anathema. In contrast, Lansing was perfectly comfortable with such matters.[46]

Two domestic departments also played an important role in intelligence gathering for Wilson. The Secret Service, which fell under the authority of Secretary of the Treasury William McAdoo, competed with the Justice Department's Bureau of Investigation under Attorney General Thomas Gregory. The turf battles between the two cabinet departments over jurisdiction do not concern us here. They both focused on internal matters, including feared German spies and saboteurs during World War I. The BI took the lead on investigating private citizens. However, they also established an Alien Enemy Bureau in the early days of the war with a brief to identify and arrest disloyal foreigners. J. Edgar Hoover, then a young civil servant in the Justice Department, headed it.

WILSON'S INFORMATION FLOW

Despite these beginnings, Wilson did not benefit from an organized intelligence structure (the CIA was still thirty years away), nor did he receive daily intelligence briefings—those would begin with Dwight Eisenhower's administration, another forty years in the future. Joseph Tumulty, Wilson's secretary, the equivalent of today's chief of staff, gave Wilson long sheets of newspaper clippings of editorials and news stories every day from several papers Wilson trusted. This included the *New York World* and the *Springfield* (Massachusetts) *Republican*. Tumulty also gave the president his mail at this time, which Wilson dealt with between 10 a.m. and 11 a.m. These included assorted letters often from cranks warning the president of various plots which one must assume Tumulty thought would amuse his boss. One man even offered to assassinate Mexican dictator Victoriano Huerta for Wilson and complained that Bryan had kicked him out of the secretary's carriage when he broached the subject. Sometimes Wilson tapped individual reporters for their opinions. For example, when Wilson discounted much of the press coverage on Mexico, a small group of reporters was called to Washington for personal interviews with Wilson for the perceived accuracy of their reporting. Among this select group was John Reed, who was reporting on Mexico for the *World*.[47]

There was no central clearinghouse. Each adviser could report directly to the president, and they could interact among themselves as well. While this seems to have been somewhat chaotic, Wilson conferred enough with his chief advisers that it rarely seemed unmanageable. Moreover, there was enough structure that it was relatively clear which of Wilson's advisers was the proper go-between. Those that tried to pass through someone else, such as a businessman with international properties who tried to contact Wilson through Secretary of the Interior Franklin Lane, would often find a less hospitable reaction from the president than if they had gone through the proper department.

There were some strengths to Wilson's approach despite its apparent weaknesses. Because Wilson's sources were both varied and decentralized, the chance of avoiding groupthink was lessened. The process, although often disorganized, especially at first, guaranteed that no single voice dominated the discussion. For example, with regard to Mexico in 1913–15, Wilson heard differing viewpoints regarding each of the Mexican factions, although he did not hear an equal amount from each: he received few reports concerning Emiliano Zapata south of Mexico City where there were comparatively fewer Americans with business interests. Nonetheless, Wilson heard a wide range of opinions and information, although the material was often a blend of analysis and data. His correspondents told the president what they had learned and included their judgments and often recommendations for action. One of Wilson's agents in Mexico, John Lind, was especially prone to trying to influence policy by suggesting courses of action, seeking to direct instead of only to inform. The president was usually wary of his sources suggesting policy. In general, when sources of information attempted to do more than convey information Wilson usually dismissed their suggestions. In August 1915, Wilson complained to Lansing about one of his representatives, reporter David Lawrence. A Princeton graduate who knew Wilson as a student, Lawrence had been sent to Veracruz. "The usual thing has happened." Wilson complained, "A man is sent down to explain our exact position and purpose and within a day or two sends us a comprehensive plan of his own entirely inconsistent with what he was sent to say."[48]

Wilson also received regular reports from his advisers and cabinet members. He often made notes among the margins and passed memos to other advisers for action or solely for information. The reports Wilson received were themselves limited in subject matter, tending to be part of a small handful of categories, military, economic, and political. The latter could be either domestic to the United States or international. Social issues were important, but generally, if they affected one of the main three categories. For example, Wilson's interest in Mexican land reform, he was a fan of John Reed's reporting from Mexico, was tied to the ongoing Mexican Revolution and U.S. involvement. To be fair to the twentieth-eighth president, these categories would also be of the most concern in intelligence reporting for his successors. After all, the intelligence community's role is not to entertain the president with exciting stories about exotic peoples in foreign lands. Wilson read *National Geographic* and could get that type of material there. Instead, the intelligence community is to report to the commander in chief on matters that affect American national security.

In 1917, as advised by Colonel House, Wilson created a private think tank called The Inquiry. It was a loose collection of mostly academic experts, mostly on Western Europe, there were fewer available on other parts of the world. Most came from five universities: Princeton, Harvard, Yale,

Columbia, and Chicago. They provided Wilson with a knowledge bank on foreign policy beginning at the end of 1917 and continuing through the Paris Peace Conference. In late 1917 they produced a memo on suggested terms for a peace treaty. Wilson and House sat down with their list to edit and reorganize. It became Wilson's "Fourteen Points" in early 1918.[49]

INTERPRETING THE INFORMATION

His preference for reading reports over oral briefings may be unexpected, as Wilson was a very slow reader. Famously he did not learn the alphabet until he was nine years old and could not read until he was twelve. He never did become comfortable reading French or German and his first wife, Ellen Axson Wilson, translated difficult German texts for his research. Wilson's biographer and physician Edwin Weinstein argued that Wilson might have had dyslexia. Whatever the cause, Wilson was a very slow reader. Nonetheless, while he did sometimes receive oral briefings, he preferred those in writing. The drawback to this is that written briefings do not allow for immediate feedback and questions.

In general, Wilson enjoyed policy discussions, at least until he had made up his mind. He was a member of the Whig debating club at Princeton as an undergraduate and debating clubs at the University of Virginia while in law school, and at Wesleyan when he taught there. As president, Wilson encouraged debate in his cabinet meetings. Crucially, however, Wilson engaged in debate only if he had not yet made up his mind on an issue, and if those with whom he interacted showed respect for his position. If he had come to a decision or believed the speaker did not know what he was talking about or was serving a private agenda, then Wilson's defenses raised, and debate was over. There are numerous examples. His female students at Bryn Mawr complained that he preferred to lecture than to teach, that he did not want to debate issues with them. African American leader William Trotter was thrown out of Wilson's office for arguing, which is to say, not showing what Wilson considered proper deference to him both as president and as a white man. Wilson's cabinet did not forget that he was president nor did the military leaders Wilson trusted forget he was commander in chief. Written reports were safe in this respect. If the writer were rude, or self-important, Wilson could put it aside or add angry comments. It would have no positive influence on his policymaking.

Wilson's interpretation of information did assume the existence of objectivity. Some of this probably came from his training by Herbert Baxter Adams and the graduate program at Johns Hopkins with its heavy influence from German doctoral programs. The program emphasized "scientific" research, which Wilson found dry and dull. He preferred writing with "style." Despite this, you can see Wilson's attempts at objectivity in some of his academic writings. For example, *Division and Reunion* was notable as an early attempt to write a history of the Civil War that did not favor either side but attempted to understand the war from both the Union and Confederate perspectives—at least the white perspectives. Race was, of course, famously a blind spot for Wilson. Wilson seemed most aware of economic factors as the most significant issue, self-gain as a threat to objectivity. While indeed a narrow view, it was nonetheless a genuine concern. While noting that an observer had a financial interest in a particular outcome was not in itself automatically disqualified for consideration in Wilson's view, it was a significant hurdle. The observer's motive in reporting on an international issue to Wilson, whether personal profit or moral uplift, was to the president an important distinction.

There were no set or established criteria for vetting sources of information. Some individuals' opinions—diplomats, military attachés, etc.—were given weight because of their position. For most other sources of information such as the press, businessmen, missionaries, and academics, Wilson and his advisers relied on their judgment of the source's reliability to weigh the information's worth. This procedure was much the same as how Wilson made his political appointments. Some of the cabinet officials he knew well, some he knew only in passing. In some cases, such as his first Secretary of War Lindley Garrison, he did not know the man but relied on the opinion of other advisers. This led, as would be expected, to inconsistent results.

Other factors played a role in influencing Wilson's judgment of his informants' reliability. He judged as most reliable those he had known for a long time, especially other academics, and clergymen. He trusted particular journalists, generally those on the political left. Former students were also a trusted source, assuming he had positive memories of them from school. Professional diplomats and military officers were judged on uncertain criteria, although one factor that was certain to spoil Wilson's opinion of them was if they were openly partisan Republicans. Wilson did not reject every person who was not a Democrat. Gen. John J. Pershing was a Republican and Wilson made him head of the American Expeditionary Forces (AEF). In contrast, Gen. Leonard Wood was a friend of Theodore Roosevelt and a vocal critic of Wilson's policies and found himself shunted aside. The source which Wilson trusted the least, aside from the obvious crank, were businessmen with financial interests at stake. This does not mean Wilson always discounted every report he received from every American businessman with overseas investments and property. However, he was far less likely to take their advice and accept their information than he was from other sources.

Wilson looked for consistent elements in this mass of information to judge their reliability. The accurate facts, he believed, would fit together as a whole, leaving the lies and propaganda aside as the chaff. The result was a crude form of content analysis. In 1915, as he weighed all the conflicting reports from Mexico, he noted in a speech,

> Things that are not so do not match. If you hear enough of them, you see there is no pattern whatever; it is a crazy quilt, whereas the truth always matches, piece by piece, with other parts of the truth. No man can lie consistently, and he cannot lie about everything if he talks to you too long. I would guarantee that if enough liars talked to you, you would get the truth; because the parts that they did not invent would match each other, and the parts that they did invent would *not* match one another. Talk long enough, therefore, and see the connections clearly enough, and you can patch together the case as a whole. I had somewhat that experience about Mexico, and that was about the only way in which I learned anything that was true about it, for there had been vivid imaginations and many special interests which depicted things as they wished me to believe them to be.[50]

This intelligence gathering and evaluating arrangement, it would stretch too far to call it a formal system, worked well enough by 1918 that it provided Wilson with the type and quality of information he needed as a commander in chief. However, what types of information were available?

TYPES OF INTELLIGENCE

While the specific organizations and specific sources of information available to the president would evolve over the twentieth century, the categories that exist today still, for the most part, were those into which the sources of 1913 can be divided.[51] In modern intelligence gathering terms, Wilson relied mostly on Open Source (OSINT) material, especially newspapers, and human intelligence (HUMINT). Signals intelligence (SIGINT) played a small role, although a critical one. For the most part, it was used by the military as tactical intelligence. However, in some cases, most notably the "Zimmermann Telegram," SIGINT was crucial in forming and influencing American strategic concerns. Of course, the means to gather such information would change. Image intelligence (IMINT), for example, in 1913 meant photos taken at ground level, or from either lighter-than-air or heavier-than-air aircraft. It was of use mainly for tactical military intelligence. It would generally not be of use to the commander in chief, except when it could inform briefings for the CinC on broader issues such as planned offensives.

For Wilson then, the most essential sources would have been OSINT and HUMINT. For both, however, the same problem persisted then as now—judging the reliability of their information. Wilson's initial opinion of the source was the most critical factor. The *New York World* was the paper he seems to have trusted the most and was his administration's outlet of choice for leaking information. Wilson wrote to the *World's* publisher, Ralph Pulitzer, in 1914, "Let me say that every day I open the editorial page of the *World* expecting to find what I do, a real vision of things as they are." In contrast, William Randolph Hearst's *New York American* had earned none of the president's trust. Indeed, Wilson distrusted much of the Washington press corps. As he wrote to a friend in September 1913, "Do not believe anything you read in the papers. If you read the papers I see, they are utterly untrustworthy. . . . Read the editorial page and you will know what you will find in the news columns. For unless they are grossly careless the two always support each other. Their lying is shameless and colossal!"[52]

Fortunately, looking in hindsight, his opinion of the *World* was reasonably accurate, especially as Wilson dealt with Mexico.[53]

CODES AND COMMUNICATIONS

Unfortunately, even the best of these small intelligence organizations that existed during Wilson's time in office did not initially see the benefit of SIGINT—this despite the usefulness for both sides during the Civil War in tapping their enemy's telegraph signals. The Army did set up small units to intercept German radio traffic in 1917–18, but this was localized tactical intelligence. Domestically the best SIGINT came from the Secret Service and BI following German and Austrian agents, tapping their phones and bugging hotel rooms. For the role of commander in chief, however, the growth of wireless had significance other than providing a new source to target. It also allowed the more rapid distribution of information without being tied to the existing telegraph network, which depended upon maintaining physical infrastructure. As a result, the information could flow to the White House much faster than before. When Wilson took office in 1913, however, the United States was at a distinct disadvantage. Britain and Germany had extensive cable systems to carry messages and were developing similarly sophisticated wireless systems. France and the Netherlands, needing contact with their overseas possessions, were following suit. The U.S. Navy and American companies such as Western Union were also building their networks, but it was not until the United States was about to enter the World War in 1917 that the United States truly began building its worldwide network independent of the other powers' systems.[54]

American intelligence was also weak on what is now called denial and deception, hiding their own side's secrets while breaking those of their adversaries. Admittedly this side of intelligence gathering was still in its infancy compared to what emerged in the Cold War and after, but even considering the era, American efforts were, to be blunt, embarrassing. The "War Telegraph Code" was a simple substitution code that was designed not to hide messages, but to save on telegraph costs. Intelligence historian James L. Gilbert notes that these codes were of no more use than the toy "secret code rings" found in cereal boxes in the mid-twentieth century.[55]

Wilson's copy of the codebook is in the collection of the Woodrow Wilson House in Washington, DC. They were still using the 1899 Cypher of the Department of State. Arranged like a dictionary, facing pages shared a page number. Code words were listed alphabetically down the left side with a two-digit number next to it. To the right of the codeword was listed its meaning, which could be a single word or a phrase. In addition, each code word was numbered, starting with number 1, for its particular page. So, for example, "harpists" was followed by "84" on page 406. So, someone decoding a cable with either "harpists" or "84406" would come up with the word "Haiti." "Harpoon" or "85406" meant "agreement between Haiti and." Both the code words and their real meanings were listed alphabetically, starting with the letter A although the first letter of the codeword did not always correspond with the first letter of its real meaning, depending on how many terms for each letter needed to be coded. There were also blank spaces in each letter section, so additional words could be added. Wilson added some codes for various Democratic officials at the end of the book. They were often pathetically easy to guess. "Dove" was the pacifist former secretary of state, William Jennings Bryan. Democratic 1920 nominee James Cox was "Swain." Wilson apparently also attempted to redo the code by reversing the page numbers, renumbering them beginning at the back of the book, and moving toward the front. So, the code for "Haiti" was still "harpists" but instead of 84406, it became 84443.[56]

CONCLUSION

Wilson's advisers and the primitive intelligence systems that served them were adequate for 1913, but its capabilities were strained, especially during World War I. The lack of a central clearinghouse other than Tumulty was part of the problem, but Wilson himself was the biggest hurdle. He saw no need for a more systematic approach and was happy much of the time with ad hoc arrangements, such as his representatives sent to Mexico in 1913–14. To be fair to Wilson, much of the government did not see the need either. Even the reorganization and reforms made to the State Department and the Department of War in Roosevelt's administration left much of the foreign and military policy apparatus of the government primitive compared to the European powers. World War I forced Wilson and his administration to move toward creating a more disciplined structure. When Wilson left office in 1921, he left behind a larger and more efficient organization than he had found in 1913, but it remained decentralized and small compared to what would come.

Wilson was notably reluctant to go to war, especially on a large scale. Historians in Mexico, Haiti, and the Dominican Republic, however, as well as in Russia, would be justified in noting that Wilson was not nearly as hesitant about smaller-scale interventions. A cynical observer might suggest it was German strength that made him hesitate at committing American troops. This would not be unfair, as it obviously would cost more American lives to defeat imperial Germany than to occupy Port-au-Prince. It must also be noted, however, that the goals in each case were also different. As the following chapters will note, the goals of the use of military force, and the moral justification for it, were the crucial elements in Wilson's decision-making. The cost of the resulting violence was an important factor, but in shaping the goals and measuring the justification, not as a reason for or against the use of force by itself. For Wilson, the military was a policy tool, a way to implement policy. In Wilson's mind, there were a number of types of force he could use as president—diplomatic, economic, moral, and military. The last one, military, was useful for creating new opportunities to enact his desired policies, but it had to be used in conjunction with the other tools at Wilson's disposal. It was never to be used for its own sake, but as part of a coordinated strategy. The fact that it did not always work—Wilson's policies did not always succeed—does not change how he viewed the use of the American military.[57]

CHAPTER 2

———◆•◆———

The World in 1912

In 1912, the United States' population was about 95 million people. In his final year as president, William Howard Taft was preparing to retain the Republican Party nomination against this old friend, now rival, former president Theodore Roosevelt. The Democrats were fighting for their nomination in a series of the new presidential primaries. The favorite was Speaker of the House Champ Clark of Missouri, but New Jersey governor Woodrow Wilson was among the strongest contenders competing with Clark. Arizona and New Mexico became states, raising the total to forty-eight. The Progressive Movement was going strong. Labor's victory in the Bread and Roses strike in Lawrence, Massachusetts, promised more for workers. The woman's suffrage movement was still fighting to win support in Congress and the states, while the Temperance Movement was gaining ground: eight states were already official dry, while another nine would join by the end of 1916.

There was little indication that Wilson thought much about his role as commander in chief in 1912. The election turned on domestic issues, particularly on economic matters such as currency reform and anti-trust laws. What wars were ongoing, such as in the Balkans, seemed unrelated to American interests. The Philippines was generally peaceful. Immediately south of the border, the Mexican Revolution was ongoing, but with an elected reform president sitting in Mexico City, the violence seemed to be unlikely to spread. Famously, not long before his inauguration, Wilson remarked to a Princeton colleague that it would be "an irony of fate if my administration had to deal chiefly with foreign problems, for all my preparation has been in domestic matters."[1] Apparently, Fate took this as a challenge and the new president would have to quickly come up to speed and construct, largely from scratch, a foreign policy apparatus on a scale the United States has not seen before.

The first decade of the century had seen a record number of immigrants into the United States. More than eight million immigrants entered into the county from 1900 to 1909, more than double the number that had entered from 1890 to 1899. By 1912, there were in excess of fourteen million foreign-born residents in the United States, many coming from southern and eastern Europe rather than from northern Europe and the British Isles. Still, the Irish American and German American communities were among the largest ethnic communities in the United States, and many midwestern and eastern cities had a Klein Deutschland. There was an active German-language press. In some areas in some states such as Ohio and Wisconsin, the schools taught primarily in German to match the language most of their students spoke at home. Politically, the Irish were a power within the Democratic Party, while the German American vote leaned Republican.

The U.S. military before 1914 was smaller than that of the other major powers, with much of American National Defense centered on the Navy. For all the services combined, including the states' National Guard Units, the U.S. military numbered approximately 200,000, roughly the size of the Serbian Army. The U.S. Navy had approximately 57,000 men in uniform, the Army about 98,000. The Navy, however, was one of the three largest in the world, about the size of Germany's, second only to Britain's. The U.S. fleet included thirty-two battleships, thirty-seven cruisers, and forty-five destroyers. Torpedo boats, submarines, and gunboats added almost another hundred warships to the overall count.[2]

LATIN AMERICA

While the United States was not in a declared war, its troops were engaged in different parts of the expanding American empire. Most American military intervention in this period was, of course, in the Caribbean. The United States had long regarded the Caribbean as being of particular interest and had long coveted Cuba. The Spanish-American War in the summer of 1898 had freed Cuba from Spain but placed it firmly into a new role as a protectorate of Washington. Likewise, Puerto Rico was taken from Spain to become a U.S. territory, and the Philippines became a colony. Between the summer of 1898 and President Franklin Roosevelt's administration starting in 1933, American Marines would be used to "restore order" and protect American property and lives in Cuba, Panama, Dominica, Haiti, Nicaragua, Honduras, Guatemala, and Mexico, usually multiple times. Wilson would be the most active of the American presidents in this era in sending troops, but he had a great deal of company.

During William Howard Taft's administration (1909–13), the United States intervened in Nicaragua between the ongoing struggle between the Liberal and Conservative factions. Primarily driven by Secretary of State Philander Knox, the administration favored the Conservatives. American policy was aimed at reducing the influence of European finance in Central America. The Nicaraguan vice president, conservative Adolfo Díaz Recinos, was open to a more significant role for American investment. Moreover, Liberal president José Santos Zelaya López was apparently negotiating with Germany and Japan to resurrect the proposed Nicaragua Canal. While Taft's "Dollar Diplomacy" emphasized the use of economic influence, it did not eliminate the use of political or military pressure. When a rebellion by Conservative General Juan José Estrada threatened President Zelaya's government in 1909, the United States deployed ships and Marines to

Nicaragua to protect American interests. They pressured Zelaya to resign, to be succeeded by José Madriz Rodríguez. Madriz attempted to establish policies independent of American interests, and was forced out in turn, to be replaced by Estrada who was in turn replaced by Díaz.[3]

When one of Díaz's generals launched his own rebellion, Taft rushed Marines to guard the American-owned railroad, part of which was controlled by the rebels. The Marines moved up the rail line, occasionally engaging in firefights with insurgent troops. The Marines soon controlled not only the rail line but the capital city, Managua, where they could guarantee the Díaz regime's hold on power. The threat to withdraw the troops, thus leaving Díaz open to being overthrown, guaranteed that he remained pliant to American interests. In 1914, he agreed to the Bryan-Chamorro Treaty, which reserved for the United States the right to build a Nicaraguan Canal, thus shutting out the European powers. The casualties on both sides as the Marines retook the rail line were light, but the United States kept Marines in Managua until 1933, and they engaged in other battles, especially in the mid-1920s.[4]

After Cuba became officially independent in 1902, the United States intervened two more times before the outbreak of World War I. In 1906, the government of Cuba's president Tomás Estrada Palma collapsed under allegations of election fraud from the National Liberal Party. Both the Conservative Palma and the National Liberals asked the United States to intervene, the former to crush the rebellion, and the latter to supervise new elections. President Theodore Roosevelt was reluctant. His administration was then trying to soothe jangled Latin American nerves and reassure the rest of the region that, despite Panama, the United States had no imperialistic designs on the region. The American expatriate community in Havana, however, was panicking and demanding intervention. Secretary of War William Howard Taft met Cuban leaders from both sides to try to negotiate a settlement. Both factions were recalcitrant. On September 28, 1906, President Palma and his vice president resigned, leaving Cuba without a government, which effectively forced Roosevelt's hand. On September 29, two thousand U.S. Marines landed and set up camp near Havana. Taft became provisional governor until Charles

Magoon replaced him. The rebels had already put down their arms, so the occupation was peaceful. New elections were held in late 1908, and José Miguel Gómez took office at the end of January 1909.[5]

The U.S. intervention of 1912 was not as peaceful. Known as the Negro Rebellion in English and Levantamiento Armado de Los Independientes de Color in Spanish, it was a peasant uprising by the Afro Cuban field workers and peasants. Mostly employed in the sugar cane industry, conditions for the workers were deplorable. When promised improvements by the government failed to appear, the workers began to form their own political party. Their new party was banned; political parties based on race were a violation of Cuban law. With their political party banned and with it the means to affect change within the system, the workers turned to armed rebellion, engaging the Cuban army, mostly in the eastern part of the island. President Gómez asked the United States to send Marines conveniently just minutes before they landed. The rebellion was crushed in a few weeks. Approximately 2,700 Marines and officers were deployed to Cuba. They were generally limited to guarding rail lines, towns, American property, and sugar fields. They engaged the rebels only once and suffered no casualties. However, the message sent from Washington to Havana was clear. Even in a case where the local military was capable of restoring order (or crushing the revolution, depending on your perspective), the United States was willing and quite able to land troops to protect American interests. "Restoring order" was not enough. American property and lives must also be protected. Cuba would find this out again in 1917.

The Mexican Revolution was the conflict of most interest to Washington. President Porfirio Díaz had ruled Mexico since 1876, arranging to be reelected every four years to at least keep the appearance of following the county's constitution. He welcomed foreign investment, especially, but not limited to that from the United States. In the political system he established he maintained a greater degree of order than during the violent half-century preceding his rule, thus keeping foreign business content. As Taft noted to his secretary of state, Philander Knox, "I cannot conceive a situation in which President Díaz would not act with a strong hand in defense of just American interests." However, the aging Díaz's regime was weakening, and he was challenged by Francisco Madero, a wealthy liberal landowner who began publishing a newspaper demanding reforms including free and fair elections. Díaz had Madero arrested and jailed, and the longtime ruler easily won a rigged election. Madero escaped from prison, fled to the United States, and proclaimed himself president of a revolutionary junta.[6]

President Taft maintained a generally neutral policy, although he refused to interfere with the revolutionaries shipping arms across the border into Mexico. With the United States signaling that it was uninterested in intervening to pick sides, many local revolutionaries throughout Mexico united loosely under Madero's leadership—if only one of temporary convenience. On May 10, 1911, the border city of Ciudad Juárez was captured by the revolutionaries. Díaz quickly agreed to negotiate. Government representatives and Madero's signed an armistice on May 21. As anti-Díaz riots spread through Mexico City, the longtime ruler resigned and fled to exile in France.[7]

Madero faced the same problem that had driven Díaz from power: ongoing rebellion. Much of the ongoing unrest had been targeted against the existing system rather than Díaz specifically.[8] Crucially, however, the most powerful enemy for the new president was not even Mexican, but American. U.S. ambassador Henry Lane Wilson (no relation to Woodrow Wilson), a political appointee and conservative, hated Madero for not being sufficiently deferential to American business interests.[9]

Madero was aware of Wilson's hostility and had instructed his minister of foreign affairs, Pedro Lascuraín—who was visiting the United States in late 1912—to ask president-elect Woodrow Wilson to recall Ambassador Wilson. Madero asked Lascuraín to inform the president-elect that Mexico had already told Washington that the ambassador was persona non grata. However, the Mexican government had not pushed the matter further because it believed the new U.S. administration would recall the Republican appointee in due course.[10]

On February 9, 1913, only three weeks before Woodrow Wilson was sworn in as the new American president, General Félix Díaz, nephew of the former ruler, attacked the presidential palace. The attack was repulsed by troops loyal to Madero, but the revolutionaries seized the city's arsenal and began the battle now known as La Decena Trágica (The Tragic Ten Days). While artillery shells and bullets landed around the city, Ambassador Wilson urged Washington to grant him control of Marines and U.S. Navy warships—that he be "clothed with general powers in the name of the president." Taft refused. The ambassador began meeting with Díaz and Madero's supposedly loyal commander, Victoriano Huerta, while also pressuring the other ambassadors to join him in pressuring Madero to resign.[11]

On February 18, 1913, Huerta's troops seized key points in the city and arrested members of Madero's government, including the president and vice president. Ambassador Wilson clearly knew it was coming. He dropped hints in his cables to Washington, his fellow diplomats, and even to American reporters. The now-president Huerta had Madero and his vice president murdered, supposedly killed in a failed rescue attempt.[12] Taft delayed extending formal recognition to Huerta's regime, to win concessions from Mexico in negotiations over some minor border disputes.[13] Moreover, Madero's supporters and allies elsewhere began to gather their resources. Several American consuls reported that some state governors refused to recognize Huerta as the legitimate Mexican president. The American consul at Nogales reported to the State Department, "A very bitter resentment here and in the state [of Sonora] resulting from the killing of Madero. The state will not submit to the provisional government at Mexico City."[14]

Meanwhile, president-elect Woodrow Wilson prepared for his inauguration in Washington on March 4. His wife, Ellen Axson Wilson, told one of Wilson's advisers that her husband hesitated to recognize Huerta's government due to his distrust of Ambassador Wilson.[15] Wilson looked for a source he could trust. In April, Wilson sent William Bayard Hale, a progressive reporter and writer, to investigate.[16] Hale traveled to Mexico City and, in June, sent back his first report. His conclusions confirmed Wilson's worst fears—Madero had been overthrown in a coup supported by those opposed to reforming Mexico. The coup would have failed if Madero's commander, Huerta, had not betrayed him. Even worse, Huerta had the active support of Ambassador Wilson.[17]

Wilson began to look for ways to oust Huerta, even quietly considering how best to support the anti-Huerta revolutionaries. His cabinet was divided. Secretary of War Garrison urged Wilson to use force to end the disorder below the Rio Grande. The only two choices, Garrison claimed, were for the United States to recognize Huerta or to intervene militarily. Wilson agreed with Secretary of the Navy Daniels that intervention would lead to "considerable" guerrilla warfare against American troops. These cabinet meetings followed a pattern that would be repeated between 1913 and 1915. Garrison was a consistent voice for military intervention. Secretary of State William Jennings Bryan advocated mediation, often backed by Daniels. Wilson usually took a position between Garrison and Bryan, although leaning toward the secretary of state. In his diary, adviser Colonel House wrote that Wilson believed Bryan overstated the dangers of intervention. Nonetheless, Wilson thought, the threat of a never-ending guerrilla war if the United States invaded Mexico made the prospect a last resort.[18] Nonetheless, as shall be covered in chapters 3 and 5, Wilson did find himself intervening in Mexico multiple times between 1914 and 1919.

Besides Mexico, the United States was also involved in Panama. Under the Hay-Bunau-Varilla Treaty (1903), Panama granted the United States the right to "act as if it were sovereign" in the newly created Canal Zone. While the canal was being built, the United States ensured that the country would remain calm and nonthreatening to American interests. Panama's military was disbanded, and only pro-American leaders were allowed to be chosen between the conservative and liberal political parties. Little changed when Woodrow Wilson took office in March 1913, except that the administration attempted to "express regrets" to Colombia, from which Panama had been taken. Besides, the United States was to pay $25 million to Colombia in what wags called "Canalamony." Theodore Roosevelt objected loudly to what he thought was an admission that the United States, and he, had been in the wrong in promoting the 1903 Panamanian Revolution. The treaty and the payment were delayed until the early 1920s after Roosevelt had died. The canal officially opened on August 15, 1914, without the international spectacle one might have anticipated. World War I garnered the world's attention. As noted in chapter 8, Wilson sent American troops into Panama on a small scale. However, his focus was preserving order, and preventing European powers from gaining a foothold there.[19]

Haiti had long been an uncomfortable neighbor for the United States. Established by a successful slave revolt between 1791 and 1804, its mere existence made Americans nervous, lest it be seen as inspiration at home. Washington did not even recognize Haiti diplomatically until 1862. It was a convenient place, along with Liberia, for Republican administrations to send black leaders as diplomats to reward service to the party. Generally, the United States only paid attention to Haiti when revolution or other violence broke out. Even after the constitution of 1868 seemed to establish a relatively stable government and economic development grew, the United States sent the Navy to Haiti to "protect lives and property" sixteen times between 1868 and 1912—ten times alone between 1902 and 1912.[20]

Haiti was especially crucial to the United States because of its excellent harbor at Môle Saint-Nicolas. The planned Panama Canal only increased Washington's desire to keep Haiti, and its harbors, out of European control. Political unrest heightened American concerns. Between 1911 and 1915, a half dozen men served as Haitian president, each of which was in their turn either killed or forced to flee into exile. This seemed to provide just the excuse and opportunity for a more powerful nation to seize control of the unfortunate country. There were several candidates among the powers. France had maintained its influence, even after the Haitian revolution. More worrying to Washington, Germany had more apparent pull in Haiti than mere numbers would suggest. Only about two hundred Germans lived in Haiti by 1910, but they controlled over two-thirds of the country's international commerce. Moreover, the Reich citizens also owned and operated utilities in Cap-Haïtien and the capital, Port-au-Prince. Germans owned the capital's main wharf and tramway, as well as one of the country's most important railroads. In response, the U.S. State Department backed a consortium of American investors organized by the National City Bank of New York. It acquired controlling interest of the nation's only commercial bank, Banque Nationale d'Haïti, which acted as the Haiti government's treasury.[21] As Wilson took office the continuing unrest and revolving door presidency continued, worrying Washington, and prompting policy-makers to continue to cast nervous glances toward Berlin, and to a lesser extent Paris, wondering if either might be tempted to seize a base on the crucial approach to the Panama Canal.

ASIA

Outside of the Caribbean, U.S. troops remained engaged most notably in the Philippines. The Filipino-American War between the First Filipino Republic and the United States lasted from 1899–1902. Fighting in the Philippines slowly ended as various guerrilla groups were either defeated or put down their arms. In the mostly Muslim south, however, resistance to American occupation continued. The Spanish had never fully controlled the southern, majority Muslim islands in the Filipino archipelago, and the United States found itself in the same situation. Known in the United States as the "Moro Rebellion," fighting in the south lasted from 1899–1913.

When the United States took the Philippines from Spain, they informed the Moro leadership that they intended to continue Spain's policies of establishing a protectorate. The Moro Sulu Sultanate rejected this and demanded a new treaty. With the American military trying to suppress the Filipino independence movement elsewhere, the McKinley administration did not want another war, so they agreed. The 1899 Kiram-Bates Treaty granted autonomy on internal matters to the Sultanate. As soon as the Filipino War was over; however, the United States abandoned the agreement and established direct control through a military government. Moro resistance to this new status was sporadic, focusing on guerrilla warfare in most cases. There were numerous atrocities, including the "Battle of Banyan" in 1902 in which American soldiers slaughtered several hundred Moro fighters, both men and women. The military governorship of Gen. Leonard Wood (1903–6) was particularly marked by brutal fighting. At the First Battle of Bud Dajo, up to a thousand Moro, including women and children, were killed, with only six survivors. The governorship of Gen. John Pershing (1909–13) was more successful than his predecessors. Contrary to lurid stories about bullets dipped in pig's blood, Pershing worked with Moro leadership and successfully transitioned the providence to civilian leadership.

The Philippines was essential to the United States, as they were to Spain beforehand, as a gateway to trade with China. The Qing Dynasty had controlled China since 1636. However, the European powers, followed by the United States and Japan, had been forcing concessions on Beijing to open territory and to grant exclusive territorial rights. Uprisings such as the Taiping Rebellion (1850–64) and losing wars against European states and Japan demonstrated how weakened the ruling dynasty had become. Efforts to reform China and follow Japan's path to modernization while protecting its sovereignty failed and the Qing were forced from power. The Chinese revolution, now known as the Xinhai Revolution, began on October 10, 1911.[22] A provisional government tried to bridge the divides between different revolutionary groups: Nationalists in Nanjing and Qing General Yuan Shikai in Beijing competed for influence. The first provisional president, Sun Yat-Sen, abdicated in favor of Yuan as the second provisional president, but China's government remained unstable. Yuan's government was recognized by most foreign powers, including the United States. Yuan died in 1916 and during the following "Warlord Era" (1916–28) there was no one Chinese government with effective control of the country.

Woodrow Wilson was very interested in China, especially in the Christian missions there. Missionaries became one of the main channels for information for Wilson. One of his cousins and one of his former students from Princeton both sent him regular reports from China. Moreover, the YMCA mission in Beijing was supported by Princeton University, and many of its staff had come from there as well. Despite the bad feelings left between Wilson and the administration at his former university, Wilson continued to support the Chinese mission and remained on good terms with professors and former students. They became an active channel for reports on China for the new president.[23]

EUROPEAN IMPERIALISM

European powers large and small were themselves engaged in extending their influence, not just in Asia, but closer to home, particularly around the Mediterranean. Italy was among the states eyeing North Africa. In 1911, Italy went to war with the Ottoman Empire over the provinces that now make up Libya. When Italy demanded that the Ottomans hand over these provinces, Constantinople offered full control of the area, but with the Ottomans retaining formal claim. This would have copied the arrangement in Egypt, which was formally still part of the Ottoman Empire while being controlled by Britain. Italy refused and declared war.

The war came at an inopportune time for the Ottomans. The Young Turks Revolution in 1908 had begun to reform their military, but it was still in poor condition and poorly trained in 1912. Italy quickly seized the major coastal cities but was unable to advance further into the interior. They also destroyed much of the Ottoman fleet in the area and took the Aegean islands that made up the Turkish province of Rhodes. Guerrilla warfare and massacres on both sides increased the casualties and the desire of both governments to end the war. The Treaty of Lausanne of 1912 (now named the Treaty of Ouchy to distinguish it from the 1923 Treaty of Lausanne) turned Libya over to Italy and returned the Aegean islands to the Ottomans. The war prompted the Balkan states to ally to take advantage of the tottering regime in Constantinople. Unfortunately, the ease of the Italian victory seems to have registered with the Balkan states far more than the cost of the war, or the realities of trench warfare at Benghazi. Before the Italian-Ottoman War had even ended, the Balkan Wars had begun.

THE BALKAN WARS

The two Balkan Wars of 1912–13 destroyed much of what was left of the region's crumbling Ottoman hold. The significant combatants, Serbia, Greece, Romania, and Bulgaria had each become independent states during the nineteenth century by expelling Ottoman rule. In 1912, they each still had unrequited claims on some of the remaining Ottoman territories and upon each other. The First Balkan War lasted from October 1912 to May 1913. Opposing the Ottomans was the Balkan League: the kingdoms of Bulgaria, Serbia, Greece, and Montenegro. The League members' militaries soon defeated the Ottoman military in a series of rapid victories. The war ended with the Treaty of London in May 1913. The Allied states of the Balkan League partitioned most of what was left of the Ottoman Empire's remaining European territories. However, the treaty also created an independent Albania, which angered Bulgaria and Greece, each of which claimed some Albania territory.

The Second Balkan War began in June 1913 when Bulgaria, frustrated with its share of the First Balkan War's spoils, attacked its former allies, Serbia and Greece. Despite having done well in the first war, Bulgaria was not successful in the second. Serbian and Greek armies drove back their former ally's troops and entered Bulgaria. Romania decided that this was the time to take the territory it wanted from Bulgaria, so it entered the war. Finally, sensing an opportunity, the Ottoman Empire took advantage of the situation to retake lost territory. Bulgaria was forced to sue for peace. In two separate treaties, it surrendered territory to Serbia, Greece, Romania, and the Ottomans.

After the two wars, the region understandably remained extremely tense, with Revanchist groups still eyeing neighboring states' territory. Serbia and Bulgaria were especially disgruntled. The military of the former dreamed of uniting all the Slavic peoples into a united Yugoslavia, while the latter resented losing what it had so recently gained against the Ottomans. Austria-Hungary, like the Ottomans, an aging and weakening empire, watched their southern neighbors with increasing worry. The fate of Ottoman control over the Balkans and Libya made it disturbingly clear what could happen to a weakened empire at the hands of more aggressive states, even small ones. Moreover, Vienna knew that Italy coveted Austrian territory along the north and east coasts of the Adriatic. In Vienna's eyes, Rome's successful war to snatch Libya from Constantinople's control might well be the first step in expanding the Italian state's borders.

Meanwhile, these wars were not the only political violence in Europe. There were multiple assassinations of heads of state and their heirs in Europe before the archduke's murder in Sarajevo in June 1914. The Serbian king, Alexander I, was overthrown and killed in June 1903, the prime minister of Bulgaria in 1907, the Portuguese king and his heir in 1908, and a Russian prime minister in 1911. The Spanish prime minister was murdered in late 1912 and the king of Greece in March 1913. The reasons for each assassination varied. Several were by self-proclaimed anarchists, one as part of a military coup, by Republicans opposed to monarchy, and in the case of the Greek king, by an alcoholic homeless man for no apparent reason. Whatever the causes, violence as a tool for political change, the anarchist "propaganda of the deed," was by the summer of 1914 a well-recognized means of attempting radical, sudden political change. Archduke Franz Ferdinand would be in good company, notable more for the after-effects of his death than by its method.

GREAT BRITAIN

Britain had its own issues. The Irish campaign for "Home Rule" was designed to create an Irish parliament that would be responsible for domestic affairs. It won the support of Britain's Liberal Party. However, it was opposed by British Tories and the Protestant Unionists in Ulster, who feared that "Home Rule" would mean "Rome Rule"—that is, domination by Irish Catholics. Earlier attempts at passing a Home Rule bill had failed due to opposition by the House of Lords. In 1911, however, the Parliament Act severely reduced the power of the House of Lords. It passed only because the new King George V agreed if needed to create enough Liberal peers to outvote the Tory opposition among the Lords. This radical change divided Britain. After two close general elections, the Liberals were only able to form new governments by allying with the Irish Nationalists on the condition that they support Home Rule.[24]

With Home Rule seeming to be a real possibility, Ulster Unionists formed their own military groups, the Irish Volunteers, and threatened to resist Home Rule by force. In the meantime, Irish Volunteers were formed in the rest of Ireland to fight against the Unionists. Many of these volunteers did not want Home Rule, but full independence. While the British military was strong enough to crush such homegrown resistance, it would mean civil war, and it was not certain how many British officers would agree to fight their fellow citizens. The Third Home Rule Bill, with some compromises designed to appease Ulster's opposition, passed the House of Commons in June 1914 and the House of Lords in July.

The bill received royal assent in September 1914 but was placed on hold until after the war. The length of the war, and the Easter Rising of 1916, meant that the 1914 Home Rule bill was never enacted. After World War I, the Irish Revolution and the following civil war made the issue moot. However, while Europe was watching the Balkan Wars, and the crisis over Archduke Franz Ferdinand's assassination, the British were also looking homeward, nervously wondering if a new civil war was about to break out.

INTERNATIONAL TENSIONS

World War I was part of, and in some cases, the culmination of other armed conflicts in Europe and the worldwide European empires. Even those conflicts not directly related to the outbreak of World War I would become entangled in it, such as the Mexican Revolution (1910–20). Like World War I, these other conflicts were modern, mechanized warfare where the entire population was mobilized. They also presaged the large-scale casualties, refugees, and ethnic hatreds of World War I.[25] These other conflicts also involved the United States to different degrees. The Mexican Revolution was the most significant for DC policy-makers because of its proximity to the United States. The Chinese Revolution interested policy-makers and the public due to the sentimental and emotional ties many Americans felt toward China as well as its effect upon American trade with Asia. The Balkan Wars and the slow collapse of the Ottoman government threatened to involve the United States because of American missionaries in the region that could be threatened by unrest and ethnic and religious violence. Of course, the balance of power in Europe was traditionally of great importance to the United States, mainly as it applied to naval power. Washington also paid attention to European conflicts if they interfered with American trade elsewhere or seemed to threaten American dominance in the Caribbean. The popularity of Alfred Thayer Mahan's writing on naval power and trade had made a strong impact on American policy-makers, especially Theodore Roosevelt, Henry Cabot Lodge, and their allies in the Republican Party, so naval policy was deemed to be of critical importance.

International tensions were reflected in the popular invasion fiction of the era. Novels and short stories centered on an invasion of one's home country by an aggressive foreign enemy were popular not only in the United States but also in Europe and Japan. The stories often turned on a decisive naval battle, in which the home fleet is defeated, leaving the nation open to invasion. This was not entirely unrealistic as far as the United States was concerned. U.S. Navy war plans centered on a decisive naval battle in the Caribbean (against a European power) or the central Pacific (against Japan). While popular fiction and the actual war planning by professionals may seem tangentially related, public fears could easily shape real-life military actions. For example, during the Spanish-American War, public fears of an unrealistically powerful Spanish fleet shelling East Coast American cities forced the Navy to deploy ships to guard the American East Coast that would have been better used hunting the real Spanish fleet in the Caribbean.[26] The ongoing naval arms race between Britain and Germany spilled over into the policies of the other naval powers, including the United States, forcing the other powers to build their naval strength so as not to fall too far behind. The popular invasion fiction did not make tensions worse, but they made war more conceivable by the great powers' populations. It had, to risk using a buzzword, become part of the zeitgeist.

The significance of the international tensions and small wars that involved the major and mid-sized powers is not that they demonstrate the inevitability of a world war. The cause and effects of World War I were nowhere near that simple. However, they did make a more extensive war more likely to start within particular regions and over particular issues. Successful wars against the tottering Ottoman Empire made future attempts to peel territory away more likely. They also made Constantinople much more apt to react with force to protect its weakened territorial integrity. The successful efforts in the Balkans by Serbia, Bulgaria, etc., to increase their boundaries also made future efforts look more doable, and therefore more attractive. Moreover, because some of the territory Serbia coveted was in Austria-Hungary, another aging empire, Belgrade was more likely to look to its north for its next acquisitions. The comparison between taking territory from a weakened government in Constantinople to taking territory from a weakened government in Vienna was obvious to Serbian expansionists.

CONCLUSION

Even at a distance the United States was not unaffected by these factors. Given the existing interests in international trade, and with the traditional American interest in the European balance of power as it related to sea power, a European war that threatened to introduce a new, aggressive Germany as a major naval power to the advantage of Britain would be of great consequence to the United States. With the addition of the Panama Canal, American desire to control the Caribbean became increasingly imperative as well. Fears of German attempts to enter the Caribbean were exaggerated, but nonetheless real. The importance of the United States as potentially the most powerful neutral state in a general European war also drew the attention of European powers who might want to see Washington as an ally or distracted by events closer to home. Hence unrest around the Caribbean basin, especially in Mexico, would become a natural target for any European power who wished to divert the United States. The result was not the inevitability of a world war, but a proliferation of potential flash points and areas where war could break out. Moreover, the worldwide spread of those potential flashpoints meant that the non-European powers, especially Japan and the United States, would be drawn in. In brief, the stage was set for a world war, but it depended on individual decisions to raise the curtain.

The following chapters will discuss Wilson's actions when the United States sent its military into World War I and other flashpoints of the era. Wilson's understanding of the role of commander in chief in early 1913 was at best rudimentary. He would no doubt have disagreed, pointing to his careful reading of *The Federalist* and his multiple sophisticated works on the U.S. government. However, his understanding of what his duties would entail had not yet developed past the organizational basics and the theoretical. The deeper understanding of being commander in chief would come with experience, the real teacher Woodrow Wilson was just beginning to face.

CHAPTER 3

———————◆•◆———————

Veracruz

Woodrow Wilson was sworn in as president of the United States on March 4, 1913. Three weeks before, a military coup had ousted the elected reformist government of Mexico. President Francisco Madero was murdered, and General Victoriano Huerta became the new Mexican president. The outgoing American president, William Henry Taft, had left the question of recognizing the new regime in Mexico City to his successor. Wilson was, however, appalled by the coup. He refused to recognize the new military government, calling it a "government of butchers." Between 1913 and 1914 Wilson continued communicating with Huerta's government through Wilson's representatives and the American chargé in Mexico City, Nelson O'Shaughnessy. Wilson also began quietly backing the revolutionaries, the "Constitutionalists." American customs officials began to be less vigilant in guarding against the Constitutionalists smuggling arms across the border from Texas. At the same time, arms shipments to the Mexican government had to be approved by Wilson, and he began to delay signing their release. The American president's policy, known as "watchful waiting," seemed to be slowly paying off. The revolution against Huerta gained strength, and Wilson sent representatives to both Huerta and the revolutionaries to attempt to arrange the Mexican president's departure and new elections.[1]

Wilson's actions in Mexico illustrate how he maintained control when military actions influenced wider diplomatic interests of the United States. Whereas in Haiti and the Dominican Republic Wilson granted a great deal of independence to the military commanders on the scene, in Mexico he maintained a tight rein over even some tactical decisions. Because intervention in Mexico threatened to spiral into a wider war against the strategic and diplomatic interests of the United States, Wilson denied his commanders the independence they may otherwise have wished for.

HUERTA DEFIES WILSON

Wilson's "watchful waiting" and support for the Constitutionalists had weakened Huerta but had not forced him from office. By early 1914 Wilson began to ponder resorting to military force. His opportunity came in April 1914. On the afternoon of Good Friday, April 10, 1914, there was a minor incident at the port of Tampico in which several American sailors were briefly arrested. Tampico was an essential port for the export of Mexican oil. Huerta's forces still held it, but Constitutionalist forces were right outside the city. Several foreign navies had ships in the harbor watching the situation, including the United States. Traveling in a whaleboat flying two U.S. flags, an American naval officer accompanied by several sailors landed at a pier in Tampico to make a routine purchase of gasoline. Mexican soldiers on the dock arrested them for being in a restricted area. The Americans were then marched at gunpoint through the town by the Mexican soldiers. When they were presented to the town's commander, he was horrified, releasing them with a profuse apology and promises of punishment for those responsible. Seemingly, the incident was over.[2]

The American commander in the area, Rear Adm. Henry Mayo, was dissatisfied with the Mexican response. There were multiple warships in

Tampico harbor, including those from the United States, Britain, France, Germany, and Spain. Mayo surveyed the commanders of the other foreign ships in Tampico Harbor: the Mexicans had not declared martial law, nor had they made the docks off-limits for foreigners. As such, the U.S. whaleboat and its small crew were within their rights to land to make a purchase. Incensed, Mayo demanded yet another apology. He also demanded the Mexicans fire a salute to the American flag to make the situation even trickier. He gave them a deadline of only twenty-four hours. Having made his demands, Mayo wired Rear Adm. Frank Fletcher, commander of American naval forces at the port of Veracruz, informing him about the situation. Fletcher passed along the message to Washington without comment.[3]

It was Easter weekend when the cable arrived and so only slowly made its way through official channels. Nelson O'Shaughnessy, the American chargé in Mexico City, embarrassingly learned of Mayo's demands when told the next day by a friend in the Mexican Foreign Office. O'Shaughnessy decided to try to calm matters as quickly as possible, anxiously seeking out Huerta, with whom he was on good terms. Huerta immediately apologized and promised additional punishment for those responsible. To O'Shaughnessy, the incident seemed to be finished.[4]

It might have ended here had Wilson not been already out of patience with Huerta. Personal anxiety also probably played a role. When Wilson heard of Mayo's demands, he was not at the White House, but at a health retreat in White Sulfur Springs, West Virginia, with his wife, Ellen, who was in poor health and getting worse. She would pass away less than four months later from kidney disease. Worried about his wife and separated from his advisers, Wilson lost his temper. He sent Secretary of State Bryan a cable, "Mayo could not have done otherwise . . . unless the guilty persons are promptly punished, consequences of the gravest sort may ensue." In a calmer light, the situation was ludicrous. The United States was now demanding that a government it did not recognize fire a salute to honor the American flag over a trivial incident. Huerta agreed to order the salute, but only if the United States agreed to fire a simultaneous salute to the Mexican flag. Wilson refused.[5]

Meanwhile, Wilson was simultaneously trying to reassure the American press that the United States was not going to war with Mexico while also asking the State Department for a memorandum on the president's constitutional right to use force. The new State Department counselor, Robert Lansing, answered with a report covering previous American administrations that used military reprisal in diplomatic confrontations. The shelling of Greytown, Miskito Kingdom (Nicaragua) in July 1854 left the largest impression on Wilson. After an American citizen was arrested on an American ship by local soldiers, the USS *Cyane* had bombarded the town, and Marines landed to burn what was left. The area was under British protection, but the British commander in the area issued only a weak protest.[6]

Having been assured there were proper legal precedents, Wilson began to plan to use the military as a tool to oust Huerta. On April 19, Huerta again refused to order the salute. On Monday, April 20, Wilson notified congressional leaders that he was determined to use force if Huerta continued his defiance. In a public statement, Wilson had decried Huerta's "repeated offenses against the rights and dignity of the United States."[7] The crisis also ended opposition to armed intervention by Bryan and Daniels, joining Secretary of War Garrison in support. Unbeknownst to Bryan and Wilson, Garrison's War Department had been planning for such an occasion. Assistant Secretary of War Henry Breckinridge noted in a letter the department's frustration, "My own chief [Garrison] has had to bear the entire brunt of fighting alone for a policy that is consistent with national dignity and military safety." The War Department and the Navy Department both prepared for a possible war. They did so quietly, fearing, with justification, that both Wilson and Bryan would have been horrified by the extent of necessary war planning during peacetime.[8]

Congress quickly took up a resolution declaring that Wilson was "justified in the employment of armed forces of the United States to enforce demands made on Victoriano Huerta." Republican senator Henry Cabot Lodge sneered at Wilson's message requesting congressional approval as "weak and insufficient, although of course well expressed." It was not the use of force that bothered Lodge and his allies, but that Wilson wanted to strike at Huerta for some minor offenses while ignoring far more significant damage done to American property elsewhere in Mexico during the revolution. Nonetheless, the House passed the resolution on the evening of April 20 by a vote of 337 to 37. Lodge delayed passage by attempting to insert an amendment that would have justified intervention against every faction in Mexico. Lodge's amendment failed, but it delayed matters long enough for the situation to be overtaken by events. While the Senate argued, the crisis came to fruition not in Tampico, but Veracruz.[9]

Veracruz

On the evening of Monday, April 20, Wilson, Daniels, and Garrison met with their military commanders to approve plans to seize not just Tampico, but also Veracruz. Moreover, the U.S. Navy would blockade both of Mexico's coasts, and perhaps even launch an expedition from Veracruz to Mexico City to oust Huerta. It would take a week for the U.S. Atlantic fleet to reach the Mexican Caribbean coast.[10] Mere hours after being approved the plan was abandoned as new information reached Washington. In the early morning hours on April 21, William Canada, the American consul in Veracruz, cabled the State Department that a German cargo ship, the *Ypiranga*, would arrive that day with a large delivery of arms for Huerta's army. Canada had informed Washington on April 18 that he had heard reports of the shipment. Now he had confirmation that the ship would land the next day. Over 1,200 freight cars and 20 locomotives, Canada claimed, were already at the port, waiting for the arms shipment.[11] As soon as Bryan read the message from Canada, he rushed to call the president. Wilson, Bryan, Garrison, and Daniels held a hastily organized telephone conference. Huerta would not be allowed to receive these arms. Under international law, however, the United States could not legally seize either the *Ypiranga* or its cargo without first declaring a blockade. Such a blockade required a formal declaration of war, but since the United States had not done so, they could not blockade Mexico, despite earlier plans to do exactly that. Moreover, until the cargo was unloaded it legally was on German territory. Seizing it would cause an international incident with Berlin. Not to be deterred, Wilson found an elaborate rationale for legally seizing the shipment. Once on the docks, the cargo belonged to Huerta's Mexican government. Since the United States did not recognize Huerta's legitimacy, Wilson decided he could legally order the shipment's seizure on the docks. At 4 a.m. on April 21, Secretary of the Navy Josephus Daniels ordered the Navy to take the Veracruz customs house.[12]

We have discussed Wilson's childhood experiences in the Civil War, and his desire not to send men into combat unless necessary. Why then did he choose to use military force in such a seemingly cavalier way in the early hours of April 21, 1914? The explanation lay in part within the intelligence that Wilson was receiving. His distrust of Ambassador Wilson was justified, and the ambassador had been recalled, and relieved of his post, earlier. Wilson's similar distrust of the American chargé in Mexico City, Nelson O'Shaughnessy, was not as reasonable.

O'Shaughnessy was friends with Huerta and did not support Washington's preference for the Constitutionalist revolutionaries, but he did his best to carry out Wilson's policies. Wilson relied on his channels of information, in this case, an amateur diplomat named John Lind. Wilson had sent Lind to meet Huerta in August 1913, not as an official diplomat, but as Wilson's representative. Lind was an unusual choice for the role. He spoke no Spanish and had some anti-Catholic prejudices. A former Republican turned Democrat over the gold/silver issue of the 1890s, Lind was a Bryan supporter. He served as Minnesota's governor from 1899–1900, and Wilson had considered him as a possible ambassador to Sweden, but Lind had refused. His main virtue was that he could be trusted to carry out Wilson and Bryan's policies. He had quickly worn out his welcome in Mexico City, and ended up in Veracruz, where he passed information of varying reliability back to Washington, urging the administration to be more proactive in helping the revolutionaries.[13]

Lind optimistically assured Wilson that the Mexican army would not fight: "To dispose of the present regular army will be an easy task. If the officers command 'break ranks' and say 'shoo' they will scatter and never be heard of again except as inmates of jails and almshouses." Wilson also assumed that Mexicans would greet as allies American military forces fighting a common enemy—General Huerta. As a result, the United States could seize Veracruz customs house with little or no resistance. Causalities would be light or nonexistent.[14] To be fair to Lind, he was not completely wrong. Much of Huerta's military did pull out of Veracruz without a fight, but after they were ordered to do so by Mexico City. Some, however, had already deployed, and they remained to fight the occupation. To Wilson's shock, it was the very people he was trying to help, Veracruz's civilian population, who did most of the fighting to stop the invasion. Wilson's naivete would be costly, and he should have known better. American ham-fisted diplomacy under Taft had already sparked riots targeting U.S. citizens living in Mexico in 1911 and 1912. As an author of multiple histories of the United States, Wilson was also aware of how Mexican resisted American invasions during the Mexican-American War (1846–48). In this instance, however, Wilson was unable to see how other actors would judge his actions. The result was costly to both Mexicans and Americans.[15]

While Veracruz was not the first time Wilson had to make military decisions, it is a good example illustrating how Wilson viewed the U.S. military as one tool to achieve broader objectives: assisting political change in another country. From the start, it was clear that Wilson and his cabinet secretaries would be handling the military differently than had Roosevelt or Taft. When Wilson decided to intervene in Tampico to enforce Mayo's demands, the decision was his alone. Bryan vacillated, and by this point, Wilson was used to Bryan's hesitancy to use force and Garrison's willingness to do so. Wilson and his cabinet members did, in this instance, consult the military first, learning more about the details of the original event at Tampico, and then on the tactics of seizing the ports. For example, they asked the General Board about the rights of foreign navies in Tampico. The report, submitted by Rear Admiral Fiske, detailed the various ways in which the Mexican military had violated standard procedure and neutral rights when they arrested the American sailors who had attempted to purchase oil. Not only was the memo read by the civilian leadership, but it was also used in dealing with Huerta. Bryan even borrowed phrases from it in his notes to Mexico City. Likewise, the State Department relied on the Navy's advice on the proper procedure for saluting another nation's flag. Was it normal, for example, for a flag salute to always be returned? Would doing so imply recognition of Huerta's government? The Navy assured the State Department that a return salute was given to the other nation and did not imply diplomatic recognition of its government.[16]

As Richard Challener noted in his book on military leadership and American foreign policy, while the General Board was able to influence Wilson's policies, at least on their edges, the commanders at the scene were given no such opportunity.[17] When Rear Admiral Fletcher was sent to Tampico in November 1913, he was explicitly told that he was under no circumstances to land his forces unless Washington approved beforehand. Even then, the admiral had first to notify Wilson and Daniels that there was no other way "to save the lives of Americans and other foreigners."[18] This tight control from Wilson to Fletcher also applied to information. Fletcher justifiably complained that the administration gave him only vague instructions. He sent a representative to Daniels to personally request briefings on American policy. Fletcher even kept an aide in the American embassy in Mexico City so as to not be blind-sided by Washington's sudden turns on Mexican policy.[19]

Wilson needed as much advice as he could find on military matters. His administration's naivete sometimes demonstrated itself clearly, as when in mid-April 1914 Wilson suggested that the United States might install a "peaceful blockade" of Mexico. The General Board informed the administration that there was no such thing as a "peaceful blockade," at least not an effective one. Shippers could simply switch their goods to ships flying the flags of other countries. Moreover, they noted that using military force would require prior congressional approval and that they did not think taking control of a customs house or two, or even the entire port, would be useful. Such actions would be an act of war and would cost lives without being effective. They recommended a full "belligerent blockade." It would "be effective and least likely to cause international complications."[20]

The General Board went further, recommending a full-scale war. The United States would occupy Tampico and Veracruz. Then the U.S. Army would march on Mexico City. Essentially, they recommended a replay of Gen. Winfield Scott's 1847 campaign from the Mexican-American War. They went further, well into the realm of what Wilson would have considered his purview. The General Board provided Fiske with additional talking points to go along with the formal memo. They suggested that even if Huerta somehow decided to meet American demands that the U.S. Navy should still remain in Mexican waters. Moreover, they noted that American demands should include reparations "for past insults and injuries to Americans and foreign persons and property." These demands should also apply to the Constitutionalists. Finally, the United States should demand that Huerta resign. These talking points went well beyond the role Wilson assigned to the General Board, crossing into diplomatic and political questions. Gen. Leonard Wood, chief of staff of the U.S. Army, thought the blockade useless, and sneered that the Navy was too worried about losing one of their precious new battleships to assault Tampico or Veracruz directly.[21]

Before the General Board's recommendations could be presented, Huerta rejected Wilson's demands, and news of the *Ypiranga*'s arrival reached Washington. After addressing Congress on the 20th, Wilson, Bryan, Garrison, and Daniels meet Rear Admiral Fiske and General Wood. By then, it was clear that the focus had switched from Tampico to Veracruz. The Army pushed to occupy the port city. What to do about Tampico remained undecided even as Mayo's ships moved south toward Veracruz. When Wilson's orders arrived at Fletcher's command, they said only to take the customs house and the nearby dock. Wilson had chosen only a minimal objective. It was up to the military to make it happen.

LANDING TROOPS

The actual landings were quickly thrown together. It was at this juncture that the administration's inexperience clashed with the hidebound nature of military planning as it existed in the United States in 1914. Wilson's expectation that there would be no resistance to the landings was certainly optimistic, but then in some respects so was the Army's established Mexican Plan. The former assumed that the citizens of Veracruz would see the Americans as helpful allies and not invading Yankees. The latter assumed that there would be an organized, recognized government in control of Mexico so a single quick campaign by the U.S. Army from the port city to seize Mexico City would end the crisis quickly. Instead, the situation on the ground was chaotic beyond even the normal chaos of battle. Not only did the United States refuse to recognize the regime in Mexico City, there was no declaration of war, and revolutionary groups controlled much of the country. Additionally, the Army had not looked beyond their own maps and organizational charts to consider the role of the State Department. Once the Marines and Bluejackets seized Veracruz, there were now thousands of Americans and other foreigners trying to flee Mexico City for Veracruz and other ports. Finally, there were no plans to keep an occupied city operating without the locals cooperating. A Mexican law dating back to 1867 made it a capital crime to Mexican citizens to cooperate with an invading force. Collecting customs, keeping the electrical system running, or patrolling the streets were not worth risking facing a firing squad with only a blindfold and last cigarette. So, there were few if any Mexicans willing to continue their civilian jobs to keep Veracruz operating. After the landing, as the military scrambled to bring some order to the occupied city, Maj. Gen. Tasker Bliss, on station along the border in Texas, sent an angry telegram to the War College blistering the unrealistic plans that had so hampered the Army.[22]

Wilson did not help matters. He apparently did not ask his military commanders how best to carry out his orders to occupy just the dock and customs house, putting Rear Admiral Fletcher in a difficult bind. Following Wilson's orders to seize the arms after they left the ship, before they were loaded onto Mexican railcars, would take precise timing, assuming they were not loaded directly onto the waiting railcars from the *Ypiranga*. To add yet another complication, if Fletcher landed his men too soon, it would alert the *Ypiranga*'s captain who could divert his ship 125 miles to the south to Puerto Mexico, in which case all the U.S. Navy legally could do is watch the German vessel sail away. Fletcher's decision to begin the occupation was forced not by the arrival of the anticipated *Ypiranga*, but by an approaching storm that might prevent his men from landing safely. As the American commander at the scene, Fletcher gave the order. Shortly before noon, American sailors and Marines launched from several American warships in the harbor. A few minutes later, they landed on the Veracruz pier. They now controlled the docks and soon held the customs house. But had they acted too early? Where was the *Ypiranga?*[23]

There was no resistance at first. Curious civilians lined the docks, including one American woman waving a small U.S. flag. Meanwhile, another storm, this time in the form of Mexican resistance, was gathering. American consul Canada had notified the local Mexican commander, General Gustavo Maass, of what the United States intended to do. Wilson told Canada to assure the Mexicans that the U.S. troops would seize only the customs house; they would not move further into the city. They hoped, Canada said, that Mexicans would not resist.[24] Unfortunately, the United States did not take General Maass seriously, judging him on his appearance. The Mexican commander looked like a Vaudeville stock version of a Latin American general with a carefully groomed mustache and uniform designed to copy Germany's Kaiser Wilhelm.[25] While his appearance may have amused Americans, Maass acted quickly. On his orders, his men began distributing rifles and ammunition to Mexican civilians and even to inmates from the Veracruz prisons. This was not quite as cynical as it may seem, leaving civilians to face better-trained American sailors and Marines. Huerta's government had trained men in the cities as reservists, supposedly to guard against an American invasion. Whether or not Huerta actually feared a Yankee invasion, or if it were a way to use an outside threat to garner support, in this instance it worked. Now there really was an American invasion coming, one announced by the Americans themselves. Once the weapons were distributed, Maass followed his orders. Some of the regular troops had already deployed, moving toward the docks, but the Mexican commander withdrew most of his forces out of the city, destroying the railway tracks behind them as they went. They formed new defensive lines about eleven miles beyond city limits.[26]

As the American Bluejackets and Marines milled about the docks wondering what to do next, Mexican snipers opened fire from nearby rooftops. A battle erupted, and the Americans found that they had to occupy the entire city to establish order. By the end of the first night, the United States controlled the customs house and the docks. They might have remained there, but snipers continued to fire into American lines. The ships from the U.S. Atlantic fleet under Vice Adm. Charles Badger arrived. Although he was the senior officer, Badger let Fletcher continue command. As searchlights from the American warship lit the seaside part of the city, reinforcements landed. The next day American forces took the remainder of Veracruz, often through house-to-house fighting. Strong Mexican positions, such as the naval school next to the docks, were effectively shelled by American warships. By the evening of the second day, the city was under American control.

At the end, there were nineteen dead Americans. More than two hundred Mexicans were killed although no official count was ever made of Mexican casualties. Under the hot Veracruz sun, both sides disposed of the bodies as quickly as possible. The Americans stacked the Mexican dead in public squares near the docks and burned them. The losses stunned Wilson. When he appeared before the press to announce the casualty figures, Wilson appeared "shaken" and "pale" to the newspapermen present. White House physician Dr. Cary Grayson remembered that Wilson told him, "The thought haunts me that it was I who ordered those young men to their deaths." Wilson had Daniels assemble a list of the American casualties including their names and ages. The list brought home to the commander in chief in unmistakably real terms the potential cost of committing troops into battle, even a small one.[27]

A WIDER WAR?

Anger erupted all across Mexico. In Mexico City, a mob pulled down a statue of George Washington, dragging it through the streets. Back in Washington, the members of the Mexican embassy in Washington asked for their passports. Secretary of State Bryan tearfully tried to dissuade them—their action, he cried, "means war."[28] The angry reaction suggested to Wilson that America might find itself at war with every Mexican faction, even with the Constitutionalists Wilson was trying to help. The spread of ever more fantastic rumors heightened the tension. The American attaché in Mexico City reported as fact a rumor that 15,000 troops belonging to revolutionary Emiliano Zapata had ridden into the capital to join Huerta. Actually, Pancho Villa and Venustiano Carranza privately decided not to attack American forces so long as the United States remained outside of Constitutionalist-held areas.[29]

The possibility of a full war with Mexico raised concerns in the White House over Wilson's order in January 1914 to lift the arms embargo, which allowed the revolutionaries to openly buy arms in the United States. If the United States went to war with all the Mexican factions, these arms could be used against American servicemen. Wilson hesitated to reinstate the ban, knowing it would benefit Huerta. He apparently hoped no one would notice. However, in an off-the-record press conference just days after the Veracruz landing reporters asked the president if the Constitutionalists were still buying American weapons. Wilson pretended not to know. The embargo was reinstated the next day.[30] Understandably, the Constitutionalists objected. The embargo hindered them and helped Huerta. A frustrated Pancho Villa suggested that Washington issue his Northern Division enough ammunition for a single battle at a time. Lind argued with Wilson and apparently reached some sort of agreement. Lind passed word to the Constitutionalists that the United States would not interfere with their shipping arms by sea. Afterward multiple ships supposedly sailing between Galveston, Texas, and Havana, Cuba, began to be "blown off course" to Tampico, now held by the Constitutionalists.[31]

Another question remained—what to do with Veracruz? While a simple immediate withdrawal would ease tensions, it would also reopen the port for Huerta's arms shipments. Fortunately for Wilson, Argentina, Brazil, and Chile—the "A.B.C." powers—offered to mediate between Washington and Mexico City. Wilson immediately accepted. Huerta hesitated. None of the A.B.C. powers had recognized his government. However, with his situation looking increasingly unstable, mediation presented at least a possibility of maintaining power through a compromise agreement. What would Argentina, Brazil, and Chile get from the talks? They favored anything that reduced U.S. intervention in a Latin American state. The

talks also opened up the possibility of establishing a compromise provisional government that would not embrace the more radical reforms
suggested by some of the revolutionaries, such as breaking up substantial
land holdings in favor of small producers. Such reforms might set an
uncomfortable precedent to the rest of the region. The conference opened
on May 20 on the Canadian side of Niagara Falls. The Constitutionalists,
while invited, did not participate.[32]

Wilson's representatives sent him regular reports. They had strict
instructions not to agree to any settlement that did not recognize the
Constitutionalists as the ruling party. Their eventual victory, Wilson
said, was "clearly inevitable." Wilson explained,

> There can be no such persons [neutrals] in Mexico among men of
> force and character. All men of real stuff must have taken sides in
> one way or another. . . . The plan, therefore, should be of this sort: an
> avowed Constitutionalist of undoubted character and ability, other
> than Carranza or Villa, should be made provisional President and
> should be personally charged with the formulation and promulgation
> of the necessary and inevitable reforms as a duty to which he would
> be definitely pledged beforehand. . . . We should in no circumstances
> outline or even suggest the details of the reforms.[33]

Constitutionalist leader Venustiano Carranza refused to accept open
American support. He sent representatives to Buffalo, New York, to meet
with the American delegates, but to keep an eye on them rather than to
join the conference. The Constitutionalists bluntly refused any American
assistance. As one U.S. member wired to Bryan, the Constitutionalist
delegates would refuse "anything from the mediators . . . even if it is
something they [the Constitutionalists] want. . . . They wouldn't even
accept it if it were offered to them on a golden platter."[34]

The conference continued, and Wilson kept a firm grip on the U.S.
military in Veracruz. Once it was safely in American hands, Wilson had
moved to quickly take "control of the situation."[35] The unexpected (at
least to Wilson) deaths and international condemnation made Wilson
pull back. Plans for a blockade of all the Mexican ports were abandoned.

When the military began to push for expansion beyond the city limits, even as far as to take Mexico City, Wilson refused. His tight leash yanked them back and gave very strict, restrictive orders to not move beyond the outskirts of Veracruz any further than was necessary. Wilson said,

> You are under no circumstances extend those limits [of the occupied city] beyond these necessities and that you do not initiate any activities or bring about of your own initiative any situations which might tend to increase the tension of the situation . . . without explicit orders and directions from the Secretary [of War]. Even should your judgment indicate that something other than what is now being done should be done you will before acting communicate fully with the department and await instructions. Of course, the Secretary appreciates that an unexpected emergency respecting our defense may arise under which you may have to act without delay, but he wishes you to clearly understand that the emergency must be grave.[36]

The Army took over Veracruz from the Navy and Gen. Frederick Funston was put in command. Funston wanted to advance further into Mexico and went so far as to send alarmist reports about nonexistent Mexican threats to American positions. He especially chafed at being forbidden to send reconnaissance patrols beyond his set position: "If a disaster should result, I must not be held responsible." Growing ever more impatient he informed Washington that a group of "foreigners and citizens in Mexico City will unite in request that U.S. troops occupy the city to prevent massacre and pillage by Zapata." "Merely give the order," Funston wired the administration, "and leave the rest to us."[37]

General Funston had an ally in Secretary of War Garrison, who was also pressing for further action. The secretary of war began investigating how to acquire troop transports, but quietly, so as not to raise concern as the A.B.C. arbitration conference had already begun. Some parts of the American press joined in, especially Hearst's chain of newspapers. They consistently blared out vivid headlines about Mexican atrocities, real and imagined.[38] Wilson probably tuned out these voices calling for intervention, having little regard for the accuracy of the press. The notable exception among the American press was the *New York World*. Frank Cobb, the *World*'s editor, met Wilson multiple times at the White House.[39] As for his own cabinet officers, while Wilson did respect Garrison's opinion, he also knew that his secretary of war would endorse intervention, just as Bryan would argue against it. Colonel House noted in his diary entry for April 28, 1914, that Wilson observed that the opinions in the cabinet "shaded off" from Garrison urging intervention as "the one extreme to Bryan on the other. Bryan had talked to [Wilson] as much concerning peace and always with the same set speech, that [Wilson] no longer had to listen."[40]

Wilson refused to allow the military to move further into Mexico, and Funston settled in to run the city. Because of the harsh laws forbidding Mexican citizens from cooperating with invaders, Funston had to staff much of the local administration with Americans. He declared martial law and raised the American flag over the city. The local market was thoroughly cleaned, and prostitution was regulated with regular medical inspections. Remaining political prisoners in the jails were freed. The occupying forces collected Mexican customs fees and taxes, which were set aside to turn over to whatever Mexican government finally established itself. They even issued their own postage stamps.[41]

On May 11, there was a ceremony and parade in New York City to honor those Americans killed at Veracruz. Wilson was determined to attend. His advisers were worried about his safety: he had received threatening letters and would be vulnerable while riding in an open carriage in the parade. Wilson insisted on attending and fully participating. It was his duty, he insisted, to honor the fallen. He was their commander in chief, and he had been the one to order them into Veracruz. On that Monday morning, seventeen coffins were unloaded from the battleship *Montana*, each placed on its own gun caisson. The solemn procession began at the Battery, with Wilson riding in an open carriage tipping his hat to the thousands lining the route. The procession stopped at New York's City Hall where Mayor John Purroy Mitchell said a few words, then laid a wreath on one of the coffins. He joined Wilson in his carriage, and they crossed the Manhattan Bridge to the Brooklyn Naval Yard for the official memorial ceremony. Secretary Daniels said a few words, then read the names of those killed at Veracruz. Wilson then spoke. He told those in attendance that the men they were honoring had died to help Mexicans find their way to freedom. Wilson described war as "a sort of dramatic symbol of a thousand forms of duty." There was no pride in death in a war of aggression, he noted, but to die in a war of service was glorious.[42]

CONCLUSION

Veracruz was a shock to Wilson, a learning experience for the inexperienced commander in chief. The determined armed resistance had been a surprise to Wilson. So, too, was the need to occupy the entire city once fighting had begun. Moreover, Wilson and his civilian leadership—Bryan, Daniels, and Garrison—did not consider the consequences of changing the military target abruptly from Tampico to Veracruz. It set a pattern that Wilson followed closely for the remainder of his administration. He relied on the military for advice about tactical matters but kept very tight control over anything that had to do with politics, diplomacy, or even a more comprehensive strategy.

What about the arms shipment? About an hour after Americans began landing, the *Ypiranga* arrived. It was met by the U.S. battleship *Utah*. An American officer informed the civilian ship's captain that they had taken the customs house to stop Huerta from receiving the arms shipment. The captain agreed to remain where he was, anchoring in the outer harbor within range of the *Utah*'s guns.[43] When the Americans examined the *Ypiranga*'s manifest they found the reports of the contents were correct. There were over 1,300 cases of arms and ammunition. To their surprise, however, most of the *Ypiranga*'s shipment was not from Europe, but had originated in New York. Huerta's regime had attempted to bypass the American arms embargo by purchasing from a New York company using a Maine packing house as a middleman. The shipment was then sent to Mexico via European ports on the Black Sea. With no legal authority to keep the *Ypiranga* in port, the German ship was allowed to leave. It docked at the southern port of Puerto Mexico (now Coatzacoalcos) where the cargo was unloaded. It was too late to help Huerta. The American middleman who arranged the shipment, John W. deKay, was never paid.

After the revolution deKay filed a claim with the Mexican-American Claims Commission for reimbursement. It was rejected.[44]

The fact that the *Ypiranga* was a German ship was vital to understanding Wilson's reasoning. It made the shipment initially appear to be an effort by Berlin to support Huerta over Washington's objection. The Wilson administration was already sensitive to fears of German influence in the Caribbean and Central America. It was not just the *Ypiranga* that worried the Wilson administration either. A few weeks later, in early May 1914, the State Department instructed the U.S. embassy in Tokyo to investigate reports that the Germans were using Japanese middlemen to ship arms to Mexico via the Hamburg-American Line. The State Department did not find evidence of such shipments.[45] Indeed, as Nancy Mitchell argued in *The Danger of Dreams*, Berlin was trying to be as accommodating as possible in Mexico, even if their ambassador to Mexico, Paul Von Hintze, sometimes went against German policy. The problem for Berlin was that they did not always understand Wilson's policy toward Mexico nor did the Wilson administration understand what Berlin was trying to do. While a detailed examination of these issues is outside the range of this study, it does reflect the poor intelligence that both sides were receiving about the other, and this would inevitably affect military policy as well.[46]

Huerta did not remain in power long after Veracruz, but military developments in Mexico decided events rather than the Niagara conference. On July 2, 1914, the conference adjourned without resolution. At that point three different Constitutionalist armies were advancing on Mexico City. General Pancho Villa took Zacatecas and General Álvaro Obregón captured Guadalajara. Huerta was running out of men, arms, and money. The loss of customs money collected at both Veracruz and Tampico prevented him from buying more supplies. The arms from the *Ypiranga* reached Puerto Mexico, but because of the different railways gauges in the area could not easily reach Mexico City. Members of Huerta's government began to flee into exile. On July 9 Huerta appointed Chief Justice Francisco Carbajal foreign minister, thus making him his successor. Carbajal was a "neutral" serving whoever was in control in Mexico City. The Constitutionalists regarded "neutrals" as collaborators and so continued their advance on the capital. On July 15 Huerta resigned, departing into exile on the German warship *Dresden* from Puerto Mexico. With Huerta gone, President Carbajal attempted to negotiate a peaceful occupation of Mexico City with the Constitutionalist armies. Back in Washington Wilson was "jubilant." He nonetheless sent a message to Carranza telling him that the United States would not recognize a new Constitutionalist government that failed to negotiate with Carbajal for a peaceful transfer of power.[47]

The situation was not as simple as Wilson seemed to believe. The Constitutionalists had been allies united against a common foe. With that enemy gone, their alliance quickly collapsed. With American forces still occupying Veracruz the revolutionaries began fighting among themselves in the "War of the Winners." The United States pulled out of Veracruz in November and Carranza's forces moved in. The arms still stockpiled in the warehouses, many meant originally for Huerta, were a windfall for Carranza's forces. Between 1915 and 1916, this war would repeatedly cross into American territory and again Wilson would order American troops into Mexico. Wilson was faced with making military decisions on America's borders that would have profound implications around the world, both diplomatic and political.

CHAPTER 4

—◆•◆—

Haiti and the Dominican Republic

I n 1914 Wilson had already committed troops to combat in Mexico. From 1915 to 1916 he would do so south of the border three more times: again in Mexico in the spring of 1916, in Haiti in 1915, and in the Dominican Republic in 1916. The interventions on Hispaniola (Haiti and the Dominican Republic) resulted in Wilson ceding more control to the military over events than in Mexico. However, as with Mexico, he backed military decisions made at the scene, reacting to events as they occurred, but then reasserted control. In each case, he allowed independent action on primarily military matters, while keeping control over the broader national security strategy for himself. In the Haitian and Dominican interventions, Wilson also demonstrated his reliance on gathering intelligence from nongovernmental sources and more official channels, including both diplomatic and military sources. Moreover, Wilson treated Haiti and the Dominican Republic differently than he did Mexico, at least in part because he regarded the latter as being more capable of self-government than either of the Caribbean nations, and as a result was more tolerant of revolutionary unrest, judging it to be the product of a peoples struggling to establish a representative government as opposed to simply looting.

HAITI IN 1914–15

Haiti in 1915 was what we would now describe as a failed state. During just the short period between 1911 and 1915, a half-dozen different men served briefly as president; each was either killed or forced to flee into exile by an interminable series of revolutions. With Haiti ruled by the upper 10 percent of the French-speaking elite, these revolutions relied on the *cacos*, a group of bandits and mercenaries, for their muscle. The term "cacos" derives from the Creole name for a cunning bird of prey that ambushed its victims. The *cacos* were not composed of a particular ethnic group or subgroup, other than being drawn from the 90 percent of the population that was of Creole extraction. Mostly young men, they preyed on the inhabitants of rural villages, especially in the north and east of the country, which were isolated and often beyond of the control of the official government in the capital. Most importantly, the *cacos* represented a convenient and experienced army for hire for would-be presidents. A pattern was set in which an ambitious Haitian general would set up control in an area to the north and east, hire *cacos* soldiers, and declare a revolution. The *cacos* brigands would then be unleashed to fight and loot their way to Port-au-Prince. Once established in the presidential palace, the new president would pay off the *cacos*, and then try to hold onto his position as best he could against the next contender.

Jean Vilbrun Guillaume Sam (1859–1915) was the last of the Haitian presidents during this chaotic time. As commander of Haiti's Northern Division, Sam was one of those who brought President Cincinnatus Leconte to power in the 1911 revolution. Leconte was killed by an accidental ammunition explosion that destroyed the presidential palace in August 1912, although stories persist that it was, in fact, an assassination. He was succeeded by Tancrède Auguste, who died, possibly poisoned, in May 1913. Auguste was briefly replaced by a reformer, Michel Oreste Lafontant.

Lafontant was ousted in a coup led by the mulatto land-owning elite. Emmanuel Oreste Zamor replaced him with the aid of Sam. Zamor held office from February through November of 1914, and was then thrown out of office in his turn in a revolt by Joseph Davilmar Théodore using *cacos*. When Théodore was unable to find the promised cash to pay his *cacos* mercenaries in February 1915, he fled the capital, to be replaced by Sam. Another revolution, led by Dr. Rosalvo Bobo, seemed likely to depose Sam, so the new Haitian president began to jail political opponents. On July 27, 1915, 167 jailed political prisoners, including former-president Zamor, were executed. A new revolution broke out in Port-au-Prince. As an angry mob stormed the presidential palace, Sam fled to the French embassy. The mob then stormed the embassy and searched until they found Sam, who may have been discovered because he could not stifle a persistent cough. He was dragged from his hiding place, beaten unconscious by the enraged crowd, then tossed over the embassy wall to be torn to pieces by those outside. Sam's gruesome end sparked two weeks of chaos (and inspired Eugene O'Neill's play, *The Emperor Jones*). It also led President Wilson to decide to send in the Marines to occupy the ports, and then the rest of the country.

The Wilson administration had been interested in Haiti from the start. Haiti had traditionally been exceptionally protective of its sovereignty, and foreigners were banned by law from owning property. Some non-Haitians worked around this by marrying Haitian women. While the Wilson administration wanted to remove this barrier for American investors, there was little interest in the United States for expanding to Haiti as there seemed to be little prospect for a good return on investment. Other nations, such as Mexico, appeared to have more promise. The most critical point of contention was the Haitian central bank. The National Bank of Haiti was originally a French corporation. In 1910 it was reorganized by an international consortium under American, French, and German control. This new bank took control of Haiti's foreign debts, and all customs collected went directly to the bank. These revenues were first dedicated to paying off the debts, then the remainder (if there was any) was issued to the Haitian government for its regular expenses. This was increasingly a sore point for the short-lived Haitian governments between 1911 and 1915, especially when it was difficult to pay the *cacos*. Washington did not like it because it guaranteed a role to France and Germany, and the United States was unhappy with the influence of European powers in the Caribbean. After World War I the German role, however minor, was especially uncomfortable for Washington. Wilson and Bryan attempted to use the bank as leverage to allow greater control by Washington of Haitian affairs. In 1914 the United States submitted a treaty to President Zamor that would allow the United States to take over Haitian customs and the town of Môle Saint-Nicolas on the northeastern tip of Haiti. The coastal town was a valuable strategic location along the windward passage to the Panama Canal. While Guantanamo Bay in Cuba was a better location for a naval base, the United States did not want a rival power to gain control of the Haitian site.

President Zamor was in an awkward position. Any leader who was thought to have signed away Haitian sovereignty would be quickly overthrown. On the other hand, the revolution launched by Davilmar Théodore was already gaining momentum. Boaz Long, chief of the Division of Latin American Affairs, submitted a memorandum to Bryan and Wilson asserting that the only way to stop the revolving door of Haitian presidents was to take over the customs houses, thus removing the financial lure of revolutions. The proposed treaty was sent to Haiti, where Zamor and his brother, General Charles Zamor, seemed desperate enough to accept it. Anticipating the adverse reaction by other Haitian leaders, General Zamor suggested that if the United States occupied Port-au-Prince, the Haitian government would accept the agreement. In effect, landing U.S. Marines would give the Zamor administration cover for accepting American demands. Such an arrangement would also put the Zamors under U.S. protection. Bryan agreed. Seven hundred Marines were dispatched from Guantanamo. The Marines were ready on July 20, 1914, when fighting broke out in Port-au-Prince. However, by agreement, President Zamor had to request them first. The president and his brother, the general, were in the field. By the time American representatives found Zamor, he was no longer interested in the treaty, as he had arranged a substantial loan from German merchants in Haiti. In October, they changed their minds again. Théodore's revolution was bearing down on Port-au-Prince. Once again American forces were sent to Haiti; this time the force included eight hundred Marines in two groups, one sailing on the transport *Hancock* from Guantanamo and the other on the battleship *Kansas* from the Mexican coast. It was too late. President Zamor resigned and fled on a Dutch ship.[1]

Haiti did not become more stable under President Théodore. The new regime's money difficulties and resentment toward the National Bank remained. So did Wilson's determination to take charge of Haiti's customs house. While the other powers with diplomats in Port-au-Prince recognized the new government—including France, Germany, and Britain—the United States did not. Bryan cabled the American minister, Arthur Bailly-Blanchard, to inform the new regime that the United States would withhold recognition until they agreed to a treaty putting the United States in charge of customs, appoint an American "adviser" to oversee their finances and to agree not to turn Môle Saint-Nicolas over to any other nation's control. Théodore and his foreign minister were considering the idea when word leaked to the Haitian senate. Angry legislators attacked the foreign minister, and he was lucky to escape with his life. Théodore and his remaining cabinet ministers (the foreign minister having understandably resigned) discussed it with Blanchard. They could not agree to American receivership of the customs. Not only would any government that agreed quickly fall from power, but its members might also well be killed. They proposed an American guaranteed loan in exchange for mining concessions and business privileges for American citizens. Wilson refused the offer.[2]

The National Bank had cut off all money to Théodore's administration as punishment for issuing paper money in violation of the agreement with the bank. The National City Bank of New York, which owned a controlling interest in the Haitian bank, asked the U.S. government to preserve the latter's assets in gold stored in vaults at Port-au-Prince—fearing that a desperate President Théodore would seize the gold. When Théodore demanded the gold be turned over, a mob gathered outside the bank. Bank managers asked that the gold be removed and stored elsewhere. On December 17,

1914, sixty-five Marines from on board the gunboat USS *Hancock* landed in Port-au-Prince, marched to the bank, and removed half a million dollars in gold used to secure Haitian government bonds. The gold was escorted by the Marines to the gunboat USS *Machias* for transport to New York. Théodore's administration was not informed until after it was done. In late January, Théodore ordered those future customs deposits be made not to the National Bank, but to specific merchants who happened to be his supporters. This allowed him to purchase a load of coal sitting in an American merchant ship to fuel Haiti's navy, two old gunboats. This would give him an advantage over the revolutionaries as Théodore would have the benefit of being able to quickly move troops and shell rebel-held coastal towns.[3]

The U.S. minister met with Rear Adm. William Banks Caperton to discuss options. They agreed that it would be wise to prepare for military intervention. The admiral ordered the gunboat USS *Wheeling* to Saint-Marc to intervene if rumors were true that Théodore's troops were planning on burning down the town. Caperton wired Washington for more troops, noting that he only had 450 men for a landing force. He asked that the battleship *Montana* be sent from Cuba with two Marine battalions. When reinforcements arrived, Caperton issued an ultimatum to Théodore ordering him to stop his attempts to go around the National Bank of Haiti. Théodore stalled for time, asking for arbitration. By February 1915, matters stood stalemated.[4]

GUILLAUME SAM

After two weeks the Marine reinforcements left, but the stalemate remained. Sensing Théodore's weakness, various Haitian factions began to attempt to enlist Caperton as an ally in another revolution. Caperton rejected these advances, but anxiously wired Washington for instructions: "I urgently request information as to the Government Haytien Policy." It is not that the admiral was opposed to intervention. Rear Admiral Caperton had already devised his plans to occupy Port-au-Prince, and he wired Daniels, "Better class Haytiens [sic] . . . desire American intervention to stabilize government but do not openly promote such ideas for fear of execution by politicians." This latter group Caperton held in disgust, calling them "scheming politicians who promote revolution for their own personal gain."[5] On February 25, the next revolutionary general, Guillaume Sam, entered the capital and became the new president. He began courting American support while also harassing his political enemies among the Haitian elite. He proclaimed martial law and began locking up the young men of the Port-au-Prince elite as political prisoners.[6]

The inevitable revolution against President Sam was much different from its immediate predecessors because both the Sam regime and his opponents knew the United States was carefully watching events. The leading would-be president was Dr. Rosalvo Bobo, who had been Théodore's minister of the interior. At first, his actions fit the typical model. With a revolutionary army, including *cacos*, he occupied Cap-Haïtien. After that initial step, however, the typical sequence of events fell apart. This time President Sam had a capable general of his own, General Probus Blot. General Blot drove Dr. Bobo's forces out of Cap-Haïtien in mid-June 1915. Fearing that the government troops might begin to loot the city and the National Bank of Haiti there, the French consulate requested French marines land to protect their property. Fifty French marines from the cruiser *Descartes* landed and took up positions around the French consulate, the bank, and a monastery operated by a French order. They were ashore for five days before returning to ship. A few days later, the *Washington* arrived. Captain Henri Lafrogne quickly paid an official call on Rear Admiral Caperton and assured him that he was not attempting to supplant American influence in Haiti. Lafrogne was well aware that his landing Marines created all sorts of diplomatic problems. The Haitian resented his landing. The Germans were, understandably, very unhappy with French marines landing in a neutral nation where Germany had financial interests. The United States was very aware of European intrusions into the Caribbean. Caperton politely and diplomatically suggested that the *Descartes* depart. Lafrogne was willing but had not yet received official orders to do so, and he was low on coal. However, he did remain respectfully in the background and let the American admiral take the lead on protecting order and foreign interests.[7]

Caperton took the initiative. He informed both sides, rebels and government commanders, that fighting in the city was forbidden. Cap-Haïtien was neutral ground, a sanctuary city. General Blot was amenable and agreed. Dr. Bobo also agreed. In reality, neither had much choice with the *Washington's* guns in the harbor backing the admiral's words. Caperton set up a radio station at a key position at the local train station. When fighting outside the city threatened to send fleeing soldiers toward Cap-Haïtien, he sent Marines to the road into the city to block the way. More Marines landed to guard the city, and the small gunship *Eagle*, a converted yacht, moved close into shore, where even its small guns overmatched any weapons the Haitians could muster. General Blot objected to what had become a much more blatant violation of his country's sovereignty, but as before, there was nothing he could realistically do. However, when Blot's troops routed Dr. Bobo's small army, the situation promised to right itself. If Bobo were defeated, then Sam's government would be secure, and there would be no need for Caperton's men to remain ashore.[8]

By mid-July it seemed that all was calm. The *Descartes* left Cap-Haïtien on the 12th. On the 15th, Bobo's defeat was confirmed. The *Eagle* left its position at the port city and went to the border area with the Dominican Republic. It returned with news that Bobo was out of money and ammunition. A second government force had joined Blot's and was chasing rebels fleeing toward the border. Rear Adm. William S. Benson, Chief of Naval Operations in DC, wired his congratulations to Caperton, noting, "We hope we will soon be able to permit you to return to your old cruising ground off the Mexican coast." Had this been a fictional tale, the reader would immediately expect some dramatic development, some shocking event. The reality in this case, fits the fictional model. With the traditional model of revolution having been stymied, at least partly because of Caperton, anti-Sam forces launched a coup within Port-au-Prince itself.[9]

On the morning of July 27, radio messages from the capital to the *Washington* carried the news of a coup within the city. Sam had ordered the arrest of any of the city's elites who were suspected of not supporting his administration. His police began arresting not *cacos* or the poor, but the sons of the elite. Hundreds were arrested while others fled to any foreign legation they could find. Still others locked themselves in their homes for fear of going out into the street where they might be arrested or dragooned into Sam's army. Port-au-Prince's chief of police, Charles Devla, arranged a simple plan from within the Portuguese legation, smuggling messages to a few followers. At 4 a.m. on July 27, about thirty men attacked the hundreds of *cacos* guarding the presidential palace. Surprised and confused, the *cacos* briefly fled, but returned to find the coup plotters had control of machine guns. President Sam fled as well. Conveniently the French legation was next to the presidential palace, with a single locked door separating the two. Sam could not open the door and was shot in the leg as he scrambled over the wall onto French territory.[10]

This would have been the end of the matter, but Sam had left orders with General Charles Oscar Etienne, the prison commandant. If there were an attempt to oust or kill Sam, he would kill all the political prisoners. Etienne did so with relish. He and his men went from cell to cell with machetes and pistols, shooting and hacking the prisoners to death, often torturing them for as long as possible beforehand. At one point they left, then returned posing as rescuers, luring survivors out to be killed. When they had finished, they fled to find refuge where they could. When the citizens of Port-au-Prince went to check the prison, they were horrified to find the bloody massacre scene. There were a few survivors, including one man who lay wounded under piles of the dead for hours. Led by the outraged families of the dead, a mob chased down the prison guards. Etienne had taken refuge in the Dominican legation, where he was killed in the doorway by a Haitian father who had found bodies of his three sons in the prison. The French ambassador convinced the mob not to storm his home to find Sam. After all, he reminded them, some of you had taken refuge here before. The mob dispersed. In the morning, however, the ambassador opened his doors and windows to let in the morning air and found a new mob flooding into his home. They found Sam hidden in a bathroom. The ex-president was dragged from his hiding place, beaten, then torn to pieces by the crowd just outside the legation walls. Caperton had set sail on the 27th as soon as he got word of the coup. However, the *Washington* arrived in Port-au-Prince late the morning of the 28th, just as Sam's body parts were being paraded through the city streets. From the bridge of his ship, Caperton watched the people parading Sam's legs, head, arms, and torso around the city. The crowds had seen the smoke from the American warship on the horizon and knew if they were to exact their revenge on Sam, it had to happen before the American warship arrived.[11]

THE U.S. NAVY INTERVENES

The reports from Port-au-Prince were horrific, and no doubt influenced the administration's willingness to intervene. As with Mexico, where the majority of American Navy ships in the Mexican Caribbean ports were at Tampico when suddenly they were needed at Veracruz, when the riots against the Sam regime began in Port-au-Prince on July 27 there were no American warships in the capital's harbor. Caperton immediately decided to land Marines and bluejackets to restore order. The landing was dangerous as the men would be entering the city at dusk, but given the chaos in the streets, Caperton felt he had little choice. Indeed, he did not receive his confirmation order to land until 10 p.m., after his men had already landed. The landing was announced beforehand by two naval representatives who went to the newly formed Committee of Safety. They were told U.S. forces were there to restore order. Civilians were to be off the streets, and no resistance would be tolerated. The landing was completed by 5:50 p.m. and was quickly met by American Capt. Edward Beach (Caperton's chief of staff) and Haitian General Ermane Robin. There was little resistance besides some desultory sniping and a mob that was quickly dispersed without firing. Soon U.S. forces had secured the National Palace and the government buildings in the capital. The next day they advanced into the foreign colony where the legations stood and secured it. Only two bluejackets died, possibly victims of friendly fire. Reinforcements began arriving a day later. By mid-August, when the USS *Tennessee* arrived, there was a full brigade with two thousand Marines ready to secure the entire country under American control.[12]

This might have been the end of it once the disorder from the revolution against Sam had finished. By now, Wilson had had enough of the violence, reluctantly noting, "I suppose there is nothing for it but to take the bull by the horns and restore order." In a memo to Lansing, Wilson compared his dilemma to that facing Roosevelt earlier in the Dominican Republic when his predecessor had taken over the customs house. Wilson fretted that he did "not have the legal authority to do what we apparently ought to do." He asked that the secretary of state contact the secretary of the navy to see if there were enough available forces to take control of Port-au-Prince and the countryside around it. The United States would inform the Haitian congress that the Americans would protect them (evidently from outraged Haitians) but that they must "put men in charge of affairs whom we can trust to handle and put an end to revolution." Finally, if necessary, the United States would step in to run elections to guarantee a "constitutional government."[13] The exact details of military intervention were left up to Rear Admiral Caperton. American Marines quickly occupied the port cities and moved into the south and central parts of the interior. *Cacos* attacks on the north in September 1915 led to an American Marine campaign that drove the Haitian resistance into the mountains along the Dominican border. Resistance would begin again in 1918.[14]

Wilson kept a close eye on the Navy during the campaign as well as on elections and the desired treaty with a new Haitian government. He reviewed the instructions sent to Rear Admiral Caperton about occupying Haiti. The instructions were not focused on military matters, however. Wilson left that to the admiral on the spot. Instead, they directed Caperton to organize and oversee the customs service collection of money. He was not to pay out any of the money except for immediate necessary expenses such as sanitation. Caperton was told to use native "reliable" Haitians as much as possible, but "safeguarded by cooperation of Naval Officers, particularly pay officers." He was to reassure the people that elections would be held when the situation was "nearly normal." Finally, the admiral was instructed when "carrying on a temporary government of affairs [to] comply with established customs and Haytian [sic] law as far as possible."[15]

ESTABLISHING AMERICAN CONTROL OVER HAITI

On August 9, Caperton reported that the Haitian Congress, including Senator Philippe Sudré Dartiguenave, had promised to "accede gladly to any terms proposed by the United States." They would cede the harbor at Môle Saint-Nicolas, grant the right to intervene "when necessary," and give up customs control. They also insisted that the United States protect any new government. Lansing answered that the United States preferred the election of Dartiguenave to the presidency rather than Bobo.[16] The revolutionary Committee of Safety tried to prevent the election by dissolving Congress. Caperton instead told the committee that they no longer had authority and sent "a force" to keep the Chamber of Deputies open, warning Washington that the committee was under the "hostile and disturbing influences of the Bobo and Zamor factions." Dartiguenave was elected president on August 12.[17]

Immediately the United States began negotiating a new treaty with Haiti. Lansing admitted that "this method of negotiation, with our Marine's policing the Haytien [sic] Capital," was "high-handed." From a "practical standpoint," however, "it is the only thing we can do." Wilson agreed. He told sweetheart Edith Galt that "the 'revolutions' of Haiti have no *political* object and no popular aims: they are for plunder purely." He also referred to Dartiguenave as a man chosen with prior approval and "therefore in a sense our man."[18]

Despite the earlier protestations to Caperton, the Haitian congress balked at the treaty. Banning foreign ownership of land in Haiti was an established part of their law, and they resented foreign control of the customs house. Wilson understood their dilemma. He noted that "these poor chaps are between the devil and the deep sea. They dare not offend us" but dared not accept a treaty so insulting to Haitian independence. The United States would, Wilson noted, "insist . . . control of the customs is the essence of the whole matter."[19] On August 30, he told Edith, "Apparently the Haitian authorities are seeking to play fast and loose with us. I am wondering whether to blame them or not!" When the Haitian Congress finally approved the treaty, several members of Dartiguenave's cabinet resigned. Wilson again wrote to Edith that he had a "sneaking sympathy" for them, but that "what we have proposed to be necessary for Haiti's salvation."[20] In effect, the treaty made Haiti an American protectorate, technically independent but under American control.

Note that the order to take over the customs house on August 18 came from Secretary of State Lansing, not from the Secretary of the

Navy. Lansing also ordered the deployment of U.S. forces to protect the American custom's collectors, which Caperton took as justification for intervening with a larger force than Washington seemed to have had in mind. Secretary of the Navy Daniels was not pleased. He asked Caperton to stop, but never actually ordered him to do so. As a result, he had to "accept successive *faits accomplis*, since to recall the Marines would entail tremendous loss of face." The admiral, however, was looking at the military situation, and as he advanced into Haiti, military rule naturally followed. So while Caperton did not create American policy in Haiti, he expanded it on his initiative.[21]

The Dominican Republic

The United States also invaded the Dominican Republic, occupying the rest of the island that the small country shares with Haiti. President Wilson had little to do with American policy toward the Dominican Republic. Secretary of State Bryan was the main driver, but Wilson did have to approve the policy and approve the occupation by U.S. Marines. The issues that lead to American occupation can be traced to the 1905 decision by President Theodore Roosevelt to approve American takeover of the receivership of Dominican customs. This stabilized the small country's debts and ensured domestic peace. Foreign debt claimed 45 percent of the collected money, and another 45 percent went to the Dominican government. The remainder covered the receivership's expenses. This not only curtailed the threat of foreign intervention to collect Dominican debts, it made it more difficult for revolutionary leaders to seize power to loot the treasury.[22]

When unrest did break out again in 1913, no one in the Wilson administration was equipped to handle it. Bryan's clearing of experts from the State Department to replace them with political hires had eliminated much of the institutional memory. The only official Latin American expert was Boaz W. Long, whose sole qualification—besides his political status as a "deserving Democrat"—was owning a business with a branch in Mexico City. Arthur Link describes the Wilson administration's Caribbean policy as "the blind leading the blind."[23] To make the situation even more of a farce, Bryan appointed James M. Sullivan, a New York boxing promoter and lawyer with underworld connections, as the American representative to Santo Domingo. Sullivan was not without connections in the Dominican capital. He was "closely allied with a group of New York financiers, the owners of the *Banco Nacional de Santo Domingo*." So, the new American diplomat's allies in the Dominican Republic were the very group that was trying to take over the country's American receiver-general, in other words, to control the country's finances. The conflict of interest inherent in this appointment would result in Sullivan having a very short career as a diplomat, but only added to an already chaotic situation, making the situation even worse.[24]

THE DOMINICAN CRISIS

José Bordas Valdez's ambitions were the immediate cause of the political crisis. Inaugurated as provisional president in April 1913, Bordas abandoned his promise of a new constitutional convention. He packed his cabinet with political opponents of the Horacistas, the political group who had chosen him as a compromise candidate for provisional president. The most notorious of these was General Desidero Arias, who desired to be president himself. Bordas then began removing Horacistas from prime patronage jobs running the national railroads and giving them to general Arias' men. Horacista leader Governor Jesus Maria Cespedes declared himself to be the new provisional president and gained support from many other leaders in the northern part of the republic. Had the State Department's experts not been purged by Bryan, American policy-makers might have understood Bordas' actions as the catalyst for the revolt. Instead, Boaz Long declared that Horacista party leader General Horacio Vásquez was to blame for the revolution. Bryan quickly concluded that this rebellion against the constitutional leader, Bordas, had to be quashed.[25]

Bryan sent Sullivan as the U.S. representative to the Dominican Republic. It would prove to be an awful choice. Sullivan was to warn Vásquez and Cespedes that Washington would not recognize their regime even if they did take power and that they would withhold customs revenue from them as well. Sullivan also advised that the rebellion would be treated as if it were led by outlaws rather than military leaders. However, the United States would be happy to help with a new, free election. Without much choice, the two revolutionary leaders agreed. For his part, President Bordas agreed with the stipulation that Cespedes would resign as governor of his province, and that the government's blockade of rebel-held ports would continue until the revolutionaries laid down their arms. Bryan was not only in favor of this response, he asked Secretary of the Navy Daniels if the U.S. Navy would help enforce the blockade. Bordas used the opportunity to strengthen his hold on power. When municipal elections were held in November, along with those for a planned constitutional convention to be held in December, Bordas made it clear he had no intention of holding fair elections. His troops arrested opposition leaders and broke up their meetings with armed force.[26]

With his policy in tatters, Bryan turned to Wilson for advice. The president decided to send election observers to the Dominican Republic, although to allow the Dominicans to save face, the observers would go as private individuals, not as an official American delegation. Despite the presence of some thirty-three American observers, Bordas continued his repression in the cities. In the interior, however, where Bordas had little power, the opposition Horacistas won overwhelmingly. Now Bordas and his military controlled the capital but were almost bankrupt and held little territory outside the main cities. With a presidential election scheduled for April, American diplomacy had achieved little but to further muddy the water. Even worse, the Wilson administration had little idea of what long-term policies it should follow besides a very general sense that they wanted to promote a stable, freely elected government. Wilson's inattention to the situation and Bryan's inability were, in short, contributing to a situation that would shortly invite military intervention by the United States.[27]

With few other choices and loath to recognize General Arias' legitimacy lest it encourage a continuing series of revolutions and coups, Wilson was forced to side with Bordas in 1914. The United States increased the Dominican government's monthly allowance from $5,000 to $7,000 for one month so that Bordas could finance his army to defeat Arias' rebellion. This seemed, initially, to be successful. Bordas' forces drove Arias back to his stronghold in the mountains in the west. Promising new elections in June 1914, Bordas won support from various Dominican factions. Sullivan reported that "there is hope for tranquility here, and I believe that in a year the professional revolutionists will have neither a home nor a habitation in the land."[28]

As Arthur Link noted, "Never did a prophet miss the mark more widely." General Vásquez returned from exile and began his rebellion, uniting the different political parties to oust Bordas. By the end of May 1914 much of the country was in complete disorder and Bordas was "totally powerless to cope." Bryan and his advisers were, in Link's words, "lost in bewilderment and ready to adopt any expedient that offered some hope of solution." They considered backing a blockade of the rebels' main port by Bordas, but the latter was unable to enforce it. They began negotiations, with representatives of the different rebel factions and Bordas' regime meeting aboard the cruiser USS *Washington* and the battleship *South Carolina*. The talks failed because Bordas refused to leave office. He was then reelected in uncontested elections held in some of the country's provinces and announced himself as the constitutional president of the Dominican Republic.[29]

THE "WILSON PLAN"

American policy was in complete tatters. Amazingly, Sullivan made matters even worse as he began to send Bryan false reports in the summer of 1914 designed to convince Washington to give full support to Bordas, and, not coincidentally, save the business investments of his brother and friends in the Dominican Republic. Fortunately, by this time the *New York World* had begun publishing a series of stories revealing Sullivan's many conflicts of interest. The *World* was among Wilson's favorite, most trusted newspapers, and the stories guaranteed that Wilson would ignore the corrupt diplomat's reports. Taking advice, at last, from the professional diplomats in the State Department, Wilson developed his plan to resolve the Dominican situation. The so-called Wilson Plan called on the competing factions to lay down their arms and pick someone other than

Bordas to act as provisional president. If the various factions could not agree on a candidate, then the United States "will itself name a Provision President, sustain him in the assumption of office, and support him in the exercise of his temporary authority." There are several points of note in this brief statement. Wilson was careful to call Bordas "Mr. Bordas" to avoid giving him any recognition of his claim of legitimacy as president. Likewise, they referred to Bordas' "present position and authority" without using a title, again to deny any appearance of official recognition. The most striking part is the blithe assumption that the United States could legitimately choose the next provisional president. The "provisional" aspect maintained the illusion that the Dominicans still had the freedom to choose their leader in a free election despite the proviso that "the Provisional president will not be a candidate for President."[30]

The Wilson Plan continued that "at the earliest feasible date" elections for a new president and Congress would be held. American observers of Washington's choosing would "observe the election . . . and that it will expect those observers not only to be accorded a courteous welcome, but also to be accorded the freest opportunities to observe the circumstances and processes of the election."[31] General Desidero Arias, now minister of war, took control of the capital with his troops. The Dominican congress, seeing which way the military winds were blowing, quickly impeached Dominican president Juan Isidro Jiménez. Refusing to recognize the impeachment legality, Jiménez called on his loyal military and demanded Arias turn over control to him. In the meantime, the auxiliary cruiser USS *Prairie*, which had participated in the American occupation of Veracruz a year before, joined the USS *Castine* in the city harbor. Both vessels had Marine units ready to move ashore. Soon fighting broke out between the contending presidents' forces, and Santo Domingo sank into chaos.[32]

THE MARINES LAND

The American occupation began on May 5, 1916. It was a bit disjointed, although "piecemeal" may be a kinder description. Two companies of Marines landed from the USS *Prairie* at Santo Domingo. They quickly seized key police and governmental positions and secured the safety of the American consulate and legation. They also seized Fort San Geronimo (or Jeronimo), which protected the western approaches to the capital city.[33] Two days later the Marines offered protection to the Haitian legation, as Haiti and the Dominican Republic had abysmal diplomatic relations. The legation was vulnerable to attack by angry Dominicans. Meanwhile, the aging Liberal guerilla movement leader Juan I. Jiménez resigned rather than continue in office while he was viewed by his people as an American puppet.[34]

The Wilson Plan was clearly failing, but the administration blamed not their unrealistic expectations, but the Dominicans. With the country sliding into further chaos, the American occupation was almost inevitably going to spread beyond its somewhat limited beginnings. On May 15, Rear Admiral Caperton's forces occupied Santo Domingo. Two weeks later, on June 1, U.S. Marines seized two port cities, Puerto Plata and Monte Cristi. While landings at the latter were unopposed, the Marines had to fight their way into Puerto Plata. Fortunately, the fire from about five hundred pro-Arias irregulars, while heavy, was inaccurate; still, the Marines sustained several casualties, including the first Marine killed in combat in the campaign. From the ports, the Marines began their systematic occupation of the rest of the country. There was little armed resistance from the ill-trained Dominican forces. The most notable exception was on June 27 at Las Trencheras. It was here that a Spanish army had been defeated in 1864, and Dominicans thought the fortification invulnerable. Dominican troops dug trenchworks on two successive hills to block the road to Santiago. American field guns covered a Marine bayonet charge on the defenders' first trench line. Dominican troops retreated to their second lines, rallied briefly, broke, and fled under the fire from the American artillery. The entire battle took about forty-five minutes. One Marine was killed, and four wounded.[35]

Meanwhile, while Jiménez had resigned, his rival, General Desidero Arias, was still in the field with his forces. In July, however, American Marines headed toward the general's stronghold at Santiago de los Caballeros. Arias agreed to cease continued resistance. The would-be Dominican president went into exile.[36] Three days later, additional American forces landed and took control of the remainder of the Dominican Republic over the next two months. On November 29, 1916, the commander of the cruiser force, Capt. Harry Shepard Knapp, imposed a military government aboard his flagship, the USS *Olympia*. Wilson approved the State Department's recommendation that Knapp impose martial law, noting it was "with deepest reluctance . . . but I am convinced that it is the least of the evils in sight in this very perplexing situation."[37] Scattered fighting continued, but by mid-December some American forces were returning to the United States. The Dominican Republic was now primarily under U.S. control. The Navy took over the occupied country's public works while Marines continued " 'anti-bandit' patrols in the countryside."[38]

CONCLUSION

In Haiti and the Dominican Republic, Wilson resorted to military force once diplomatic and political efforts had failed. In both instances these failures were, if not inevitable, highly probable. The flow of intelligence to Wilson from both countries was inadequate and tainted by other interests, especially from American banks with financial interests at stake. The diplomats on the scene were often amateurish, especially Sullivan in the Dominican Republic. Even if they had been professionals and able to influence the Wilson administration's decision-making, their ability to change events was limited. Wilson had yet to learn that other countries' domestic politics were not always responsive to American policy preferences. Wilson's idea of "moral force" had little power to shape overseas events in either Caribbean nation. Nor could diplomacy and the promise of official recognition carry as much policy weight as Wilson desired. Only the blunt instrument of military force proved to be sufficient to impose American will on its smaller Caribbean neighbors. Ironically, even as Wilson was learning the limits of diplomacy in encouraging another nation to move in the direction he desired, the revolutionary Venustiano Carranza government in Mexico was trying to steer Wilson's policy toward his own country. As a result, Mexico and the United States ended up fighting an undeclared border war that repeatedly threatened to become a much bigger conflict.

Bryan drove American policy in the Dominican Republic more than was usual. It was Bryan who picked the American envoy, James Sullivan. The amateur diplomat influenced Bryan's policy by sending numerous misrepresentations designed to get the United States to intervene in such a way as to protect Santo Domingo's largest bank. The different Dominican factions did their best to win the secretary of state's support by promising that they were the ones to bring a "responsible and representative" government to the nation. It is no accident, as Bryan biographer Michael Kazin noted, that once Bryan left office in the spring of 1915, Wilson "abandoned the gentler approach [to the Dominicans] altogether." In Haiti, Bryan followed much the same policy, switching between factions and listening to the reports of an American with financial interests. At least in the case of Haiti the reports came from Roger Farnham, who, although he had substantial financial ties in Haiti, seemed to genuinely have the Haitians' "best interests at heart." Bryan was, in Kazin's words, less inclined to use the "syrupy idealism he vainly sprinkled on the Dominicans." Simply put, Bryan had less confidence that the Haitians could rule themselves than he had for the Dominicans.[39] Security considerations played a role, of course. Even discounting the far-flung fantasies of a German-French alliance to seize Haiti in 1915, just the threat of European intervention in the Caribbean on the route to the Panama Canal would make any American administration wary, regardless of idealistic factors.[40]

Wilson kept the military on a very tight leash in Mexico. Why did he not do the same in Haiti and the Dominican Republic? There he allowed the military not total autonomy, but much more freedom than they enjoyed in Mexico. Why the difference? The key lies within Wilson's view of how societies develop the capacity for democratic self-government. Wilson believed that societies would evolve through multiple stages with representative democracy at the top. Different societies reached each level at their own pace. Wilson believed that every society was capable of reaching the highest stage, that of democratic self-government. However, this did not mean he thought all societies or groups of people would reach the highest level at the same pace, or even in a short time frame. They each had to develop at a pace determined by their history, their leadership, and from the influence and tutelage of those that had reached the higher levels already. Haiti and the Dominican Republic in 1915 were what we would now describe as failed states. In contrast, while Mexico was in revolution, it had been developing economically until the very recent past. The 1911 presidential election had been fair and free. While Wilson would not have described Mexico in early 1913, before Huerta's coup, as having reached the highest level of participatory democracy, he would have described it as further along the evolutionary path than Haiti or the Dominican Republic at the same time. In short, Wilson would have seen Mexico as more civilized than either Caribbean nation and as such was willing to resort to military force, allowing the military to expand its mission beyond the initial reaction to violence on the respective Caribbean capitals. Still, Wilson kept a hand on the reins regarding diplomatic issues, including the choice of new leaders. The military could use force against "bandits" without Wilson's interference, but when it came to political decisions, Rear Admiral Caperton had a voice as one of several advisers. A free rein in military matters did not mean freedom from oversight elsewhere.

CHAPTER 5

The Border War

Between 1915 and 1916, the United States and Mexico fought an undeclared border war as the Mexican Revolution spilled over into its northern neighbor. Different Mexican factions competed for American support, smuggled arms and supplies over the border, and worked to hinder other factions from acquiring such resources. At the same time, a struggle between several different intelligence services—notably American, British, German, and Mexican—worked to aid whichever faction their government favored at the moment while attempting to obstruct the others. The outcome, as one might expect, was chaos. Pancho Villa's March 1916 raid on Columbus, New Mexico, and General Pershing's pursuit of him into Mexico are only the most well-known events of this largely forgotten struggle, but they were by no means the only such raids. As a result, Wilson and his administration had to deal with a fluid situation often involving multiple competing factions in a kind of proxy war.

During this entire period, military actions were overshadowed by diplomatic considerations. Moreover, while there was an overt and apparent military function for the various instances of hot pursuit of Mexican raiders across the border, much of the military maneuvering and postings approved by Wilson were shaped by the diplomatic messages he wished to send. Of course, such messaging can be dangerous, as it can easily limit the military actions each side considers appropriate. Signs of strength or saber-rattling can eliminate delaying further military action as a possible response. They can also elevate the scale of military action each party may consider appropriate. Backing down from the use of force might be interpreted by an opponent as weakness—the same applies to a small-scale, limited use of force. Even if the opposing actor does not take advantage of what they perceive as weakness the first time, the original actor may decide on the next occasion that they must use force lest they be seen as continually only bluffing. Both Wilson and Carranza played the same game, threatening force and moving troops around, risking a war.

CARRANZA AND THE PLAN DE SAN DIEGO

The Wilson administration extended de facto recognition to Carranza's government in the autumn of 1915. Wilson believed that Mexico was capable of establishing a stable government despite the chaos, in contrast to his assumption that Haiti and the Dominican Republic needed a firmer hand to guide them. Carranza proved difficult to deal with, and to the Wilson administration he seemed stubbornly unwilling to accept friendly advice. Hence, the recognition was granted reluctantly and only in the wake of an unwieldy conspiracy. Named the "Plan de San Diego," the conspiracy was an uprising aimed at the United States; it was launched by others, but used by Carranza to pressure Washington. So-named because it was supposedly written on January 6, 1915, in San Diego, Texas, the plan called for an uprising of Mexican Americans in the Southwest. Allied with Native Americans in the region, plan supporters called for a new country to be carved from American territory taken from Mexico in the 1840s. African Americans would get their own independent nation as a buffer state northeast of Mexico. Except for the very elderly, all white males over the age of sixteen in the territory would be killed. Finally, if it were so desired, the new nation could ask to be annexed by Mexico, a twist on how Texas entered the United States after its rebellion. The revolution was scheduled to begin on February 20, 1915.[1]

In 1915 Villa, Carranza, and other Mexican factions were trying to gain American support, so some of Villa's supporters reported the activities of a Huerta supporter named Basilio Ramos to American authorities. Ramos had been recruiting volunteers in Texas for the planned rebellion when he was arrested. Justice Department officials examined the documents seized with him. Alarmed, they tried, unsuccessfully, to arrest additional conspirators named in Ramos' papers. The U.S. Army increased patrols along the border. However, February 20 arrived and nothing happened except the release of a second manifesto calling for revolution. By May of 1915 the plan had apparently fizzled. A judge reduced Ramos' bond from $5,000 to $100. Ramos quickly posted bail and fled to the protection of Carrancista officials across the border.[2] That was not the end of the plan, however. Carranza saw it as an opportunity to pressure Wilson to recognize his government. Taking advantage of Mexican anger at American high-handedness to his advantage, Carranza used his subsidized newspapers in Mexico to inspire bitterness against the United States. Carrancista papers in border towns, such as *El Demócrata* and *El Constitucional*, published sensationalized stories about the supposed successes of the Plan de San Diego rebels, including a stunning assault on Brownsville, Texas. Americans along the border did not have to believe the stories were true to understand that the Mexican press was printing what they wished would happen.[3]

In July 1915 approximately thirty Mexicans began three weeks of guerrilla raids in southeastern Texas. They killed civilians, burned train trestles, and cut telegraph wires. By August, groups of Mexican soldiers numbering up to fifty attacked targets as far as seventy miles north of the border. When pursued by the American cavalry, these guerrilla groups fled across the border to find sanctuary in Carranza-controlled territory.[4] Carranza kept a discreet distance from these attacks. He did not want another American invasion. Publicly turning a blind eye to the attacks, he cautiously and surreptitiously encouraged them. Some of his commanders armed the raiders, and sheltered them from American reprisals. Carranza's goal was simple enough: to pressure Washington into granting him recognition in the hopes he would establish a Mexican government that could restore order along the border.[5]

HUERTA RETURNS

The Plan de San Diego was not the only active conspiracy, however. Supporters of the former Mexican dictator, General Huerta, hoped he would return from exile in Europe. During his Spanish exile, Huerta maintained contact with other conservative émigrés from the old regime and plotted his return to power. Hoping to tie up the United States with Mexico, Germany offered to aid the former leader and his exiled allies. In February 1915, a German naval officer and intelligence operative, Captain Franz von Rintelen, visited Huerta in Spain and offered to back a counterrevolution. Huerta saw that the victorious revolutionaries had fallen out among themselves into civil war. Encouraged by Villa and Carranza's continued fighting, Huerta sailed for New York, landing on April 12. His reception must have heartened the general, as he was met at the docks by a crowd of supporters. Everywhere he went he was met by applause from the Mexican exile community. When he entered one café, the band played the Mexican national anthem. Undoubtedly casting himself in that role, Huerta told reporters that only a "strong man" could control Mexico.[6] The Germans promised to supply Huerta with arms, money, and diplomatic backing. They would provide 10,000 rifles and an initial credit of $10,000. In return for being restored to power, Huerta agreed to start a war with the United States. This would, of course, make it more difficult for the preoccupied United States to aid Britain and its allies in their war against Germany. Once a Mexican-American war began, the Germans promised, they would continue to supply Huerta via U-boats.[7]

In Washington, Villa's representative reported to the administration that numerous former Huertista officers were on their way to El Paso from their places of exile in the United States. On June 24, 1915, Huerta took a train from New York to San Francisco, switching mid-trip to one bound for El Paso. On June 25 Huerta was arrested by United States marshals as he stepped from his train in Newman, Texas, only a few miles from the border. The ex-dictator, referring to Wilson's policy, commented wryly, "efficient watchful waiting."[8] His supporters— including General Pascual Orozco, who was waiting in a car to drive him across the border—were also arrested. To keep him secure from possible rescue attempts by his exiled supporters, the former and would-be dictator was held prisoner on a U.S. Army base. He died of alcoholism complications a few months later.[9]

THE ABC CONFERENCE

Broader strategic considerations that the state of the Mexican government played a critical role in Wilson's policy in mid-1915 as relations with Germany were perilously poor. Secretary of State Robert Lansing kept a detailed daily schedule that illustrated how Mexico was a persistent and unwelcome distraction from what he believed were more significant problems. An examination of his activities from June through September 1915 shows Mexico taking up approximately the same percentage of the time, about 25 percent, as issues concerning Germany. Mexico was fast solidifying its role in Lansing's mind as the distraction that prevented the United States from dealing with what Lansing considered the more critical issue, the war in Europe.[10] Lansing was not alone. The president wrote Colonel House, "I feel, with . . . Lansing, that the Mexican situation grows ominously worse and more threatening day by day, and I have felt, the last few days, as if it were more likely to draw me soon back to Washington than even our correspondence with Germany." Wilson dealt with this problem by returning to a familiar and comfortable alternative—proposing mediation and an international conference with Latin American states whose representatives in Washington had indicated an interest in the issue as well as Mexico. This conference included Argentina, Brazil, and Chile, along with Bolivia, Uruguay, and Guatemala, which Wilson referred to as the "A.B.C.-B.U.G." countries.[11] Holding a Pan-American conference would, Wilson believed, serve several purposes. It would help defuse feelings throughout Latin America over U.S. intervention in Mexico. It would also, Wilson felt, draw the Latin states closer to the United States at a time when Washington was worried about German attempts to expand its influence in the region. Moreover, a conference would give Wilson domestic political cover if it became necessary to recognize a Mexican faction unpopular in the United States, particularly Carranza's.[12]

The conference met for the first time on August 5 in Washington. Secretary of State Robert Lansing represented the United States. Their ambassadors in Washington represented Argentina, Brazil, and Chile while Bolivia, Uruguay, and Guatemala sent their embassies' ministers.[13] As Wilson read the daily meeting transcripts, it was clear to him that the Latin American states were opposed to the Mexican Revolution and Carranza. Even his secretary of state had little respect for the revolutionary leader. Lansing reported in a letter to Wilson that "there was unanimous agreement that Carranza was impossible, that even if he triumphed it would mean continued disorder." Wilson wrote a marginal comment, "You will also see (I am afraid I do) their lack of sympathy with the revolution and their sympathy with the exiled reactionaries."[14]

Wilson feared that Lansing would guide the delegates away from the strongest revolutionary faction, Carranza's, which could open the door for a counterrevolutionary leader to win the conference's support. Accordingly, Wilson sent a memo to Lansing instructing his secretary not to exclude Carranza from consideration as the legitimate Mexican leader:

> I think it would be unwise for the conference to take for granted or insist upon the elimination of Carranza. It would be to ignore some very big facts. It seems to me very important that the plan now formed should leave the way of action open in any direction and not assume beginning over with a clean sheet of paper to write on. Carranza will somehow have to be digested into the scheme and above all the object of the revolution will have to be in any event conserved.

Immediately upon receiving Wilson's message, Lansing reversed course. He told the conference, "We must be careful . . . that the factions organizing the government, together with those that may adhere to it, represent a sufficient body of Mexicans to insure stability. . . . We must not take a very small body of men that do not represent . . . the body of the revolution." Lansing continued, "For that reason we cannot eliminate consideration of the Carrancista element which is apparently a great body of the revolution at the present time."[15]

True to his long-standing refusal to allow outside interference in internal Mexican affairs, Carranza rejected even a purportedly Pan-American-centered influence on Mexican affairs. Carranza replied to the invitation to the conference that it could only legitimately "consider the question whether the governments there represented shall recognize or refuse to recognize as the de facto government of Mexico the one I represent as the First Chief." Moreover, Carranza waited six weeks before declining the invitation.[16]

Wilson was still hesitant to extend recognition to Carranza's government, unconvinced that he was the man for the job. He wrote to his future wife, Edith Galt, "It must be said that there may presently be no feasible course left open to the United States but to recognize that very trying and pig-headed person, Carranza." "The other 'chiefs,'" Wilson wrote, "are all in a more or less demoralized condition. Only Carranza has political authority over any considerable portion of the country."[17] Moreover, Wilson now believed, correctly, that Carranza's forces were behind at least some of the cross-border raids. Recognition might give Wilson more opportunity to pressure the Mexicans into ending the violence. As long as Carranza remained merely an unrecognized factional leader, Wilson's influence seemed limited.[18]

RECOGNIZING CARRANZA

In August, while the conference dragged on, a German submarine torpedoed a British passenger ship, the *Arabic*, killing several Americans. On the same day, the *New York World* began publishing a series of Austrian and German documents leaked by the administration. The papers demonstrated German and Austrian complicity in subsidizing propaganda in the press, fomenting strikes, and even in sabotaging munitions plants in the United States to impede the arms shipment to the Allies. Faced with the possibility of a diplomatic break with Germany, Wilson knew he must end the upheaval on America's southern border. No other Mexican revolutionary leader had emerged from the factional infighting; it was Carranza or continued chaos.[19] On September 13 Wilson told Lansing that he should ensure that the conference grant Carranza de facto recognition as the Mexican government leader. Wilson made the same comment to his adviser, Colonel House, laughing bitterly as he remarked that the Mexican leader had "once or twice put one over on us."[20]

As it became clear that Wilson was about to decide who to recognize as the legitimate leader of Mexico, representatives of rivals Villa and Carranza in the United States launched their last wave of lobbying. Villa's representatives argued that recognizing Carranza would only prolong the unrest because he was unacceptable to either Villa or Zapata. Villa's newspaper, *Vida Nueva*, reported that Carranza was directly supporting the Plan de San Diego raids. Carranza would see recognition as rewarding the attacks.[21] However, even as the lobbying effort continued, the conference concluded that "the stronger of the Mexican governments at present . . . is that of Carranza." When the conference met for the last time in October, the only remaining question for the delegates was whether to agree to extend recognition to Carranza's government or to continue ignoring the obvious. On October 9 the group agreed to recognize the Carranza faction as the de facto government of Mexico. His was the authority in place and in control. They announced publicly that on October 19, 1915, the United States, Argentina, Brazil, Chile, Bolivia, Uruguay, and Guatemala would officially recognize Carranza.[22] On the same day that Wilson issued recognition of Carranza he renewed the arms embargo for Mexico, exempting Carranza's government. Two days later, the border raids suddenly dwindled to a tiny fraction of what they had been as Carranza ordered his commanders to suppress any further actions. The few remaining cross-border attacks were probably genuine bandit activity unaided by Carranza's military.[23]

Villa's Reaction

Villa denounced the decision to recognize Carranza and vowed to continue the war. In his last interview given to a U.S. newspaper, the angry revolutionary leader lashed out at those he blamed for causing his defeat:

I have no words to express my disgust for the men (and we know who they are) who without risking their lives on the line of fire, remaining a good distance from danger, have attacked the U.S. in a more deadly way than all the armed, with wicked money. These men, refugees outside our country, sustained by economic interests allied to foreign lands, have given not their blood, but their gold to the end of weakening our forces and blinding our cause.

Finally, Villa warned, recognizing Carranza would only "bring revolution after revolution" and that "compared to such revolution, the war of the last four years will be like child's play."[24]

Having recognized Carranza's government as the de facto Mexican government, Wilson soon had a new problem. Villa was angered by what he felt had been a betrayal by the United States. He had met repeatedly with Gen. Hugh Scott, had protected American property and lives, and had seemed open to American guidance. Indeed, had Villa been militarily victorious over Carranza, it is likely that Wilson would have recognized Villa's government. However, having been defeated in several significant battles by Carranza's forces, it seemed clear to Wilson that the stern Constitutionalist leader was best able to restore order in the form of a constitutional government. When Villa learned of the diplomatic recognition and discovered that Wilson had allowed Carranza to move troops across American territory before the Battle of Agua Prieta, he was determined to lash out.

On January 10, 1916, Villa's forces stopped a train at Santa Ysabel, removed eighteen American miners, and killed seventeen of them. Much of the American press, most notably the Hearst papers, called for a military response, "We ARE too proud to fight. . . . Why even a little, despicable, contemptible bandit nation like Mexico murders our citizens, drags our flag in the dirt and spits at and defies this Nation of ours with truculent insolence."[25] Neither Carranza nor Wilson wanted a war over the incident, precisely what Villa intended. Wilson was determined not to repeat the mistakes of Veracruz. He reiterated an earlier State Department warning against Americans traveling in Mexico and pressed Carranza to act. Mexican government troops quickly moved troops into the area and, by January 13, had engaged Villas forces, killing two of his commanders and capturing numerous prisoners. Democratic leadership in the Senate defeated attempts by Republican senators William Borah and Henry Cabot Lodge to pass a resolution authorizing Wilson to use force in Mexico. The Democrats' decision to oppose a resolution authorizing him to use force in Mexico may seem counterintuitive. He could have kept it in reserve, allowing him a freer hand to use force should another such outrage against Americans in Mexico occur. However, the president probably understood the resolution was an effort to force his hand or at least embarrass him. Both Borah and Lodge were bitter enemies of Wilson, and the resolution would have highlighted the president's refusal to use force. Instead, Wilson attacked the interventionists as pushing for a war that would benefit American businesses and hurt Washington's efforts to rebuild trust in Latin America, especially after taking Veracruz in 1914. The issue was defused for the time being, but not everyone in the United States was satisfied, and a desire for the administration to use force against Mexico still bubbled under the surface. In a speech on January 27, Wilson noted with some sarcasm, "Nobody seriously supposes . . . that the United States needs to fear an invasion of its own territory." Irony has a way of listening to such words, however, and Wilson's snide remark would quickly come back on him.[26]

Reports of a possible raid on the border town of Columbus, New Mexico began to reach the American military along the border. Unfortunately, they were contradictory—sometimes placing Villa near Columbus, sometimes as much as fifty miles away. Moreover, some reports had him moving forces away from the border town, while others claimed he was moving closer. Other messages from those in contact with Villa claimed that he wanted to come to Washington, DC, to meet with President Wilson personally. While some of the reports were reasonably accurate in hindsight, they were lost amid all of the noise of inaccurate reports. Besides, continued alerts of coming cross-border raids that never occurred resulted in a somewhat reduced alertness of American forces along the border.[27]

Just before dawn on March 9, 1916, Villa and about 480 men attacked Columbus, New Mexico. The 13th Cavalry was based there to protect the town. Although caught by surprise, they rallied and drove Villa's forces off with heavy losses. Several of the town's buildings were burned. Ten cavalrymen were dead along with eight civilians, as compared to more than one hundred of Villa's men. Villa and the rest escaped over the border.[28] Major Frank Tompkins and thirty-two of his men pursued Villa for about three hours, going as far as fifteen miles into Mexico before breaking off pursuit. The pursuit over the border violated War Department orders but was excused as necessary and appropriate under the circumstances. Major Tompkins was awarded the Distinguished Service Cross for his cross-border counterattack, which caused more casualties among Villa's men, scattering them and their supplies over a wide area.[29] Indeed, Tompkins' actions would not have been remarkable earlier on, as the Porfirio Díaz regime (1876–1911) and the United States had an agreement allowing cross-border pursuit of raiders and bandits.[30]

THE PUNITIVE EXPEDITION

Wilson learned of the attack later that morning. Secretary of State Lansing informed him by telephone, and they agreed that there was now no choice but to send American forces into Mexico. Lansing warned Wilson that this was precisely what Villa wanted. In such a case, Carranza, he apparently hoped, would either be forced to resist the American invasion by force or allow the violation of Mexican sovereignty. Both cases would weaken Carranza and recast the ongoing Mexican political turmoil, possibly to Villa's advantage. The president replied, "I know that is so and I will do what I can to avoid any trouble of this sort."[31] Wilson's response would have to be a careful mix of the military and the diplomatic. The military objective was clear and straightforward—to either kill Villa or to scatter his forces to eliminate their ability to threaten the United States again. The diplomatic objective was also straightforward: to avoid a diplomatic break and a war with the Mexican government. Unfortunately for Wilson, not only were these goals in conflict, but it was also entirely possible that reaching one strategic objective would require abandoning the other. In this case, war was not an arm of diplomacy, but a hindrance to it with its own needs and logic. Wilson justified the use of force by its intent and its scale. In this case, the intent was military. However, the scale remained uncertain and Wilson kept a careful watch on the military to make sure it did not grow further than Wilson believed it could without endangering his diplomatic strategy. As such, he kept an eye on the size of the military force used and how far it could go into Mexico in pursuit of Villa. In Wilson's words, the military was instructed to give "scrupulous respect for the sovereignty of that republic" and hoped they would enjoy "entirely friendly aid of the constitutional authorities in Mexico."[32]

As it happened, the cabinet included the new secretary of war, Newton Baker, who was suddenly thrust into a dramatic, dangerous situation on his first day on the job. Baker quickly demonstrated his calm demeanor and willingness to listen to the experts. "I call for the General Staff," he wrote his wife, "and preside over a council of grizzled veterans in determining what to do next. The decision is up to me, but these fine soldiers help enormously through their long experience and frank helpfulness."[33] Following his staff officers' advice, Baker recommended Brig. Gen. John J. Pershing, commander of U.S. forces along the section of the border that included Columbus, to command what became known as the Punitive Expedition. Pershing's orders were more comprehensive than the "Catch Villa" of the headlines. He was to break up Villa's forces, cooperate with Mexican government troops when possible, and draw whatever supplies of additional men he needed.[34]

However, Carranza was more protective of Mexican sovereignty and far less willing to cooperate than Wilson had hoped. Immediately after Villa's raid, the first chief had ordered his military to pursue the rebel leader. Perhaps they could catch or kill him before the United States could send forces too far into Mexico. As for the American request to send forces after Villa, Carranza proposed an agreement allowing both sides to cross the border in "hot pursuit" of raiders such as Villa. This did not explicitly approve the current U.S. attempt, but it did provide an opening. In the meantime, however, Mexican border garrisons began preparing to resist an incursion by the United States. In response, Baker moved more U.S. units to the border, including four cavalry regiments. The U.S. Army War College recommended that Wilson follow their war plans and call for 400,000 volunteers. Chief of Staff Major General Scott recommended to Baker that Wilson should, at the very least, call out the National Guard and send 150,000 men to the border. It appeared Villa's attempt to spark a Mexican-American war might be working as both sides began preparing for a wider conflict.[35]

Wilson disapproved of the military's war planning. Nonetheless, the Army and Navy had to prepare for different contingencies for the use of armed force. Their war plan for Mexico, known as Plan Green, copied the Mexican-American War (1846–48) with an invasion force taking Veracruz before moving on Mexico City, and a second force crossing near Brownsville and heading to Monterey. The plan was modified as the Mexican Revolution began and then descended into a civil war. By 1916, Plan Green called for thirteen different divisions (four regular infantry, two regular cavalry, seven volunteers) to invade from several points in the north from near Brownsville and El Paso and take the port of Tampico while the Navy blockaded both Mexican coasts. The Army alone would commit 250,000 men. The invasion force had three tasks:

- capture Mexico City
- destroy the Mexican army
- occupy the entire country, securing supply lines amid a hostile populace

Plan Green assumed a full-scale war, which Wilson emphatically did not want. The far more extensive plans were shelved. The American military had to arrange for a smaller, mobile force, deal with the possibility of an extended supply line, and guard the border from further raids.[36]

Pershing crossed the border on March 15, 1916, with five thousand troops. Carranza's new minister of war and navy general, Álvaro Obregón, had agreed to let U.S. troops cross the border to pursue Villa. Moreover, he ordered local military commanders to cooperate with U.S. officers. Still wanting to keep the mission on as short a leash as possible, Wilson issued specific orders to Funston and Pershing to forestall even a chance of a new Mexican-American War:

Given the great distance between the seat of Government and the forces in the field, the President regards it as of the utmost importance that General Funston and all officers in command of troops of the United States clearly understand the exact nature of the expedition of our forces into Mexico, and he therefore directs obedience in letter and in spirit to the following orders:

ONE. If any organized body of troops of the de facto Government of the Republic of Mexico are met, they are to be treated with courtesy and their cooperation welcomed, if they desire to cooperate in the objects of the expedition.

TWO. Upon no account or pretext, and neither by act, word or attitude of any American soldier, shall this expedition become or be given the appearance of being hostile to the integrity or dignity of the Republic of Mexico, by the courtesy of which this expedition is permitted to pursue an aggressor upon the peace of these neighboring Republics.

THREE. Should the attitude of any organized body of troops of the de facto Government of Mexico appear menacing, commanders of the forces of the United States are, of course, authorized to place themselves and their commands in proper situation of defense, and if actually attacked they will of course defend themselves by all means at their command, but in no event must they attack or become the aggressor with any such body of troops.

FOUR. Care is to be taken to have in a state of readiness at all times the means of rapid communication from the front to the headquarters or the General commanding the Department, and, through him, to the War Department in Washington; and any evidence of misunderstanding on the part of officials, military or civil, of the de facto Government of Mexico as to the objects, purposes, character or acts of the expedition of the United States, are to be reported to the Department with the utmost expedition with a view to having them taken up directly with the Government of Mexico through the Department of State.[37]

The overall thrust of these orders was clear: the administration did not want a war with Mexico. As the commander on the ground, it was Pershing's responsibility to make sure that his command was not to be an aggressor, nor was it to do anything that might be construed as making the United States appear to be an aggressor, a difficult task, given that American forces were crossing an international border. Wilson knew how President Polk in 1846 had used an alleged Mexican crossing of the U.S. border to start the Mexican-American War, which Wilson considered an act of aggression. Mexico could be expected to be wary of such a pretext being used again. Note in Point Four that "misunderstandings" by the Mexican government were to be forwarded "with the utmost expedition" to the State Department—and not the War Department—to be resolved. To Wilson, the military was one of a set of tools with which to achieve his foreign policy goals. Pershing's mission had a clear military function, but it was secondary to diplomatic considerations.

Despite General Obregón's reassurances, President Carranza had not given overt, open permission for Pershing's mission. His was a delicate balancing act. If his acceptance of American military intervention was too open, he risked being ousted by angered nationalistic Mexicans and fulfilling Villa's fondest plans. Too firm a refusal, on the other hand, risked a war with the United States that Mexico, weakened by six years of revolution and civil war, could ill afford. For Carranza, the United States might eliminate Villa and withdraw quickly, doing away with a troublesome rival and cementing Carranza's control of the country while placating his more powerful, and somewhat touchy, northern neighbor. Thus, both Wilson and Carranza were trying to walk exceptionally fine lines between eliminating Villa and falling into a war neither man wanted.

Pershing did have some early success. On March 18, Villa was caught between American forces to the north and Carranza's forces to the south. He escaped the trap by slipping through the more widely spread Mexican lines. On March 29, some of Pershing's men caught Villa at Guerrero. Villa escaped again, but his chief general was killed and the Americans rescued a number of Carranza's men being held as prisoners for execution. Interestingly, the U.S. cavalry knew Villa was at Guerrero thanks to intelligence passed to them by some of Carranza's troops. They reported that Villa had been wounded earlier and evacuated to that place. The reports were accurate, but Villa managed to slip away again.[38]

The intelligence relationship between Carrancistas and Pershing's expedition was kept quiet by both sides. Pershing was not known as a subtle tactician, but he was an avid consumer of intelligence who relied on multiple sources, particularly HUMINT. In the Philippines he used both American and Filipino sources, often using local sources who were willing or who could be coerced into cooperating with the Americans. Katherine Bjork points out that this tactic was in common use in the Indian Wars, in which Pershing and his superiors all participated. During the wars against the Native American tribes, Pershing used Indian scouts from other tribal groups. In the Philippines, he used Filipino scouts. In Mexico, he tried as much as possible to use Mexicans as informants.[39]

Pershing's covert actions went beyond gathering intelligence. He also approved an effort proposed by several Japanese to assassinate Villa by poisoning him. There was a small Japanese community in Mexico and several of its members had worked for Villa as personal servants. The Bureau of Investigation had rejected an offer by the Japanese to poison Villa, but their BI handler apparently passed them on to Pershing. Two Japanese agents code-named "Dyo" and "Fusita" put some poison (it is unclear what specific type) into Villa's coffee, but he had diluted it with more coffee, and it had no effect. The two Japanese fled before they could be discovered. Word got back to Washington and Attorney General Thomas Watt Gregory asked Secretary of War Baker to investigate. Baker ordered Funston to do so "with as little publicity as possible." With the assistance of the chief of the Army's Military Intelligence Division, the whole sordid mess was quickly shoved into a desk drawer and forgotten. It is likely Wilson never heard of the attempt. He would have strongly disapproved and would have at the very least, severely reprimanded Pershing and may have revoked his command.[40]

On March 18 Congress passed a resolution authorizing Wilson to use force to capture Villa. The resolution also reassured Mexico that the United States did not intend to violate its sovereignty or interfere in its domestic affairs. Given that the United States was not only sending a large number of U.S. Army units into Mexico, and that by attacking Villa the United States was, in effect, taking sides in the ongoing Mexican civil war, Mexicans could not be blamed if they remained less than reassured by both the U.S. Congress and Wilson's promises.[41]

Carranza had sent a note objecting to Pershing's border crossing on March 17 while hoping the American general would quickly be victorious and then leave. The longer Pershing remained, and the further into Mexico he penetrated, the more tensions increased. On March 19 Mexico's secretary of foreign relations Candido Aguilar proposed an agreement that limited hot pursuit for both governments to sixty kilometers (approximately thirty-seven miles) inside each nation's borders. Wilson saw both messages at the same time on March 20. He proposed accepting Aguilar's suggestion for future interventions, but not applying it to Pershing, who was already well past the sixty-kilometer point. A second message to the foreign secretary proposed no limits on distance. However, it noted that "in no case will the pursuing forces establish themselves or remain in foreign territory for a time longer than is necessary."[42] The Mexican Foreign Office replied with a proposal which, while not limiting in distance, proposed limiting the duration to eight days. It had been ten days since Pershing had crossed the border. Again, Wilson was agreeable, telling Lansing on the 30th that such an agreement was acceptable, but not applicable to the current pursuit.

Flirting with a Wider War

By April some of Pershing's forces were five hundred miles inside Mexico. He was sending various cavalry units farther south to probe for Villa's forces. On April 12 Major Tompkins rode into the town of Parral. Some of Carranza's commanders had led Tompkins to believe that he would be able to buy supplies there. When Tompkins arrived with 8 officers and 120 men, he entered the town and quickly realized that the population there was hostile. The local Carrancista garrison was not threatening, but their commander warned Tompkins he had better leave. Tompkins agreed. As they marched out of the town, the townspeople began to yell "Viva Villa!" As soon as they had exited the town, more than five hundred Carrancistas attacked the outnumbered American column. With sheer numbers weighing against him, Tompkins had to keep moving, fighting a rearguard action for eight miles before finding refuge in a fortified town, Santa Cruz de Villegas. Facing a possible siege, the major sent out dispatch riders for reinforcements. Early the next morning the 10th Cavalry, one of the "Buffalo Soldiers" units, arrived and the Mexican government forces withdrew to Parral. The Americans suffered two dead, six wounded (including Tompkins), and one missing. Mexican losses numbered as many as seventy.[43]

Pershing was having difficulties with his communications; he was relying on couriers, cables sent by American consuls in larger Mexican cities, and when conditions permitted, wireless radio. So, word of the fight at Parral reached Washington before it reached Pershing's headquarters less than one hundred miles from Parral. When Pershing received a sharp note penned by Secretary of War Baker and forwarded to him by Funston, it was a nasty shock. Baker wrote,

> We are, of course, without information as to why the commander of American troops entered Parral without consent of Mexican local authorities. The Secretary of War directs that you send general orders to all commanders of troops in Mexico calling their attention to the importance of maintaining the most harmonious relations with all local authorities of the de facto government and urging the utmost consideration for the feelings and sensibilities of such authorities and the people in Mexican towns and villages.
>
> Newton D. Baker, Secretary of War[44]

Funston immediately came to his subordinate's defense, noting that Pershing had issued strict orders "on the subject of relationship with Mexicans generally." He then suggested—rather diplomatically, considering—"I am strongly of opinion that it would be better to await official reports before assuming that our troops were in the wrong at Parral." Funston continued, reminding Baker—and through him, Wilson—"No towns are being occupied or have been occupied by our troops, but they must go through them, or they can go practically nowhere as the towns are naturally on the roads." Furthermore, Funston added, "If any stubborn or hostile Mexican commander so wills, he can tie up the expedition provided we are dependent on the consent of such official before going through a town."[45]

The frustrations inherent in the limitations set by Wilson and Baker were coming to the surface. Baker had reacted too quickly in judging the actions of Pershing's men. But then, Wilson and Baker would have added, they had to remember the broader context. On March 24 a German U-boat had attacked a cross-channel ferry, the *Sussex*, mistaking it for a minelayer. Twenty-four Americans were among the eighty dead, and the crisis threatened to pull American closer to war with Germany. Now the Mexican government was objecting loudly and insistently to American forces engaged in a battle more than five hundred miles within Mexico. This battle furthermore was against government forces, not Villa's. Carranza quickly admitted his forces were at fault, but noted, correctly, that the longer American forces stayed in Mexico, the higher the chances for further conflicts escalating out of control. While Funston and Pershing resented it, Wilson and Baker thought it was time to pull back on their reins.

In fact, Pershing was sending angry messages to Gen. Eulalio Gutierrez, military commander of Chihuahua, demanding the arrest and punishment of those Mexican officers responsible for Parral. Fortunately, he sent the message through the American consul in Chihuahua, who had the sense to notify Secretary of State Lansing first. The secretary told him to hold onto it. Pershing then withdrew northward to establish a new headquarters. From there he sent a long message to General Funston complaining about Mexican government forces being of little help, and of not much use in restoring order. He suggested that he be allowed to seize the city and state of Chihuahua, and all the state's railroads. Pershing then released his complaints about Carranza's forces to the American press, announcing that, given the Mexican government's lack of cooperation, he was suspending his hunt for Villa.[46]

Pershing had let his temper overrule his judgment. Had the United States adopted his suggestion, it would have meant an open war with Mexico. Wilson and Baker dispatched the chief of staff, Major General Scott, to confer with Pershing's superior, General Funston. After their meeting, Scott sent his recommendations to Washington. First, he and Funston recommended that they abandon the hunt for Villa, without withdrawing totally. "It is evident," Scott wrote, "Carranza troops concentrating to oppose our southward advance." As a result, there "are three courses open":

1. "Drive through by force," including seizing the main north-south railroad. However, this would not guarantee capturing Villa, who could run as far south in Mexico as he wanted, or even go to Yucatan.
2. Pershing should concentrate his forces near Colonia Dublan. This would cover the road to Columbus as well as the railroad. It would allow Pershing to protect American Mormon colonists. It would also act as a goad to motivate Carranza to catch and eliminate Villa finally.
3. Pull Pershing out entirely. There was little chance of catching Villa, especially as the Mexican population was "friendly to him and daily becoming more hostile to us."

Scott recommended the second option. The other two were out of the question. Wilson approved Scott and Funston's recommendation immediately. It was not a surrender, which would have been humiliating, and it did not dramatically increase the risk of war. After only a month, the purpose of Pershing's expedition had dramatically changed.[47]

If Wilson hoped the Mexican government would accept this new status as an acceptable compromise, he was wrong. When Obregón began a new series of talks with Funston and Scott, it was clear his only interest was compelling the Americans to pull all of their forces out of Mexico. On May 1, Carranza sent a message to Wilson, saying, "It was inconceivable to him that the American government would insist on maintaining troops in Mexico."[48] Wilson would naturally have recalled them, "unless he had decided 'to wage an unjustified war against us.'"[49] Scott and Funston warned the president that they expected a "flat ultimatum to get out of Mexico at once or take the consequences." The problem was that this acquiescence to the Mexicans would "be a complete victory for Mexicans over the United States in the eyes of the Mexican people already arrogant and encourage further aggressions."[50] Wilson continued,

Your telegram fully considered. This Government cannot withdraw troops from Mexico until it is satisfied that danger to our people on the border is removed. Ask for further conference with General Obregón, urge again considerations in previous telegram of Secretary of War, and urge that they be submitted to General Carranza, as matters of so great gravity should be determined by the respective Governments. This will show whether General Obregón is acting independently. If General Obregón declines to consider any other course than that already announced by him and a break in your conference therefore becomes necessary, announce to him that you feel obliged to say to him quite frankly that the United States will, in your opinion, retire its troops to a place suitable for the protection of the borders of our own country and maintain them there until we are satisfied that the danger is past; that while there, they will of course in every way scrupulously respect the dignity of the people and of the De Facto Government of Mexico and do nothing to give offense, but that if our troops, so disposed, are attacked or their operations for the protection of the people of the United States are obstructed, the consequences, however grave, will rest upon General Obregón. Safeguard your own persons in retiring from the interview; and if it terminates in such a break as above outlined, concentrate the American troops in position thoroughly prepared for defense. On no account give excuse for attack. If attacked, take all necessary steps to make answer decisive and speedy.[51]

Wilson and his advisers were not sure how responsible Obregón was to Carranza as rumors swirled that the two men had broken their alliance. However, the Mexican general was still loyal to Carranza's administration, and Major General Scott realized that so long as talks were held openly, his Mexican counterpart had little wiggle room. Scott had several mutual friends independently suggest to Obregón how undesirable a war with the United States would be for Mexico. Scott and Obregón then held a marathon meeting that lasted more than twelve hours, ending early on the morning of May 3.[52]

Their agreement stipulated that since Villa's forces had been scattered—none of his forces were within four hundred miles of the border—and Carranza's government was committed to controlling the border areas, the United States would begin withdrawing its forces. The crisis seemed to be over. Before the agreement could be announced, on the night of May 5 and 6, some two hundred Mexican irregulars attacked Glenn Springs and Boquillas, Texas. They were not Villistas, but that was unknown at the time. The Mexican irregular cavalry crossed and attacked a U.S. cavalry post, killing three and wounding two. The Mexicans looted and burned several buildings in the town, took some prisoners, then attacked the nearby town of Boquillas. Once again, they were pursued across the border by U.S. cavalry, who advanced one hundred miles into Mexico before outrunning their supplies. They retreated back across the border, but had forced the raiders to release their hostages and spent ten days in Mexican territory. Carranza declared that the Glenn Springs raid showed the United States and Mexico had "common enemies," but Mexican government forces also began to mass around the Americans—another reason they retreated back to the United States. This American pursuit into Mexico forced Carranza to abandon the newly minted agreement.[53]

Meanwhile, Pershing's expedition created a diplomatic morass and generated a logistic nightmare for the small U.S. Army. Scott and Funston had hoped to be allowed to use Mexico's railroads to supply the expedition, an optimistic wish indeed. While the use of the rails was sometimes granted, for the most part Pershing's men had to be supplied by trucks leaving from the expedition's base in Columbus. Hundreds of trucks along a route stretching for hundreds of miles had to be guarded. The logistics stretched the Army beyond its peacetime capabilities. It could not support Pershing and guard the border at the same time; it simply did not have sufficient men. Moreover, raids from Mexico across the U.S. border continued, often smaller raids aimed at large ranches. A larger attack on Terlingua, Texas, was apparently thwarted by the preparations made by the small U.S. cavalry unit based there, including setting up two machine-gun posts. Fortunately, reinforcements were coming. Unconvinced by Obregón's assurances, General Funston, commander of the Southern Command, and General Scott, Army chief of staff, on May 8 had sent a cable to Washington asking that National Guard units from Arizona, New Mexico, and Texas be activated so that additional men would be available to watch the border. On May 10, Wilson ordered that the respective National Guard units be called up. The Guard units mobilized in their respective states and moved to the border as quickly as possible. They were only the beginning.[54]

Unfortunately, this first call-up showed the uneven quality of the National Guard units and how unfit for duty many of them were. Those from Arizona and New Mexico were in especially poor shape. The two territories had only become states in 1912, and both were relatively poor. Their units tended to be understrength, short on equipment, and more often than not, poorly trained. Both states scrambled for men and equipment. Recruiting proved to be a struggle. In Arizona, officials resorted to trying to sign up "transients passing through" Tucson. In New Mexico they resorted, to their chagrin, to recruiting in Texas. The latter's units were in only slightly better condition. The *New York World* snidely noted that while Texans bragged that they could handle Mexico without help from the other forty-seven states, when their Guard units were called up, they were found to be "standing at the bottom of the list in efficiency at the latest inspection of the War Department." Slowly, the three southwestern states' units began to report for duty, freeing regular Army units to protect Pershing's supply lines.[55]

DEFUSING TENSIONS

In the spring of 1916, there were several military operations going on simultaneously:

- Pershing was well inside the state of Chihuahua.
- Other regular Army units were engaged in defending against other raids by various Mexican groups.
- The National Guard was being called to duty to guard the border.
- The Army truck convoys continued entering Mexico, supplying Pershing.

While interrelated, the first three each had independent components. Even if Pershing had not gone into Mexico, the Army was still overextended guarding the entire border, and it is likely the Guard would have to have been called up at some point. They also involved overlapping but distinct powers of the commander in chief. First, there was command of the regular armed forces and their use in foreign engagements. Nevertheless, the use of the National Guard was distinct from that, and both reflected the different aspects of how the Constitution put limits on the president's powers. Using the military in Mexico required congressional approval, even if Wilson sent the troops into Mexico before Congress officially approved its use. Given the nature of the raid, however, there was no doubt Congress would approve. Calling up the Guard did not take congressional approval, but it did require the cooperation of the various state governors. Given the American outrage over Villa, there was little doubt the state governors would approve, especially the governors of the border states. Nonetheless, it does illustrate the different authorities Wilson had to deal with to intervene in Mexico.

Wilson believed the president had the lead role in diplomatic matters, and the use of the military was a related aspect of that power, which, although primary, was not absolute. As Pershing's mission continued, the diplomatic facet grew increasingly important. Even after the Glenn Springs affair had destroyed the withdrawal agreement, Wilson was determined to limit the use of the military in Mexico. Ray Stannard Baker, a reporter who later served as Wilson's official biographer, recalled an interview with Wilson:

> He said his Mexican policy was based upon two of the most deeply seated convictions of his life. First, his shame as an American over the first Mexican war, and his resolution that there should never be another such predatory enterprise. Second, upon his belief in the principle laid down in the Virginia Bill of Rights, that a people have the right "to do what they damn please with their own affairs." (He used the word "damn.") He wanted to give the Mexicans a chance to try. . . . "It may prove," he said, "that we shall have to go in finally and make peace." He . . . said that the most significant trouble was

not with Mexico, but with people here in America who wanted the oil and metals in Mexico and were seeking intervention to get them. He referred to the Mexican boundary as one of the longest in the world and declared with shut jaw that he would not be forced into war with Mexico if it could be avoided. He does not want one hand tied behind him when the nation may need all of its forces to meet the European situation. He emphasized the enormous undertaking it would be to pacify Mexico: "Five hundred thousand men at least."[56]

His interview with Baker illustrates Wilson's view of the broader context, "the European situation." He was well aware that a war with Mexico would hinder the American ability to respond to Germany.

Meanwhile, talks continued. Obregón hoped for an agreement for withdrawal and was undoubtedly relieved when Scott and Funston said the United States was still willing to apply it. Washington was convinced that Carranza was making "noises" for domestic consumption. Scott reported that Mexico City was moving new forces to Coahuila and Chihuahua to deny the area to Villa. Thus, Pershing could remain in a defined area to guard the border and the nearby American Mormon colonists. That ignored the fact that by moving troops into the area, Carranza hoped the United States would withdraw, not just limit their forces to a somewhat smaller zone. On May 16 Baker informed Wilson and the cabinet that, according to Scott, the border situation was the best it had been since the Columbus raid. However, while the situation had improved, it was still willfully optimistic as an acceptable status quo as even an improved situation still risked war with Mexico.[57]

While Wilson and Baker grew complacent, Carranza was preparing an ultimatum. It was published in the Mexico City newspapers on May 31 simultaneously with being delivered to the U.S. government. The message cast doubt of America's reasons for the Punitive Expedition. The United States claimed the troops would be recalled once Villa's forces were scattered. But while the Villistas had indeed been dispersed, Pershing remained. Instead, Carranza charged, the expedition was being kept in Mexico for domestic American reasons. A large number of forces, including artillery, indicated that it was intended to be used against Mexican regular forces. While Carranza insisted that his government had been willing to cooperate with the United States to defend the common border, Washington's actions demonstrated that Washington was only interested in protecting its interests in the area. The solution was simple. The best indication of American intentions was to withdraw all of its troops. Wilson canceled a June 2 cabinet meeting in a deliberate sign that he was not concerned. While Wilson took his time writing a reply, other members of his administration were furious. Lansing called it "insulting." State Department counselor Frank Polk told Wilson it was "impertinent." The assumption in Washington was that Carranza wrote it for Mexican home consumption. Otherwise, why release it to the Mexican press simultaneous with delivering it to the United States?[58]

Wilson did ask Funston if Pershing was too far into Mexico, and he dispatched another 1,600 troops to the border. Then on June 16, sixty Mexican raiders crossed into the United States forty miles from Laredo, Texas. They attacked an American patrol, killing four and wounding another half dozen. Once again, the United States pursued the raiders across the border in hot pursuit despite being warned by the local Carrancista commander not to cross the border. Four hundred American cavalry withdrew back to Texas the next day after a short skirmish with an unidentified Mexican force. Tensions were heightening. The Mexican commander in Chihuahua warned Pershing that he was to resist the American movement into Mexico in any direction except northward back to the U.S. border. Pershing replied that he would move in any direction he felt necessary. Major General Scott ordered the War College to prepare plans for an invasion of Mexico via the northern railroads. Mexico began recalling reservists in Ciudad Juárez.[59]

Wilson and Baker met and decided for a full call-up of the National Guard—those from Arizona, New Mexico, and Texas having already been called to service. Up to 125,000 guardsmen would be placed along the border, freeing up 30,000 regulars. Secretary of the Navy Daniels sent more American warships into Mexican waters. Mexican government forces fired on an American naval party in Mazatlán harbor, inflicting several casualties and one death among the Americans. The U.S.

representative in Mexico City asked the British chargé to look after American interests in Mexico City. Major General Scott noted in his diary, "It looks to me as if the war will be on in a few days."[60]

As both sides prepared for war, Wilson continued his diplomatic efforts which still took precedence as a tool over the use of force. Wilson's stubborn streak was showing. His latest message repeated what had been said previously. The United States denied interest in anything except border security. If the Mexican government showed it could guarantee the stoppage of further raids across the border and protect American lives and property in Mexico, then the United States would withdraw Pershing. This note was released to the other Latin American diplomats in Washington at the same time it was sent to Mexico. Wilson could engage in his own signaling as much as did Carranza.[61]

CARRIZAL

The closest the United States and Mexico came to an actual war was probably on June 21 at Carrizal. Pershing had sent two troops, about one hundred men total, from the 10th Cavalry on a scouting expedition. On the way, the two groups had to pass through Carrizal, a small town about ninety miles south of El Paso. Their commander, Capt. William T. Boyd, was warned by an American living in the area that there were about four hundred Carrancista troops in the town and that Boyd should go around Carrizal rather than through it. The Mexican commander, General Félix Gomez, also warned Boyd. The American captain was determined not to be turned aside by the Mexicans and insisted he had orders to go through any town he came across. Pershing's orders to Boyd were verbal, so whether Boyd was telling the truth is unknown, but it is known that Pershing had ordered him to avoid conflicts with Carranza's troops. When Boyd attempted to move through the town, the Mexicans resisted, and a firefight began. When it was done, twelve Americans were dead, including Boyd. Another ten were wounded, and the Mexicans had taken twenty-four prisoners.[62]

It took several days for Pershing to learn the details, although word of the fights—and the Mexican victory—spread throughout Mexico and the United States quickly. Meanwhile, Mexican men signed up to fight the Americans and newspapers throughout the United States called for war. Believing Carranza's forces had initiated the fighting, Wilson considered asking Congress for authority to send more forces into Chihuahua, perhaps tempted by Pershing's earlier suggestion of taking the Mexican state over to bring order and eliminate the Villistas. The draft of Wilson's address to Congress lays out his rationale in authorizing the use of force, but explicitly not declaring war. Wilson's premise is that the United States was not going to war with the Mexican people, but to protect the U.S. border because the "de facto government" was "unable or unwilling to protect our territory against violence from their side of the border." This was a duty "that should go with a regularly constituted and freely employed control." While the term "failed state" did not yet exist, that is essentially what Wilson was labeling Mexico, a state without a legitimate government in effective control.[63]

Wilson's prepared speech accused Carranza's forces of starting the conflict at Carrizal, an accusation based on the initial erroneous reports. When he received details from the Army that it had been Captain Boyd who had initiated hostilities, not the Mexicans, Wilson abandoned the address to Congress. Wilson did not want to repeat the actions made by President Polk in 1846, marking the United States as the aggressor. Moreover, as he told his secretary, Joseph Tumulty, he was well aware of German attempts to entangle the United States in Mexico: "Germany is anxious to have us at war with Mexico . . . and thus give her the liberty of action to do what she pleases on the high seas." So, when Carranza demanded the United States withdraw its forces, Wilson refused, but rather than threatening war said he would not take any action until Mexico returned the captured men and their equipment.[64] In a speech on June 30 before the Press Club of New York, Wilson explained his position:

> The easiest thing is to strike. The brutal thing is the impulsive thing. No man has to think before he takes aggressive action; but before a man really conserves the honor by realizing the ideals of the Nation, he has to think exactly what he will do and how he will do it. Do you think the glory of America would be enhanced by a

war of conquest in Mexico? Do you think that any act of violence by a powerful nation like this against a weak and destructive neighbor would reflect distinction upon the annals of the United States? Do you think it is our duty to carry self-defense to a point of dictation into the affairs of another people?[65]

Wilson's demonstration of his awareness of how the United States would be perceived is striking. Rather than seeing the use of force as conferring honor, he weighs the force used against a weaker neighbor by proportionality. Military force was to be used in sufficient strength to finish its assigned task, not to prove the United States was the stronger nation. There was, Wilson would say, no glory in being a bully.

In July, the Mexican government suggested the two countries form an international commission to discuss their shared grievances. After mulling it over for a week, Wilson agreed. Of course, Mexico wanted to begin with the question of a quick withdrawal of American troops, but the United States wanted to emphasize border security and protection of American property. The commission began meeting in Connecticut in early September. The talks demonstrated the gulf between the two party's intentions, between withdrawing American troops and securing the border. Neither side would budge, and they moved the talks to Atlantic City in the hopes a change in scenery might help. The ongoing presidential election campaign only hindered matters, as the Republicans attacked Wilson's Mexican policy. Indeed, Carranza's representatives seemed more aware of Wilson's domestic political restraints than the Americans were of the domestic political restraints on the Mexican government. Taking a break for the election, the delegates began meeting again in December, this time in Philadelphia. Nothing changed, and the talks officially came to an end in January 1917 without resolution. The Mexican delegates signed a protocol that recognized a U.S. right to move troops across the border, basically the "hot pursuit" the United States had demanded all along. Carranza, not unexpectedly, rejected it. At best, the talks helped reduce tensions for a few months. In addition, Carrizal's American prisoners were released to the United States as a sign of good faith by Carranza.[66]

The embarrassment at Carrizal persuaded Pershing to deploy his forces more carefully. He settled in at his camp at Colonia Dublan, approximately 150 miles southwest of El Paso, near an American Mormon colony. Pershing allowed his men to remain occupied in ways that Wilson would never have approved had he known, including sanctioning brothels for the men, the women being registered and screened by Army doctors. Villa's military victories in the fall of 1916 made Pershing nervous, and he suggested being allowed to actively pursue Villa again. Wilson refused. A victory by Carranza's forces over Villa at Torreón allowed Wilson to declare that the situation was under control and Pershing could return to the United States. The Punitive Expedition began to wind down. On January 31, Wilson extended full diplomatic recognition to Carranza's government, instead of the earlier, limited recognition as the de facto government. That same day Germany announced the beginnings of unrestricted submarine warfare.

CONCLUSION

Although they unknowingly came close once, when an American patrol passed close by a cave in which the wounded revolutionary was hiding, the U.S. forces did not catch Villa.[67] Ironically, the intervention ended up strengthening him. In early 1916 Villa had lost a great deal of support. Even the areas such as Chihuahua, where he had a broad base of support, were turning away from him. Then came the Columbus raid and Pershing's expeditionary force. After Pershing entered Mexico, Villa's support rapidly and dramatically increased. Even among government forces, support for Carranza's rival increased. Obregón ordered his commander in Chihuahua to have any soldier who shouted "Viva Villa!" to be shot. Soldiers began to desert Carranza's army for Villa in sufficient numbers for the de facto president of Mexico and his commanders to worry. As one government official reports, "These strong sympathies for Villa are the result of the penetration of American troops, and they are certainly due to the fact that Villa is seen as being the enemy of the Americans." By the end of 1916, even as Pershing still had troops in northern Mexico, Villa's army numbered as many as 10,000. Villa's forces seized Chihuahua city and Torreón, allowing them to capture large amounts of supplies. Avoiding Pershing also allowed Villa time and opportunity to practice hit and run raids, something he had not had to use much before 1916. He continued attacking Carranza's forces, relying on the Mexican government's inability to coordinate effectively or openly with the United States lest they lose even more popular support.[68]

Carranza's use of the Plan de San Diego was successful in pushing Wilson to recognize his regime at first. Harris and Sadler note that he "played Woodrow Wilson like a violin in 1915."[69] However, when Carranza tried again to use cross-border raids from June to July 1916 to pressure the United States, it almost backfired severely. Rather than encouraging Wilson to pull Pershing out of Mexico, it prompted the American president to move 150,000 National Guard troops to the border and to prepare a message to Congress, allowing him to intervene even more in Mexico. Carranza misjudged how Wilson would interpret the chaos at the border. In 1915 Carranza correctly calculated that Wilson would want to recognize a government in order to restore order. In 1916, however, the renewed raids convinced Wilson that there was no such appropriate party. Only when it looked like Carranza was able to restore some order did Wilson relent and pull Pershing out. Of course, the coming war with Germany played a critical role as well.

Both Wilson and Carranza had nationalistic groups within their respective nations, clamoring for the use of force. In Wilson's case, several factors helped mitigate the risk somewhat. First, Wilson was well aware that Germany wanted the United States to get into a war with Mexico. Such a war would hinder America's ability to aid Britain and France through arms sales or by entering the war against Germany. Second, Wilson was not a leader who would go to war for reasons of reputation. Recent studies in international relations have looked at what is referred to as "self-monitoring" and a concern for appearance of resolve. Individuals who rank high in self-monitoring carefully watch and control their "self-presentation in social situations." More aware of social cues than low self-monitors, they carry themselves to maximize the effectiveness of their "status-enhancing behavior." In diplomacy, they are more likely to be wary of actions that make them appear "weak" and are more likely to act to maintain "face." Wilson was a low self-monitor, more interested in maintaining his sense of self than in how he appeared to others. He was less likely to act militarily to save face, although it was not impossible. As Wilson famously stated in a speech on maintaining American neutrality against Germany, "There is such a thing as a man being too proud to fight."[70]

In addition, the election of 1916 played a role. Recent studies on the idea of a "democratic peace" have noted the importance of domestic political groups in determining when a democratic state decides to go to war.[71] In the summer of 1916, Wilson ran for reelection with a theme of "He kept us out of war." It was the opening address at the convention that gave Wilson his election theme. Former governor of New York Martin Henry Glynn stirred the crowd into a happy frenzy with his address. He defended Wilson's policy of neutrality toward the war in Europe by citing examples of when four American presidents—Washington, Lincoln, Grant, and Harrison—had avoided wars by relying on diplomacy. Glynn briefly defended Wilson's Mexican policy as well, and the message was clear: he would rely on diplomacy rather than war. The crowd loved the speech, at times demanding the speaker repeat a particularly good point.[72]

The address ignored much inconvenient history, such as the Mexican-American War and several centuries of Indian wars, and Glynn completely neglected to "Remember the *Maine*." Regarding Mexico, he blamed Taft for not backing Madero's presidency, which lead to further revolution and civil war.[73] The thrust of the argument was evident, as was its popularity. Wilson would choose negotiation over war. While this did not eliminate the possibility of Wilson asking for a war in Mexico, it did create the political space Wilson could use to restrain further military action. On the other hand, Wilson could not refrain from sending signals that he considered the use of military forces. Of course, there were national security considerations; he could not leave the border undefended. Nevertheless, there were also political realities. While "he kept us out of war" was popular among his base, Wilson faced a Republican opposition that accused him of being too passive in the face of provocation. Had Wilson not made military threats, such as calling up the National Guard, further attacks on the United States across the border would have made him appear weak. Wilson thus had a delicate balancing act.

Likewise, for Carranza, he walked the line between going to war with the United States and creating chaos that Villa could use, versus not going to war and sparking a nationalistic reaction that would strengthen Villa. Fortunately, both Carranza and Wilson managed to avoid making an irreparable overt act that would result in open warfare. But while Mexico remained officially at peace with the United States, the situation in Europe was quickly reaching the point where events would force Wilson's hand. General Pershing had little time to relax back in Texas after leaving Mexico before he would be called on again.

Wilson, however, despite his early instructions keeping a tight grip on the military, ended up allowing a relatively free hand to his generals, especially Pershing. The president relied on their judgment not to provoke a wider war. Pershing's actions tested the wisdom of this policy as he pushed more than once for expanding the war against Villa to where it risked war with the Mexican government as well. Nonetheless, he remained in good stead with Wilson and Baker and would quickly be called upon for an even greater task, commanding the American Expeditionary Force in Europe.

CHAPTER 6

World War I

When discussing Wilson as the commander in chief the most obvious example is, of course, World War I. The focus of this chapter is not the battles. Wilson and Baker trusted Pershing to fight the war. However, Pershing would come into repeated conflict with the Allies, and occasionally other American commanders. It is those conflicts that engaged the president and his secretary of war. Hence, those conflicts are the focus of this chapter. Wilson and his secretary of war backed Pershing in his political battles with both the Allies and with the War Department. In return they expected their general to use his best judgment to win the war with Germany while leaving diplomacy to Wilson and his administration. Of course, it was not always easy, or even possible, to draw such fine distinctions, but Pershing and his civilian leadership managed to maintain a harmonious working relationship throughout the war. In anything, Wilson, and Baker sometimes maintained too much of a hands-off policy.

AMERICAN NEUTRALITY

As the European war broke out in the summer of 1914, then spread to the colonial possessions of the combatants in Africa and Asia, the United States remained officially neutral. American imperialism had focused on North America and the Caribbean before 1898, and then in the Pacific. However, Washington remained resolutely aloof from European conflicts and the constant mélange of treaties, saber-rattling, and imperial contests. Roughly a third of Americans were either foreign-born or had at least one foreign-born parent, so the loyalties of the public toward the war were mixed, depending upon where you or your parents came from originally. As the war progressed, American neutrality took a decidedly pro-British tilt.[1] Some of that was a simple reflection of the reality that because of the British fleet, the Allies could buy mass amounts of war material and food from the United States, from which Germany was cut off. London and Berlin had both ordered a blockade of the other, which affected the United States. However, while both the British blockade and the German U-boat war violated American neutral rights, Germany's belligerence was killing people. In contrast, Britain's actions only killed some American trade and Britain was America's best customer. Moreover, because Britain cut the telegraph lines from Germany at the very start of the war, the United States was hearing mostly Britain's side of the war, a propaganda advantage of which they took full advantage. While news reports that passed British censors often included outright lies about German conduct, Germany did commit enough of what later generations would label as war crimes to give British propaganda wide acceptance. Stories of Germans bayoneting babies, or the German soap factories using human beings for their fat, were made up, but sinking the *Lusitania* and the shooting of Belgian civilians were not.[2]

A "preparedness" campaign aimed at increasing the size of the armed forces was taking root in the United States. Wilson gave it some support, half-hearted according to his political enemies, such as Theodore Roosevelt. However, by 1916 Congress had allowed the Army and the National Guard to increase their respective size, and the Navy began an ambitious plan to build new warships. Wilson's reluctance to embrace an ambitious "Continental Army" plan led to Secretary of War Garrison's resignation. Nonetheless, Wilson's support for rearming went further than some congressional pacifists were comfortable with, and it being an election year, Wilson was happy to lead "preparedness parades" in DC, leading the way with the American flag flying at his side.

Wilson also was well aware of the German sabotage campaign in the United States. Numerous German violations of American neutrality had come to light in 1916. These included efforts to foment strikes in arms plants and the construction of incendiary devices in interned German ships in Baltimore. These latter devices were then smuggled aboard Allied ships carrying arms to Europe. The most dramatic event was the explosion at Black Tom on July 30, 1916, in New York Harbor. Detonating an entire railyard full of explosives bound for the Allies, the explosion killed four people and destroyed some 20 million dollars-worth of military goods.[3]

Despite these provocations, Wilson's heart lay with finding a peace to end the war, not with rearming. His efforts to use America's status as the only neutral world power to negotiate peace were thwarted by both the Allies and the Central Powers, as well as by foot-dragging by his own advisers, especially Colonel House and Secretary of State Lansing. Moreover, Wilson himself seemed unsure at times of how to proceed even when the warring nations showed interest in American mediation.[4] After the failure of his "Peace Without Victory" initiative in January 1917, it was increasingly clear to Wilson that only American participation as a combatant would guarantee Wilson's place at the peace table and for there to even be a peace conference before each side bled the other dry. However, Wilson was reluctant to go to war and kept looking for halfway measures to protect American neutral rights, such as arming American merchant ships.

THE U.S. ENTERS THE WAR

Germany forced the question in early 1917. First, at the end of January, they announced unrestricted submarine warfare. Neutral ships no longer had even nominal protection from sinking in the war zone around

Britain. When German submarines torpedoed American ships, Wilson broke off diplomatic relations. Still, he did not go to war. Then came the Zimmermann telegram. Germany's offer to act as Mexico's ally in a war with the United States, with Japan joining in (apparently switching sides in the war with Germany) in return for which Mexico would reacquire Texas, Arizona, and New Mexico was almost enough to convince even Wilson to go to war. Still, he hesitated. His entire cabinet, even Baker and Daniels, voted for war in a cabinet discussion. American public opinion was largely in favor. In the end, Wilson's desire for a place at the peace table made the difference. On April 2, Wilson wrote his war speech, played golf to calm his nerves,[5] then went before a joint session of Congress that evening. He asked Congress to declare war on Germany (but not Germany's allies) and make the world "safe for democracy." On January 6, Congress approved, and Wilson signed the declaration of war.

After the initial excitement, reality set in. The United States was in no way genuinely prepared for war on such a scale. Preparedness campaigns were all well and fine for election campaigns, and they did help improve the American military a little bit, but far too little had been actually accomplished to prepare the United States to fight Germany. The situation in DC ranged from mildly confused to complete chaos. Even the idea that the United States would send troops to Europe was shocking to some members of Congress. Famously Senator Thomas Martin of Virginia exclaimed, "Good Lord! You're not going to send soldiers there, are you?"[6] Wilson did expect to send troops, but it was unclear how many would be needed. However, sending men to fight in France was necessary for Wilson to have a place at the peace table alongside the French and British. The question for Wilson as commander in chief was who was to command them in the field. It had to be someone Wilson trusted to wield authority without much oversight from Washington. Wilson firmly believed that Lincoln had interfered too much with his commanders in the Civil War and he did not want to do the same.[7] There were several candidates from which Wilson could choose. The existing major generals were Leonard Wood, J. Franklin Bell, Thomas Barry, Hugh Scott, and Tasker Bliss. Bell, Barry, Bliss, and Scott were all in their sixties and ready to retire.

That left Wood and Pershing (who was not yet a major general, but was senior enough to place in command).

PERSHING

Pershing was the only choice for Baker and Wilson. Both he and Wood were Republicans, but the latter was also a good friend with Theodore Roosevelt and had made a nuisance of himself criticizing Wilson and the lack of preparedness to enter the war. Neither Wilson nor Baker liked Wood, nor did they trust him. The secretary of war called him his "insubordinate subordinate," and Wilson told Baker, "Personally I have no confidence in either General Wood's discretion or in his loyalty to his superiors." Baker judged that Wood wanted to be both a great soldier and a great politician at the same time, a combination Baker felt was inappropriate in the United States. Wood was assigned to New York, but that put him in close contact with Roosevelt as well as the center of the American press. The Army reassigned Wood to the Southeastern Department to oversee the construction of training camps, and later he received his own division. In March 1918, when he was about to leave for France with his division, Wood was removed from command at Pershing's request and sent to San Francisco to take charge of the Western Department. His politicking and constant pushing of the boundaries of insubordination cost him a chance to command in the war.[8]

In contrast to Wood, Pershing paid attention to the chain of command. While he could be "prickly and aloof," he had accepted Wilson and Baker's instructions in Mexico to avoid a wider war even though his actions at time flirted with insubordination. He was not chosen immediately when the United States declared war in April, however. Despite the unmistakably clear signs that war with Germany was coming, Wilson and his administration did little of the obvious preparation, such as picking a commander. Pershing probably first knew he was being considered when his father-in-law, Senator F. E. Warren, sent him a telegram that read, "Wire me today whether and how much you speak and write French."[9] Pershing had struggled at West Point with French but assured his father-in-law that he had studied the language when he was in Paris in 1908, spoke it "quite fluently," and could read and write it well. He exaggerated but did put in the effort to improve his skills.[10]

Moreover, unlike Wood, Pershing was vocally supportive of Wilson in April 1917. He sent a message to Wilson praising his war address before Congress. Pershing also gave speeches supporting the war effort, including a draft. His father-in-law passed copies of press reports of the better ones to Baker. When the congressional delegation from Texas rebelled against a proposed draft, Pershing lobbied the state governor James Ferguson and convinced him to urge his state's representatives to support conscription. When the law passed, Pershing praised it to the press: "It means that every man will have a role to play. To have a hand in affairs and know that he is part of the system will make a better citizen of every man." A cynic might take this to be buttering up the boss for an appointment, but Pershing praised the president to his Republican senator father-in-law in private. "I think Woodrow Wilson is going down in posterity as the greatest man of this time." That surely was not a sentiment one Republican would be expected to express to another, even in a private letter. Pershing genuinely agreed with Wilson. The war was about autocracy versus democracy, and it would require sacrifices on the part of the American people, including conscription.[11]

The choice then between Wood and Pershing was no choice at all. Baker, like his president, liked to hear from experts. The secretary of war asked Major General Scott his opinion. Scott recommended Pershing. Baker sent that recommendation to Wilson. On May 2 Scott sent Pershing a telegram: "Under plans under consideration is one which will require, among other troops, four infantry regiments and one artillery regiment from your department for service in France, if plans are carried out, you will be in command of the entire force." The details were left to Pershing. He would pick the regiments and would choose his own staff. Sorting his decades of experience in his mind, Pershing left for Washington to meet with his superiors putting together the first American combat division to fight in a European war. His experiences in Mexico had allowed him to watch many of the junior officers in action—which ones impressed, which were lacking.[12]

Pershing arrived in Washington on May 10, meeting first with Major General Scott at the State, War, and Navy building next to the White House. Scott explained why the handful of more senior officers had been passed over and then discussed the situation in Europe. Pershing learned that the War College Division of the General Staff had presented several recommendations. One called for the draft law. Other recommendations had to deal with supplies and equipment. The hastily organized war plan was vague on most details, but it called for an army of a half million men. Pershing described himself as more chagrined than astonished to realize so little had been done in the way of preparation when there were so many things that might have been done before. The coming of war was certainly not a surprise. Yet, only general plans had been made beforehand, and even after the declaration of war, the War Department, in Pershing's words, "seemed to be suffering from a kind of inertia." There were, Scott noted, just two basic plans circulating. One by the War College was only five pages long. The second was written by Baker and had been approved by Wilson. Both called for a small division, about 12,000 men, to be sent to France. Neither specified the necessary details for organizing, transporting, and deploying troops overseas.[13]

Pershing then met with Baker. The secretary of war did not impress Pershing much physically at first. The diminutive secretary's feet did not even meet the floor when he sat in his office chair at his desk. However, in talking with him, Pershing quickly gained a "distinctly favorable impression" of the man, which boded well for their working relationship. Baker told the general that he would be commanding a division, which had to be quickly organized. It was not until the next day that Baker informed Pershing that President Wilson wanted him to be the commander in chief of the entire expeditionary force sent to Europe. The new commander was to pick a capable staff and head to Europe as quickly as possible to begin discussions with the British and French as to deploying an American army on the western front. Many essential details were still undecided. Baker told Pershing he would have several divisions, but the specifics were not yet developed. The numbers depended on how many troops transports were available, which was still unknown for the foreseeable future.[14]

Baker and Wilson's regard for Pershing's opinions were quickly demonstrated when Baker asked the general about recruiting four divisions of infantry volunteers. Pershing was opposed. He felt an expanded regular army was sufficient, with its numbers increased through a draft. The regular Army had a low opinion of volunteers in a war. Pershing referred to "the evils of the volunteer system in the Civil War," particularly when it came to picking officers. One of the most awkward moments for the volunteer division issue came when former president Theodore Roosevelt sent letters to Wilson and Baker on May 18 asking permission to raise two or even four divisions to go to France. His request was met, at least behind closed doors, with horror. The former Rough Rider was in his late fifties, overweight and in poor health. The thought of him leading a charge, à la San Juan Hill, against a German trench must have seemed like a nightmare. Moreover, it was no secret that Roosevelt wanted to run for office again, and no Democrat wanted Roosevelt the war hero of yet another war running in 1920. Pershing greatly admired Roosevelt but had little respect for amateurs' ability to command troops in a war. Wilson turned his rival down, although he tried to do so in as gracious a way as possible, noting, "It would be very agreeable to me to pay Mr. Roosevelt this compliment and the Allies the complement of sending to their aid one of our most distinguished public man [sic]." However, the president continued, he could not spare the experienced officers that Roosevelt wanted. They were needed to train the many men that the draft would bring into the military.[15]

On May 24, Pershing met with Wilson along with Baker. The meeting went well. Wilson had been familiarizing himself with Pershing's record and praised his performance in Mexico. Wilson also told Pershing that the United States was to try new things to break the stalemate on the western front: " 'Delaying actions' were not the way to win." This fit perfectly with Pershing's attitude that the United States could break the stalemate. However, the problem was that the general's ideas of how to break the stalemate ignored the Allies' experiences to date, rather than profiting from them. Pershing would concentrate on American troops being fresh and of high morale; he focused on riflemen rather than building on what the Allies—and the Germans–were learning about the use of new technologies in combined operations. The United States would learn, but it would be a very steep learning curve. Crucially at the end of the meeting, Wilson promised, "You shall have my full support."[16]

After the meeting, Baker gave Pershing his official orders, quoted here in full:

1. The President designates you to command all the land forces of the United States operating in continental Europe and in the United Kingdom of Great Britain and Ireland, including any part of the Marine Corps which may be detached for service there with the Army. From your command are excepted the Military Attachés and others of the Army who may be on duty directly with our several embassies.

2. You will proceed with your staff to Europe. Upon arrival in Great Britain, France and any other of the countries at war with the Imperial German Government, you will at once place yourself in communication with the American Embassy and through its agency with the authorities of any country to which the forces of the United States may be sent.

3. You are invested with the authority and duties devolved by the laws, regulations, orders, and customs of the United States upon the commander of an army in the field in time of war and with the authority and duties in like manner devolved upon department commanders in peace and war, including the special authorities and duties assigned to the commander of the Philippine Department in so far as the same are applicable to the particular circumstances of your command.

4. You will establish, after consultation with the French War Office, all necessary bases, lines of communication, depots, etc., and make all the incidental arrangements essential to active participation at the front.

5. In military operations against the Imperial German Government, you are directed to cooperate with the forces of the other countries employed against that enemy; but in so doing the underlying idea

must be kept in view that the forces of the United States are a separate and distinct component of the combined forces, the identity of which must be preserved. This fundamental rule is subject to such minor exceptions in particular circumstances as your judgment may approve. The decision as to when your command, or any of its parts, is ready for action is confided to you, and you will exercise full discretion in determining the manner of cooperation. But, until the forces of the United States are in your judgment sufficiently strong to warrant operations as an independent command, it is understood that you will cooperate as a component of whatever Army you may be assigned to by the French government.

6. You will keep the Department fully advised of all that concerns your command and will communicate your recommendations freely and directly to the Department. And in general, you are vested with all necessary authority to carry on the war vigorously in harmony with the spirit of these instructions and toward a victorious conclusion.[17]

The instructions gave Pershing a free hand on military matters. The two key provisions were, first, he was to maintain an independent American military once his forces were strong enough (rather than parceling it out to the British and French), and second, he was to maintain lines of communication with both the War Department and the State Department. The former was to be expected. No secretary of war would be willing to let their commander overseas have a completely free hand. The importance of keeping the State Department in the loop demonstrated that the military action was to coincide with American diplomacy. The Wilson administration's goal was to earn a seat of influence at the postwar peace table. This required an independent U.S. Army fighting on the western front and regular lines of communication between Pershing and American diplomats.

THE AEF AND THE ALLIES

Maintaining an independent American Expeditionary Forces is critical to understanding Wilson's goals. As early as April 6, the day Congress passed the declaration of war against Germany, Wilson wrote to Colonel

House that requests from Britain and France to send individual delega-
tions to discuss the war efforts was "in some degree [to] take charge of us
as an assistant to Great Britain."[18] This section also answered Pershing's
concern over the amalgamation of the AEF into the Allies' militaries.
While not quite a blank check, Pershing's orders gave him extraordinary
independence in his command.

After receiving his initial orders, Pershing then received a second set
of written orders. This one came through Baker from the acting chief of
staff, Maj. Gen. Tasker H. Bliss:

DEAR GENERAL PERSHING:

In compliance with the orders of the President assigning you to
the command of the United States forces in France, the Secretary
of War directs that you proceed, with the necessary staff, to Paris,
France, via England.

The Secretary of War further directs that, upon your arrival in
France, you establish such relations with the French Government
and the military representatives of the British government now
serving in France as will enable you effectively to plan and conduct
active operations in conjunction and in cooperation with the French
armies operating in France against Germany and her allies.

As a preliminary step, the Secretary of War deems it desirable
that you have a thorough study made of the available bases, lines of
communication and camps of instruction, so that you may direct
preparations for the arrival of successive contingents of our troops
in France. The equipment and training for active service of the
troops under your command in the trenches or on the firing line
should be carried on as rapidly as possible. While the entrance of our
forces into the theater of active operations will be left entirely to your
judgment, it should not be unduly hastened. Yet it is believed that
the purpose of your presence in France will be materially advanced
by the appearance of our troops upon the firing line.

The Secretary of War desires that you keep the department fully
advised of all questions of importance concerning the operations of
your troops and that you submit your views from time to time upon

such questions, as well as upon matters pertaining to the general situation in Europe. He also expects that, as the superior military representative of the United States in France, you will exercise such general authority as will best contribute to the fulfillment of your mission in France.[19]

Pershing noted in his memoirs that he "never understood why there should have been two letters of instructions emanating from the same authority." Fortunately, they did not contradict one another. However, the second letter was not as strong in its instruction to keep Pershing's forces separate from those of the Allies although it did leave the decision to Pershing. As it turned out, he needed the flexibility and did assign some American units to both the British and the French when he felt it advanced his mission.[20]

American inexperience showed in Pershing's trip to Europe with his staff on the *Baltic* from New York on May 28. The trip was supposed to be a secret. The ship had dodged two German torpedoes on the voyage from Britain to the United States. One successful torpedo strike on the trip back to England with Pershing, and his staff onboard would decapitate the entire AEF military leadership along with their French and British liaisons. Nevertheless, when Pershing and his party arrived at the dock, there sat their boxes of equipment and supplies, out in the open, carefully, and clearly stenciled "AEF—General Pershing's Headquarters." A party of ladies waited to see the group off, and as the *Baltic* left, an artillery battery on shore fired a ceremonial salute. The AEF commander growled that this just "made the announcement of our departure complete."[21]

Fortunately, the *Baltic* arrived in Liverpool safely on June 8. It had sailed alone, following a defensive zig-zag pattern in the danger zone near Britain, until being met by two U.S. destroyers on June 6. During the voyage, Pershing's staff continued planning how to deploy American forces and meet with the Allied liaison officers. The meetings and planning continued as the Americans were welcomed and feted in Britain. *At last, the Yanks have begun to arrive!* Pershing also had some diplomatic tasks. His small mission contributed nothing to the Allies' military effort in terms of strength, but it was a valuable propaganda exercise to bolster

British and French morale. Senior AEF staff made the rounds of receptions and meetings, showing the flag and assuring the Brits that American help would soon be on its way. Pershing even got a personal meeting with King George V, extending greetings from President Wilson. For the most part, however, the reception was reserved. There were no cheering crowds waving flags, and British officers seemed annoyed that the Americans seemed to focus their attention on the French.[22]

After ten days in Britain, Pershing and his party landed in Boulogne, France. There they were met by deliriously joyful crowds, including a French band that played "The Star-Spangled Banner," not once, but three times, while the American officers faithfully, if a bit impatiently, stood at attention. Then they played "La Marseillaise" several times. One of Pershing's aides joked that a French officer with one arm must have lost the other by holding it in a salute so long while his national anthem played repeatedly. Alas, he learned to his chagrin, the French officer had lost his arm trying to throw away a German grenade to protect his men.[23]

In Paris, Pershing met with the senior French general, Henri-Philippe Pétain. The two men got along well, although their tactical visions were the opposite of the other. Pétain emphasized the defensive to keep the exhausted French army from collapse. Pershing, as noted, favored a vigorous offensive. Nonetheless, the two men worked well together, although Pershing must have been concerned when his French counterpart expressed his gratefulness that the United States had, at last, entered the war, but finished, "I hope it is not too late." There were diplomatic missions as well. Pershing met the French president, Raymond Poincaré, and appeared before the French Parliament. One of Pershing's staff officers, Colonel C. E. Stanton, stood by the grave of Marquis de Lafayette and famously proclaimed, "Lafayette, we are here!"[24]

As a senior representative of the United States, Pershing could not help but be involved in American diplomacy from the start. An Allied war conference met in Paris on July 25. Wilson was reluctant to appoint a representative. He believed that since the United States was only at war with Germany, and not Berlin's allies (the United States did not declare war on Austria-Hungary until December 1917 and never declared war on

Bulgaria or the Ottomans) it was inappropriate for the United States to be involved in discussions of the war against the three junior Central Powers. Moreover, he did not want it to appear that the meeting would be discussing a postwar settlement. U.S. ambassador to the United Kingdom Walter Hines Page asked if General Pershing and Vice Adm. William S. Sims (roughly Pershing's Navy equivalent) could attend. Wilson preferred they not do so, suggesting that "all necessary naval and military information can be obtained after the conference." Wilson seems not to have considered that their presence at the meeting might be needed to coordinate actions between the various Allies, reflecting Wilson's inexperience with military matters, especially in conjunction with other nations. Sims and Pershing did, however, attend separate meetings of military representatives.[25]

THE NAVY: VICE ADMIRAL SIMS

There was no exact counterpart to Pershing for the Navy, but the closest, especially in his own mind, was Vice Adm. William Snowden Sims. Sims was tall, thin, and dignified. More than a bit of an iconoclast, he was not popular with many of his superiors as he was often more forthright in his opinions than diplomatic or political. He was competent, however. As inspector of target practice under Roosevelt, he "brought about a considerable improvement in the efficiency of gunners." A strong Anglophile, in 1910 he had given a speech at Guildhall in Britain in which he proclaimed that if Britain were threatened, "you may count upon every man, every dollar, every ship, and every drop of blood of your kindred across the seas." The remarks were publicized, embarrassing the Taft administration. He was then "exiled" to the Naval War College. The Guildhall speech could have easily derailed his career permanently, and Daniels informed him that he had been appointed despite his Guildhall remarks, not because of them.[26]

As early as March 1917, as it was clear the United States was drawing ever closer to entering the war, the Wilson administration had begun a few preparations. Wilson approved an increase of 157,000 men for the Marines and Navy. The U.S. fleet moved to Chesapeake Bay from Guantanamo Bay, and Secretary of the Navy Josephus Daniels was told to begin planning how to cooperate with the British Admiralty. Unlike the Army, the Navy would be working closely with and often under the command of the British navy. Wilson was clearly not concerned that subordinating the U.S. fleet, at least partially, to those of the Allies would diminish his place at the peace table. The battle that Pershing had to fight to keep an independent U.S. Army in the field simply did not exist for Sims.

On March 26 Daniels ordered Sims and an aide to travel undercover to London. They traveled in civilian clothing under assumed names. When an alert steward noticed that the monogram on a pair of pajamas did not match the passenger's name, he reported Sims and his aide, Commander John V. Babcock, to the ship's captain. The captain, who knew the officers' real identities, reassured the sharp-eyed steward that the two men were not German spies.[27] Sims and Babcock arrived on April 9 at Liverpool. The only excitement was when their ship was damaged by hitting a mine near the harbor entrance. Once safely on shore, the officers were greeted warmly by the British. Sims set up an office in the American embassy at first.

Daniels had, however, not set the chain of command. He never did straighten it out. Was Sims the equivalent to Pershing, answerable directly to the appropriate civilian secretary? Was he under the command of Vice Adm. Henry T. Mayo, commander of the Atlantic Fleet? Were the naval attachés in the U.S. embassies in London under his command or not? What about the attachés in the other European capitals? Did Sims command the destroyer force based in Queenstown, Ireland? What about those who worked with the French based in Brest? How about those in the Mediterranean? Sims assumed command of all naval forces in the European theater one by one, while Mayo assumed Sims answered to him. The conflict went on through the entire war, Sims adding to his portfolio while Daniels did little to clear up the confusion. While it seems to have had little effect on the U.S. naval war effort, in the end, the situation sheds light on Daniels' struggling to grasp the details of military command and the necessity of keeping clean lines of responsibility.

The most critical issue for the naval war in 1917 was submarines. Wilson wanted to strike "the hornets" in their "nest" by attacking the submarine base at Bruges. Wilson was not alone in this desire, but as Vice Admiral Sims explained, it simply was not possible. The base was too well defended by German artillery. How then to defend against the submarine threat before Germany could sink enough ships to force London to come to terms? There were numerous suggestions from well-meaning amateurs, including a plan to have Thomas Edison invent some new gadgets to do the job.[28] Sims had to explain why each method had a weakness. For example, could the Allies lay a mine barrage across the North Sea? Yes, but German minesweepers could clear a path, and until 1918 the technology did not exist to make the mines sufficiently reliable to be an effective barrier. What would immediately help in the war against the submarine was for the United States to send as many destroyers and small subchasers as possible, and for the Allies to switch to the convoy system. Sims' task was to argue for both solutions, for which he had some support from Washington.

Wilson and Daniels had supported a large-scale buildup of the American Navy. However, it was heavily weighted toward larger capital warships, battleships, and cruisers. The Navy Secretary realized this early in 1917 and modified the naval bill passed in 1916. Battleships were placed on hold while shipbuilding capacity was geared toward destroyers and other antisubmarine craft. It would take a while for the ships to be built, so the United States was initially limited to the forty-seven destroyers they already had in 1917. There were another fifty or so under construction or on order, but few were finished before the end of the war.[29] Daniels' diary indicates how desperate the need was. He investigated buying destroyers from Argentina. He considered plans for an electric net to be spread across the North Sea. When a submarine hit it, a light would be triggered along with an alarm that would sound for ninety minutes, alerting Allied patrol boats.[30] Moreover, the entire fleet was not ready to go to war. Many of the ships needed repairs, including at least half of the destroyers, and many had only partial crews. Gunnery skills had improved, but none of the thirty-seven American battleships (only six of which measured up to the German or British first-class standards) were ready for war when the United States entered the conflict. In short, Daniels had not seen to his charge's readiness for war. Fortunately, he did rise to the occasion once the war began, and he had done an excellent job regarding training. One officer noted that "personnel were in a remarkably well-trained state of efficiency and readiness."[31]

Despite his shortcomings, Daniels had a better grasp of what was needed to defeat Germany at sea than did some of his commanders. He understood that defeating Germany would take both a way to neutralize the submarine threat and to field an army of significant size in France. The latter required the Navy to supply and guard troop transports and supply ships for Pershing's AEF. The Navy Secretary even claimed that the Navy's "most important task [would be] to land American soldiers on French soil." Daniels was a "Big Navy" man by 1917 but understood the need for destroyers and antisubmarine craft for the short term. The big battleships and cruisers would be needed after the war, to make sure that the U.S. fleet was the equal of Britain's.[32]

One problem for Daniels was political. He could not send every available American destroyer to aid Britain. A significant portion of the fleet had to remain to guard the American East Coast. An enemy invasion of the United States from the Atlantic had been a staple of war novels for well over a decade, often by a barely camouflaged fictional nation that looked a lot like Germany. Indeed, the official American war plans for a war with Germany, Plan Black, called for a mostly defensive war with the American Navy guarding the East Coast. In reality, the German High Seas Fleet was bottled up in port by the British fleet, and the American coast was too far for most German submarines to operate efficiently. However, to leave the East Coast open to even a hypothetical German attack was unthinkable. So, a significant portion had to be held back, out of the actual war in the operational zone around Britain and France.[33]

The argument over deploying U.S. destroyers to Britain and France would drive a large part of Sims' struggles with Washington. As soon as he reached Britain and was briefed on the submarine war situation, he realized how much danger Britain was in to lose the war. London issued cheerful reports for home consumption to keep morale up, but they were an example of lying with statistics. The total number of ships sunk was low in comparison to the total number entering British ports. However, the latter number included numerous small coastal craft, useless in bringing in supplies from the United States and Canada. Moreover, Germany could now turn out three new submarines a week, and the British had only managed to sink or capture fewer than sixty during the entire war to date. Reports in the British press of German submarines voluntarily surrendering were fakes, made to bolster British morale and depress that of Germany. At the current rate of loss, Britain would, Sims was told, be unable to continue the war after the first of November.[34]

Sims' messages back to Daniels tried to raise the alarm without seeming panicked. In his April 21 cable he noted the tonnage sunk in the preceding weeks (408,000 tons). He recommended the immediate sailing of all available destroyers, followed at the earliest moment by reinforcement of destroyers and all light draft craft available. "Fuel is available on this side." Daniels ordered six destroyers to leave immediately.[35] They arrived at Queenstown on May 4, 1917, which became the first U.S. destroyer base for the British Isles as the destroyers were soon followed by more, as well as supply and repair vessels. The American destroyers participated in the existing patrols looking for German submarines in the most heavily traveled sea lanes. However, Wilson and Sims agreed on the need for a convoy system, which Sims argued strongly for in Britain. Daniels was ambivalent, and the Navy brass in the United States opposed the idea. From 1914 until well into 1917, ships sailing to Britain came alone. The British were convinced that it would be more difficult for German U-boats to find individual ships on the ocean. Convoys, they believed, merely collected targets for the Germans into a convenient group. Moreover, a convoy could only sail as fast as its slowest members. Sims argued that the patrol system in which destroyers and other antisubmarine craft went hunting for submarines was a failure. Submarines could see patrols coming and slip away easily. Often the only way a patrol knew where a submarine was located was when a civilian ship was attacked. Indeed, in May 1917, the American patrols out of Queenstown attacked only two U-boats. Both attacks failed. Convoys, the United States argued, would not only allow the merchant ships to be protected by destroyers, but they would also force the U-boats to come to them. Under pressure from the United States, Britain began to reconsider the matter.[36]

Wilson's instincts about convoys were correct, as was his frustration with the British Admiralty's reluctance to switch to convoys. However, he drew at least one erroneous lesson from the issue. As he noted in a speech in August on the battleship *Pennsylvania*, "This is an unprecedented war, and therefore, it is a war in one sense for amateurs. Nobody ever conducted a war like this, and therefore nobody can pretend to be a professional in a war like this." On the surface, he was correct. Fighting World War I was a learning experience for every side. However, the idea that those untrained in military science had an advantage in learning from the ongoing war was more than a little presumptuous.[37]

The British had been using convoys and destroyer escorts in limited circumstances since the start of the war. Destroyers protected the capital ships of the Grand Fleet. They escorted convoys to the Netherlands, and troop ships from overseas and from Britain to France. Finally, at the end of April 1917, they adopted the convoy system for all ships sailing under fifteen knots from the western hemisphere to Great Britain. Wilson and Sims' insistence played a role, but the most significant factor in convincing the British Admiralty was that with the United States entering the war, there would be sufficient escort ships to make it work. Ironically, there was still resistance within the U.S. Navy. In June, even after the British had begun trial convoys, the U.S. Navy was still considering having ships meet in a mid-ocean rendezvous and sailing together in convoy to Britain. Almost to the end of the war, they opposed westward-bound convoys, accepting the idea only after Wilson finally intervened.[38]

THE AEF UNDER FIRE

While the U.S. Navy was cooperating in a convoy system administered by the British, Pershing was continuing to struggle to keep American forces under his command and not have to parcel them out to the British and French as reinforcements. In mid-October 1917, the 1st Division was trained and in place on the front. They were stationed in Somerville, picked because it was a tranquil portion of the front, perfect for easing an

President Woodrow Wilson and Gen. John J. Pershing at a review of troops during the Paris Peace Conference. Wilson is wearing a kangaroo fur coat given to him by the Australians.

Col. Edward M. House and Woodrow Wilson in June 1915. Wilson was wearing a black armband in mourning for his first wife, Ellen Axson Wilson, who died in August 1914.

William Jennings Bryan (*left*) and John R. Silliman. Wilson and Bryan employed Silliman, the American vice consul at Saltillo, to pass messages to Carranza.

Secretary of State Robert Lansing

Secretary of State Bainbridge Colby (*left*) and Assistant Secretary of State Frank Polk, 1920

Lindley Miller Garrison, Wilson's first secretary of war, 1913–16

Secretary of War Newton Baker and Chief of Staff Maj. Gen. Hugh L. Scott

Secretary of War Newton Baker (*in rear left with silk top hat*) preceded by Gen. John J. Pershing (*left*) and Gen. Peyton C. March (*right*)

Maj. Smedley D. Butler in his U.S. Marine Corps uniform. This photo was taken before his mission in Haiti.

General Venustiano Carranza de la Garza

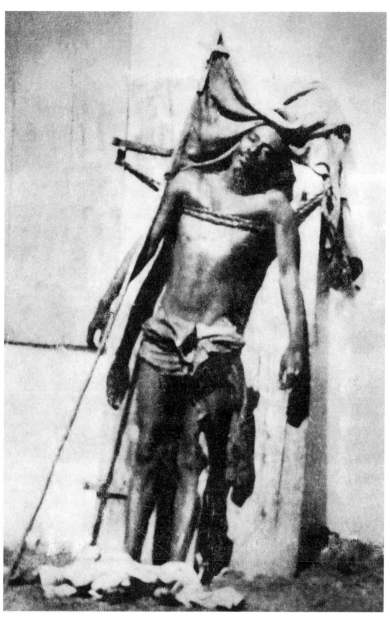

The body of Haitian nationalist leader Charlemagne Péralte. His body was fastened to a door following his killing by members of the U.S. Marine Corps. The photo was published in Haiti to demoralize Péralte's remaining followers, November 1919.

An American soldier stands atop a boxcar in Siberia during the intervention into Russia's civil war.

inexperienced American division into the war on the western front. At 6 a.m. on October 23 the first American artillery shot of the war was fired by Battery C.[39] After ten days, the 1st Battalion was rotated back, and the 2nd Battalion was put into the line. On November 3, the Germans greeted the AEF with a fierce artillery barrage and a night raid, killing three doughboys and wounding several others. They also took eleven prisoners. The French general in that sector put on an elaborate ceremony at the funeral for the three dead Americans. The AEF had gotten a bloody nose in a small action in a quiet sector, but the draft and the hurried efforts to put together training camps back home were starting to pay off. A week after the night raid on the American lines at Sommerville the 165th U.S. Infantry Regiment, part of the 42nd "Rainbow" Division, landed at Liverpool. The flow of U.S. troops to the front was starting to pick up.[40]

As commander in chief, Wilson was in charge of not just the regular U.S. Army, but the AEF consisting of National Guard units and the "National Army" made up of draftees. The Rainbow Division was made up of National Guard units from across the United States (hence, spreading across the country "like a rainbow"). Twenty-six states were represented. The idea was that of Col. Douglas MacArthur, who believed it would guarantee that every section of the country would believe it had a stake in the war. The 42nd underwent training in France to survive trench warfare, and then at the end of February 1918, the 165th Regiment, mostly made up of men from New York City, took over a quiet French sector near Lunéville. On March 1 they stormed a small section of the German trenches, the first ground gained by U.S. troops. It was a tiny portion, but it was a start. American troops were at least in action, albeit in small numbers. The Germans were about to launch their last series of major offensives to defeat the Allies before the AEF could arrive in numbers sufficient to make a difference. The rest of the spring of 1918 would be a race between German advances and offensives and American troops being rushed to the front.[41]

In December 1917 the United States informed the British, French, and Italian governments that it would participate in the Supreme War Council, which was to coordinate the Allies' war efforts to an unprecedented degree.[42] The need to better coordinate was made clear by the military situation. The British had lost far too many men for too little a gain in the Battle of Passchendaele, the Russians were clearly about to withdraw from the war, and the Italians had suffered the disaster of Caporetto. Britain's Prime Minister David Lloyd George pushed for the council's creation. The French agreed, but with reservations, fearing the council would dilute the Allied forces on the western front to bolster British efforts in Greece and the Middle East. Each of the three Allies was represented by its respective prime minister and a second member of the government. Meeting in Paris, each also appointed a permanent military representative. The United States was a member, but the American representatives acted within very stringent limits set by President Wilson. Not wanting to sacrifice his freedom to negotiate a postwar peace treaty, Wilson appointed the American ambassador to France as an observer to meet with the political leaders. France's Premier Georges Clemenceau snidely referred to him as being "ears but not a mouth." Additionally, Colonel House met with the council when he was in Europe as Wilson's representative. Gen. Tasker Bliss was the American permanent military representative and participated fully in military discussions.[43]

In December 1917 the British and French were still pressing Wilson to have Pershing deploy parts of the AEF under British and French command. In a cable dated Christmas Eve, Baker suggested to Pershing that he consider deploying some of his forces "nearer the junction of the British and French lines which would enable you to throw your strength in whichever direction seemed most necessary." Baker continued, "This suggestion is not, however, pressed beyond whatever merit it had in your judgement." He was passing it along from the president to "acquaint you with" the British and French suggestions; it was entirely up to Pershing. He was still authorized "to act with entire freedom in making the best possible disposition and use of your forces for accomplishing the main purposes in view."[44] The issue of amalgamation of American forces would continue to return. Wilson and Baker were still relying on Pershing's judgment, but they were under tremendous diplomatic pressure.

Pershing replied to the suggestion of sending American units to the French and British about as one would expect, with a no. He noted,

"Do not think an emergency now exists that would warrant our putting companies or battalions into British or French divisions and would not do so except in grave crisis." Baker approved. In his cover note to Wilson on Pershing's reply to the secretary, he noted it would "be difficult" to get loaned American units back from the Allies. Moreover, it would lead to a "weakening of the forces under General Pershing's command for independent operations."[45] Wilson and Baker would pass along the Allied suggestions, but they still gave Pershing the final say. The AEF commander's comment about "emergencies" would provide a loophole—one fitting with his original orders, but a loophole nonetheless.

The first four AEF divisions were sent to quiet sectors of the front for final training in early 1918. The 1st Division took over part of the French lines in Toul. This section of the line was marshland, with the Germans holding the high ground. Next came the 26th Division, made up of the New England National Guard, followed by the 42nd Rainbow Division. The latter went to the line in late February. Like the area near Tours where the 1st Division was initially stationed, the 42nd Division's area, the Baccarat sector near Lunéville, was used for training American units through the war. The fourth of the early divisions was the 2nd, which had both regular Army and U.S. Marines. They were sent to a less quiet area near Verdun along the St. Mihiel salient. A fifth replacement division, the 32nd, made up of National Guard from Michigan and Wisconsin, was stationed in the rear.[46] There was an exception to Pershing's refusal to allow the amalgamation of American units into French ones, the assignment of four "colored" infantry regiments in January 1918. Four infantry regiments of the 93nd Division were offered, although they did not have all of their necessary components, including either a brigade or a divisional organization. The French accepted.[47] The division never did acquire its missing components, such as artillery. The four component regiments served with three different French divisions in the French Fourth Army, all sharing the same truncated administrative staff.[48]

By March 1918, there were 300,000 American troops in France. Secretary of War Baker visited France that month to consult with Pershing. The two men liked and trusted each other and enjoyed a good working relationship. Pershing took Baker to visit Marshal Joseph Joffre. Baker may have passed on Wilson's concerns that the old French marshal had too much influence on Pershing, which strained American relations with General Pétain. The next several days were spent touring the port facilities built by the Americans—assembly yards, warehouses, rail lines, and training schools with French instructors. It was all awe-inspiring and demonstrated how the supply problems of 1917 were being overcome. New hospital trains were ready to treat the wounded from a large campaign. Baker may have been a bit chagrined when touring the airfields, as the American pilots and aircrews were flying and fixing French aircraft and firing French weapons using French ammunition. At least the U.S. military was shipping in vast amounts of raw material to make the weapons.[49] There were still problems. Not every warehouse, repair yard, or cold storage plant was completed. However, there was clear progress being made. Baker even visited American troops at the front, although his handlers were careful to steer him to a quiet sector. Under the guidance of a French commander, he visited with a unit from Iowa serving in a French area. One of the American officers with him worried that a lucky German shot might hit "the right spot." He noted later that "the most rigid of salutes would not quite atone to the Commander-in-Chief for the loss of a Secretary of War whom he had found so satisfactory." On the way back, speeding down a section of road that German gunners knew well, a four-inch shell passed over the car's hood to explode just beyond it. Baker could truthfully then say he had been under fire.[50]

March 21 was Baker's last day for the tour in France, highlighted by a luncheon at General Pétain's headquarters. On the way, they could hear a sound that grew louder and louder. It was German shelling, far beyond the usual daily "hate" shelling each side indulged in. It was so loud and steady when they arrived at the French headquarters that it was clear what was happening. The long-awaited German offensive had begun. Still, everyone acted as if there was no emergency and enjoyed the luncheon. As Baker's escort later noted, there was nothing for them to do until each officer's chief called for him. It did no good to run about. Better to stay calm, get some food, and prepare for the long hours to come. Afterward,

Baker left for London, traveling past British troops rushing into battle. The German offensive was directed at the place where the French and British armies met, just where Baker, in his December message, had suggested that Pershing deploy some American troops.[51]

The 1918 Ludendorff offensive that began that March morning was the German effort to defeat the Allies before the United States could bring its full strength to bear. The defeat of Russia freed approximately fifty German divisions from the eastern front, giving Germany a temporary advantage. Their goal was to break through the Allied lines in the region where the British and French militaries met. If the Germans could cut off the British from their supply ports, Britain would be forced to sue for peace. With Britain defeated, France would then have to surrender. Initially the attacks were very successful, advancing for miles across areas where men struggled for months to advance a few hundred yards. The German stormtrooper tactics worked well, but their advance troops outran the German supply lines. The German army succeeded in making the furthest advances either side had made on the western front since 1914. However, it was, in many respects, a pyrrhic victory. They suffered heavy casualties, used up scarce supplies, and captured ground with little strategic value that would be difficult to defend. By midsummer of 1918, with more American troops pouring in, the Allies regained a numerical advantage, and the Germans withdrew from much of the territory they had won in the spring to form more defensible lines.

The German spring offensive caused great consternation among the Allies, increasing the pressure on the United States to allow its forces to be integrated into the British and French forces as replacement troops. Pershing made some concessions to the demands, understandable given the situation, but held firm on continuing training and importing entire divisions to form an independent American army on the western front. The most dramatic change came with Gen. Ferdinand Foch's appointment as the supreme commander to coordinate the Allies' war efforts. While he did not have the power to order Pershing to deploy troops to certain areas, he could make strong suggestions. He could coordinate, but not command. Baker heard the news while dining with Britain's prime minister David Lloyd George. Lloyd George was pleased, but Vice Admiral Sims asked why it had not been done earlier. The British prime minister noted that any British government that accepted an overall French commander earlier would have been quickly removed from office. The nature of the German offensive, however, made it not only necessary but possible. Baker noted that President Wilson had earlier supported the idea and would be supportive now.[52]

Baker headed back to France rather than returning to the United States. Only a few U.S. troops were initially in the battle, some engineers working on railway tracks for the British who joined in. Three regiments of engineers were offered to British Gen. Douglas Haig for support. Pétain was told that the four U.S. combat divisions ready for the front were at his disposal. The Supreme War Council passed a resolution, with the support of American representative General Bliss, that the United States agrees to "temporary service of American units in Allied Army corps and divisions." "Those reinforcements," however, should be "obtained from other units than those American units which are now operating with the French." The council also agreed that the United States only send over infantry and machine-gun units for the time being. This was the British position, which Pershing opposed in favor of also continuing to bring over artillery, support, and other units needed to make full divisions for a genuine American army in France. Baker kept President Wilson updated with daily reports and quickly sent a cable to Wilson about the council's decision. Baker recommended the president's approval, with the stipulation that it would be temporary to preclude the formation of an independent AEF. Wilson agreed. Pershing went directly to Foch to offer American troops. By that time, the initial German drive was stalling. German troops were exhausted. However, another offensive was anticipated to be launched soon.[53]

The antisubmarine war was making progress, and there were more troopships available to bring more soldiers for the AEF. On April 24 Pershing met with the British officials in London. They agreed that in May the British and Americans would transport six divisions of American combat troops. They would not bring their artillery, and the British would finish their training. The French were not happy. They needed reinforcements! Foch protested to Pershing. He insisted that the AEF release the divisions to them. Pershing refused. The British wanted Pershing to completely give the divisions to British command. Pershing refused. The French requested that 250,000 infantrymen be sent to them in June and July. This would prevent Pershing from having enough support troops to man his supply lines. He refused. At any rate, the London agreement was abandoned after roughly a week. The divisions that the British would train would go to quiet sectors of the French lines to free up French troops for the battle. Given the emergency of the German spring offensives, Wilson and Pershing weakened their opposition to dividing American forces to aid the Allies, but there were limits.[54]

While the western front was the most critical area, it was not the only one. Italy had come close to collapse at the Battle of Caporetto. French and British units had to be deployed to help their ally hold a new line. The Italians were also now asking for American troops. Wilson ordered Baker to Italy. Should the United States send some troops, a small number at least, to Italy to boost their morale? Eventually, a single regiment was sent to Italy by rail so the Italians would see American troops coming to their aid. Requests for troops for the Greek front were, however, refused. As will be seen in the next chapter, Wilson also agreed to sending American troops to revolution-torn Russia.[55]

The first of the German spring offensives, Operation Michael, had driven the British back, but had only briefly been able to partially separate the British and French. The second offensive, Georgette, attacked a section held by tired and weakened Portuguese troops. The Germans made early advances, but as with Michael, supplies could not keep up with their advancing forces. It had, however, put a scare into the British. On April 11 British Expeditionary Force (BEF) commander Field Marshal Sir Douglas Haig issued an "order of the day": "With our backs to the wall and believing in the justice of our cause, each one of us must fight on to the end." The Georgette offensive allowed the Germans to advance about nine miles, but they failed to threaten the British ports on the channel. Counterattacks forced the German command to end Georgette on April 29.

The third of the spring offensives, Blücher-Yorck, was designed to pull British troops farther south, away from the channel ports, leaving them vulnerable. The German assault began May 27 between Soissons and Reims. The area was primarily held by four weakened British divisions, exhausted from earlier battles, and sent to this "quiet" sector. Lacking local reserves, the Allied lines collapsed. German troops advanced to the Marne River. Paris seemed to be within reach. The capital's civilians began to flee to the south, and the French government began planning to withdraw to Bordeaux. Pershing asked his French counterparts for reassurance and was told that even if Paris fell, the war would continue. Once again the German advance stalled, but it had gotten closer to Paris than any time since 1914 and had punched a hole twenty-five miles wide in the Allied lines. American troops participated in this battle in appreciable numbers for the first time. To capitalize on Blücher-Yorck's success, Operation Gneisenau launched on June 9. Intelligence from German POWs allowed the French and Americans to prepare. Still, the Germans advanced nine miles until stopped by a French counterattack on April 11. On April 12, the Germans called off the offensive. The initiatives had failed in their overall objectives, but they had broken through Allied lines in multiple spots.

The Germans launched the Second Battle of the Marne on July 15, 1918. Once again, the Germans assaulted French (and now American) lines to threaten Paris, hoping to force the Allies to pull troops away from the British channel ports. By July 17 the attack had stalled and Allied troops, including parts of the AEF, counterattacked. On July 20, the Germans began a strategic withdrawal, abandoning much of the ground the spring offensives had gained. Moreover, the AEF was now fully engaged. The German efforts to end the war before the AEF threw its weight into the fight had failed. Pershing had his army to command, and as it would be soon be joined by a second, the AEF could make a radical difference in the fighting on the western front.

The pressure on Pershing, Baker, and Wilson was not just to place troops under British and French command. The European members of the Allies also called for a far larger AEF, thinking that the war would continue well into 1919, if not 1920. On June 23 the French pressured

Pershing to have a full one hundred divisions deployed in France by July 1919. Keep in mind that an American division was twice the size of the French, British, or German divisions, which at full strength numbered about 12,000—and by 1918 many of their divisions were severely under-strength. American divisions had approximately 27,000 men with another 13,000 for support. Pershing promised to have forty-six divisions deployed in France by October 1918, incrementally increasing their numbers until reaching the full complement of one hundred by July 1919. He did so without engaging the War Department, and Washington balked at the unrealistic expectations. However, the war planners agreed to provide an additional eighty divisions and 3.2 million troops by July 1919. This was the number Pershing preferred, although he privately wondered if they could manage to train and ship as many as sixty-six. Even at that scaled-down promise, the AEF by itself would have rivaled the German army in manpower.[56]

In July, Foch sent Pershing confirmation that the American general was to form an American field army under his own command. The First Army would consist of at least thirteen solely American divisions that were then trained and combat-ready. Furthermore, eight divisions then under French army operational command would revert to Pershing's control as they rotated out of the front line. The French would provide the artillery where needed, as well as aircraft and tanks. Pershing would then operate with General Pétain, commander of the French Armies of the North and Northeast. Pershing later wrote that Foch "went on to say that in order to bring victory to the Allies it would be necessary for them to have an incontestable numerical superiority." Therefore, the French leader pressed, "the number of American divisions [should be] increased as rapidly as possible."[57]

POLITICAL BATTLES

While fighting the Germans, Pershing also had a political battle with the new Army chief of staff back in DC, Peyton March. When the war began, Major General Scott was chief of staff. He was replaced by Gen. Tasker Bliss, who served from September 1917 until May 1918, most of which time he was also the American representative to the Supreme War Council. Pershing had held the dominant role during that time, believing that he answered only to the secretary of war and the president. In reality, the chain of command was unclear. Unfortunately, Wilson and Baker left it so. Scott believed that the chain of command went from the secretary of war through him. That would place Pershing under his command. He retired, however, and General Bliss saw himself as an assistant to the commander of the AEF, Pershing. Baker believed that the field commander was supreme. "Select a commander in whom you have confidence," Baker wrote, "give him power and responsibility and then . . . work your own head off to get him everything he needs and support every decision he makes."[58]

When Peyton March left his command in France to become chief of staff, he saw the role of overseeing the Army as a whole, and not just the AEF. His view was much closer to Scott's than that of Bliss. Pershing had, in effect, set up his own War Department in France, and March was determined to rein it in. The two men, the AEF commander and the chief of staff, clashed immediately over matters as minor as the style of belt American officers in France wore, as well as more serious issues, such as promotions to general rank. Pershing submitted lists of men to promote, choosing only officers serving in France. March took a more comprehensive view, and the list he submitted to Wilson included some of Pershing's choices as well as other men serving capably stateside. When this happened a second time, Pershing sent an angry cable to Wilson requesting promotions halt until he could submit another list. March did not forward the message, which went through the War Department, to the president.[59]

March was not Pershing's only rival for authority. In late 1917, as supply problems threatened the effectiveness of the AEF, George Washington Goethals was appointed acting quartermaster general. Goethals accepted, but only after Secretary of War Baker promised him full authority and that he would not be interfered with. The new quartermaster general straightened out the most apparent deficiencies—a lack of specialized personnel (most of whom had been sent to the front) and a decentralized organization with numerous overlapping uncoordinated functions. He hired civilian industrialists (the "dollar-a-year men") who were experts in transportation and supply lines. In April 1918, Goethals became assistant to the chief of staff of the Army and was in charge of all Army procurement, not just for the war effort. As a result, he was not Pershing's subordinate, threatening that the AEF commander would have to relinquish control of his supply lines.[60]

Pershing was not pleased. Now he had two rivals, March and Goethals. Moreover, Wilson and Baker left the specific chain of command fuzzy. As far as Baker was concerned, the issue was "purely technical" and "unimportant."[61] Pershing was happy to be left to his own devices. In his memoirs he wrote, "No American general in the field ever received the perfect support accorded to me by Mr. Baker. His attitude throughout the war, insofar as it concerned me personally and the Army in France, is a model for the guidance of future secretaries in such an emergency."[62] March, meanwhile, treated Pershing as a subordinate, which irritated the AEF commander. However, March's manner irritated a great many people. He was known to be uncivil in his push for efficiency, a "real sonofabitch." Baker later remarked how much time he had to spend repairing the damage his chief of staff did to others' feelings. March was effective, and that made up for a great deal for both Baker and Wilson.[63] As for Goethals, Pershing's staff improved. He replaced his head of supply of services (SOS) with Brig. Gen. James Harbord, who straightened out many of the logistical headaches. This satisfied both Baker and Wilson and removed the immediate danger to Pershing's authority that Goethals would take over the SOS in France, divorcing it from the AEF. Goethals, however, still expected to go to France. When he prepared to leave in the summer of 1918, he had to wait until Pershing approved. Goethals knew this would not happen. He was stuck at his desk in Washington.[64]

In early September 1918, Baker set sail for France again, to meet with Pershing and Foch. While the secretary was en route, Pershing sent cables back to March demanding to know how many troops would be sent each month into 1919 and calling for more motor vehicles than even American industry could provide. When Baker met with Pershing, he found that the AEF had very different plans for how many men he would need in

1919 versus what the War Department was planning. Pershing demanded even more men and supplies than could be provided, or even shipped if available. March called Pershing's plan "impossible to carry out." "Should it be possible" to go beyond the eighty divisions the War Department was planning, "it will be done, and you (Baker) will be advised." March was correct. Including the necessary support troops for the SOS, Pershing's dream, which had increased to as many as 110 divisions, required more than 6 million men in the AEF in France. Fortunately, Foch had a more realistic view. When Baker asked the Allied commander how many American divisions he would need to win the war in 1919, Foch replied, "Forty." Baker thought he misheard or was mistranslated and asked again. "I win the war with forty," Foch answered.[65]

As the Allies pressed Germany further, Pershing finally delegated some authority with the creation of the Second Army in the AEF in October 1918. By the beginning of the month, the AEF had over a million men in France with hundreds of thousands in the pipeline in the United States. Spread over approximately a one-hundred-mile front, engaged in multiple offensives, it was far more than one general could handle. Pershing had broken down at one point, crying out his late wife's name with his head in his hand, "Sometimes I don't know how I can go on." On October 10, Pershing created the Second Army, with Maj. Gen. Robert Lee Bullard in command. Lt. Gen. Hunter Liggett took over as commander of the First Army. Pershing remained the overall commander in chief of the AEF, and he still tended to try to manage affairs below the level that should have concerned him. Now on the same level as Haig and Pétain—a group commander—Pershing set up a new headquarters. Pershing's tendency to micromanage did not disappear with the creation of his new role; he still spent far too much time at First Army Headquarters.[66]

The War Ends

Even as Baker was returning to the United States, the Central Powers began to collapse. Bulgaria sued for an armistice, as did Turkey. Austria-Hungary was falling apart. Germany was interested in discussing peace based on the Fourteen Points, but Wilson refused until Germany pulled out of occupied France and Belgium. The German army began to fold when the Allies breached the Hindenburg Line. The German navy mutinied rather than fight a glorious if useless final battle against the Allied navies. Unrest spread to Germany's cities, and the kaiser abdicated and fled to exile in the Netherlands. To everyone's shock, the war ended suddenly in the autumn of 1918, not after an Allied push into Germany in 1919.

The end of the war generated a disagreement between Wilson and Pershing, one the general had no hope of winning. When the Allies were debating German peace feelers to Wilson based on the Fourteen Points, Foch called a meeting of the commanders at their civilian leaders' request and asked their opinion. Haig thought the Germans could still resist, that the Allies were exhausted, and the Americans still too inexperienced. As a result, he did not want to demand unconditional surrender, which might motivate the Germans to continue the war. His suggested terms would leave the Allies on the German border, but not occupying German territory, particularly the west bank of the Rhine. Pétain, however, argued the Germans were beaten, and the Allies and the AEF were in better shape than Haig was crediting. He proposed terms for an armistice that called for German troops to pull out of the occupied territory. Like Foch, he wanted not only the Allies on the left bank of the Rhine but also bridgeheads on the other side. With the additional surrender of all German rolling stock (trains), the Allies would be in a good position to restart the war should Germany balk at the peace talks. Pershing wanted not just an armistice, but German unconditional surrender. Pershing called for Germany surrendering her U-boat fleet (to which Haig sniffed that was the Admiralty's problem, not theirs). Pershing also called for Germany to withdraw to the east bank of the Rhine and the occupation of the western bank by Allied forces. The meeting adjourned without resolving the issue.[67]

Pershing wired his conditions to the president. Wilson's reply indicated that he thought some demands were too strident. For example, he thought the withdrawal of the U-boat fleet to neutral waters was sufficient. He also opposed the occupation of the Rhine's left bank and beachheads and the immediate return of Alsace and Lorraine to France. On the other hand, Wilson suggested that Germany be required to surrender its heavy

artillery, something Foch and Pétain wanted. Baker told Pershing that
Wilson wanted an armistice "rigid enough to secure us against renewal
of hostilities by Germany but not humiliating beyond that necessity
as such terms would throw the advantage to the military party in Germany." Wilson was, Baker noted, "relying on your counsel and advice."
He would "be glad to have you feel entirely free to bring to his attention
any consideration he may have overlooked." The problem for Pershing
was that Wilson's "harsh but not too harsh" armistice was what all the
commanders wanted. The disagreement was over how best to achieve that
end, such as whether or not it required the occupation of the Rhine's left
bank. Pershing was closer to what Foch and Pétain, as well as Premier
Georges Clemenceau, wanted than Wilson (or Haig) desired.[68]

On October 30, Pershing sent a lengthy memo to the Supreme War
Council. He argued that the Allied armies could continue to fight. Their
morale, he said, was high, and more American troops were arriving
regularly. The German army was, in contrast, suffering from collapsing
morale. A facile armistice, Pershing argued, would allow the Germans
time to recover. It would help German morale and allow them to reorganize and prepare to fight again. An armistice would weaken the victors'
efforts to win a peace treaty that would ensure world peace. Only by
continuing the offensive until Germany was forced to surrender uncon-
ditionally and even then, the terms given be such that Germany could
not renew the war. Pershing was, in effect, trying to undermine his own
president, fearing the politicians would decide based upon considerations
other than military factors.[69]

Pershing's message could easily have been a bombshell, a clear act
of insubordination had Wilson chosen to view it that way. Events had
already overtaken Wilson and Pershing's positions. An excessively lenient
armistice was no longer in consideration, if it had ever been a real possibility. Wilson's adviser, Colonel House, in meetings with Lloyd George
and Clemenceau, had already agreed to the occupation of the Rhineland.
For their part, the Allied leaders and Colonel House were both annoyed
and disdainful of Pershing's memo. Clemenceau read it and called it
"theatrical." Lloyd George sniffed, "Politics. . . . Someone put him up to it."

House noted in his diary that they all thought it was a political document, designed to position Pershing for the 1920 presidential election. Nonetheless, the president's adviser had been blindsided by Pershing's memo, as had General Bliss. When questioned by House, the AEF commander backtracked, and tried to explain the document as "purely military." He and the president's adviser came to an understanding, and the general apologized for not consulting House first before sending the memo. House cabled Wilson that the matter was settled.[70]

Back in Washington, things were not so settled in the War Department. Baker had sent a copy of Pershing's memo to President Wilson, noting how it upset March. March also believed it was the result of Pershing having political ambitions for 1920 and probably saw a chance to weaken his rival. Baker wrote a reprimand to send to Pershing and sent a copy to Wilson. The president had been assured that the matter was settled and told his secretary of war not to send his message chastising the AEF commander. Meanwhile, Foch told Pershing that while he would not demand unconditional surrender, the armistice terms would be "approximate to" one. Pershing had risked damaging his status to fight a battle that had already been won.[71]

CONCLUSION

Wilson and Baker both gave Pershing a great deal of support against the demands of the Allies, and from within the American military itself. To some degree, they had little choice. For example, abandoning and replacing Pershing due to the Allies' pressure would have required admitting they were right about the weaknesses of the command of the AEF. This would have weakened Wilson's position at the eventual peace talks. The more significant the role the United States had in defeating Germany, the more influence Wilson would have. Replacing a commander for reasons of competence would have been a nightmare for Wilson's ambitions for a peace treaty. There were other considerations, as well. There was no obvious replacement, although there were other capable generals, such as March. Wilson and Baker also did not have the same issues with Pershing that the Allies did, especially regarding his desire not to incorporate American forces into the British and French armies more than was needed for training and emergencies. Of course, there were domestic political pressures as well. Replacing the Republican general would have simultaneously angered his supporters among congressional Republicans and made Wilson look incompetent. Finally, Pershing was getting results. The United States was losing more men than necessary due to incomplete and inappropriate training, but the AEF was winning. Nothing wins a commander's support from his political superiors quite like winning battles.

Where Wilson and Baker did a poor job was in allowing the unclear chain of command to continue. Neither man was comfortable with the military, reflected by their hands-off approach. They also did not understand how the professional officers thought of their roles. Baker may have considered the conflict between Pershing and March as "technical," but it added difficulties to an extraordinarily complex operation that need not have existed. Ironically, Pershing replaced March after the war, and he made sure to straighten out the chain of command. No other general was going to be as independent as Pershing was allowed to be in the field. In the meantime, there were still the peace talks, and Pershing met with Wilson in person for the first time since May 1917. Meanwhile, American troops were engaged in the civil war in Russia, and Americans were going to be occupying part of the Rhineland. The American military role begun by World War I was not over on November 11, 1918.

CHAPTER 7

———◆•◆———

Russian Intervention

When the firing stopped on the western front at 11 a.m. on November 11, 1918, there were still American troops engaged in Russia as part of the Allied intervention after the Russian Revolution. There were two such interventions, thousands of miles apart—in Archangel in northwest Russia, and in Vladivostok on the Pacific coast. While both were part of the chaotic situation in Russia during its revolution and civil war, Wilson had different reasons for sending troops in each. In both cases, Wilson had a diplomatic rationale, which was more important than military purposes. In both, the decision to send troops came only after heavy diplomatic pressure from the Allies in the war against Germany. "I have been sweating blood," Wilson told Colonel House in the summer of 1918, "over the question of what it is right and feasible to do in Russia. It goes to quicksilver under my touch."[1] Wilson wanted to encourage Russia to develop its own democratic government, refrain from alienating Britain and France by not supporting their anti-Bolshevik policies, and maybe even keep German troops engaged on an eastern front. He also wanted to prevent Japan from using intervention as an excuse to expand into eastern Russia, or even further into China along the Russian border. Finally, he wanted to help the Czech Legion, a Czechoslovak army working its way across Russia to try to join the war against Germany. These goals, however, as Wilson eventually found, were as confusing as they were contradictory.

THE BOLSHEVIKS

Both interventions were driven by the Bolshevik coup in November 1917, which ousted the provisional government that had taken over when the Russian Czar Nicholas II abdicated ending the Romanov dynasty in March 1917. The provisional government had attempted to continue fighting Germany and Austria-Hungary as an ally to the French and British. However, the war had become so unpopular, and it had so strained Russian society, that support for the provisional government grew ever weaker. The Bolsheviks had opposed continuing the war, claiming there was no difference between the imperialists on either side of the conflict. Once they had taken power, the new government asked for an armistice and began negotiating a treaty with Germany.

The British and French reaction was little short of panic at the collapse of the eastern front. If Russia withdrew from the war, Germany could move multiple divisions to the western front, perhaps enough to tip the balance against the Allies. Germany might also seize the tons of supplies waiting for the Russian army in Archangel and Vladivostok. In the former city alone waited a million tons of coal and other supplies, including 14,000 tons of valuable copper. Another 600,000 tons of supplies awaited in Vladivostok.[2] Moreover, Berlin might have been able to seize raw materials and food from a defeated Russia. Some of the more paranoid Allies even wondered if the Germans might recruit or impress Russians for their military. Even Pershing worried that the Germans might find recruits among the Russian peasants.[3] Accordingly, the British and French began to look for a way to keep Russia in the war, or at the very least, find enough proxy troops to continue some semblance of an Eastern Front.

Wilson wanted to ignore the new Bolshevik government to let it fall or stand on its own. The British and French looked for a means to arm the anti-Bolshevik Russian Whites, perhaps even restore the pro-Allied provisional government to power. They found willing ears with Robert Lansing and the State Department. Colonel House, however, feared that intervening in Russia would force the Bolsheviks closer to Germany. Wilson was hearing a cacophony of voices advising him on Russia, and his usual method of gathering intelligence broke down. In 1915 while referring to the Mexican Revolution, Wilson claimed, "Things that are not so do not match. If you hear enough of them, you see there is no pattern whatever; it is a crazy quilt, whereas the truth always matches, piece by piece, with other parts of the truth."[4] Wilson's intelligence gathering, in this case, left him adrift. As a result he held back, avoiding making any concrete choices, refusing to intervene, and refusing to recognize the new Bolshevik government. He continued collecting information, and gradually he was, step by step, convinced to accept at least small-scale intervention.

One set of voices that Wilson listened to insisted that the Bolsheviks were German agents doing Berlin's bidding. Of particular importance was a journalist, Edgar Sisson, who had gone to Russia as part of the American effort to promote pro-war propaganda to convince Russians to stay in the war. Their efforts, part of George Creel's Committee on Public Information (CPI), arrived too late to win public support for the provisional government before it was overthrown. Sisson remained working in Russia, however. While in Petrograd he acquired a collection of more than sixty Russian language documents that purported to prove the German General Staff had hired Vladimir Lenin and Leon Trotsky, "that . . . Lenin and Trotsky and their associates—are German agents . . . that the Bolshevist revolt was arranged for by the German Great General Staff and financed by the German Imperial Bank and other German financial institutions."[5] Sisson purchased the documents in February for $25,000. (George Kennan notes that he received copies from Raymond Robins, who did not disclose their source to Sisson). Convinced he had the scoop of a lifetime, he smuggled them out of Russia through Finland and Sweden and then into the United States. By May, Sisson was in Washington, where Wilson read the documents on May 9.[6]

Unbeknownst to both Sisson and the president, the documents were forgeries that had circulated in Russia and Europe for months. A newspaper in Paris had published at least some of them in early February, but on the whole they were ignored as bad forgeries. Neither the British or French governments were impressed by them, nor was the American State Department. Even the ousted Russian government of Alexander Kerensky rejected them. Wilson, however, was convinced they were authentic, and the CPI first released them to the American press on September 15, then published them in a booklet for the public to read. Lansing, who had not been consulted, and doubted their veracity, was appalled. Most of the U.S. press accepted them, but the *Evening Post* in New York found them clumsy forgeries. The documents sometimes referred to events that had not yet occurred at the time of their alleged writing, and even though the documents were supposedly German, they all used the Russian calendar.[7] While the Sisson documents were seized upon by those in the United States who wanted to intervene in Russia, Wilson used them as an argument against intervention in the spring of 1918. The Allies were trying to get the Bolshevik government to approve, maybe even request, intervention to prevent a German takeover in Russia. Wilson argued that this could be a trap and that the Bolsheviks could lose power when it was discovered they were German agents.[8]

The U.S. ambassador was still in Russia even though the United States did not recognize the new Bolshevik government. In early November 1917, Ambassador David Francis sent a cable to Washington, asking if the United States would send "two or more divisions" to Russia if he could get the Russian government to request it. He was apparently still thinking of a re-created Eastern Front, noting that "the moral effect of American troops on the Russian Front" would be valuable to the "millions of sensible Russians" who only needed "encouragement to organize."[9] His voice joined that of the British and French calling for military intervention, both from their governments and their representatives on the Supreme War Council.

What to do with the new Russian government baffled the United States and the Allies. Colonel House suggested the council members issue a joint statement of war aims following the Bolshevik's "no indemnities, no annexations" model. There was no way the British, French, and Italians would go along with such a suggestion that would have negated the secret treaties in which they had so much invested. Instead, each member was to deal with the Bolsheviks individually. They also looked for alternatives: non-Bolsheviks to support militarily and diplomatically, who might oust Lenin's new regime. They were driven not only by the Bolshevik promise to withdraw Russian from the war but by the fears that they were "assisted and controlled by the Germans." The council's Joint Note no. 5, "The Situation in Russia," expressed several specific concerns. The Germans would be able to get supplies from Russia, specifically wheat and oil from southwestern Russia. Controlling Russian resources would break the Allied blockade of Holland and Scandinavia by providing them with food. Moreover, Germany might use access to Russian wheat to "force the Swiss to concede a free passage to their armies." The Allies should, the note continued, support "all national groups who are determined to continue the war must be supported by all means in our power." They suggested that the best way to establish "direct communication" with their Russian "friends" was "by way of Vladivostok and the Siberian railway, or by operations in Turkey." The note was signed by the military representatives of Britain, France, and Italy, but not by General Bliss, the American representative. Bliss was never as enthused about intervention in Russia as the Allied representatives.[10]

The idea of supporting Russian "friends" through Turkey never came to fruition, and the Allies' early hopes for Cossack General Aleksei Kaledin in southwestern Russia did not last long. As the Bolsheviks negotiated with Germany what would become the Treaty of Brest-Litovsk (March 3, 1918), the Allies began a sustained campaign to convince President Wilson to join in a military intervention. The French began on January 8, formally suggesting an inter-Allied force mainly made up of Japanese to occupy the Trans-Siberian Railroad to Irkutsk, a full 1,500 miles west of the road's terminus at Vladivostok. Secretary of State Lansing refused. The United States worried that using the Japanese would inflame the

Russians, driving them closer to Germany. It was not just intervention that the United States opposed, specifically it was the occupation of the vital railway by the Japanese, and Tokyo would not agree unless the United States did not object.[11]

THE BRITISH

The British decided to try to convince Wilson by going through Colonel House. Wilson's adviser was vehemently against intervention in early 1918. London instructed Sir William Wiseman, who was friends with House and was often used as a backchannel to the White House to use his influence to persuade Colonel House to support intervention.[12] Wiseman was unsuccessful but lobbied House to abandon the idea of recognizing the Bolshevik government. The British representative argued that the Bolsheviks did not deserve recognition because they did not control the entire country, and recognition would prevent the Allies from sending aid to the anti-Bolshevik Whites who were willing to continue the war against Germany. However, what ended Wilson and House's consideration of recognition was probably the Russian acceptance of the harsh German conditions at the Treaty of Brest-Litovsk, which appeared to confirm fears that Russia would become a source of supply for the Germans.[13]

In March, Wilson began to reconsider some limited intervention. The British warned that Germany could seize the tons of war materials in Vladivostok, and the Japanese seemed ready to land to take control of the Trans-Siberian Railroad. Wilson and Lansing wrote a message saying the United States did not object to Japan acting as the Allies' agent. House objected strongly enough to convince Wilson to reverse course, and the president did not send the note. House noted, "The French have come to hate the Russians, and do not care what ill fate befalls them. . . . The English that are in power have such an intense hatred for Germany that they have lost their perspective." Wilson now wrote a new note, opposing intervention. However, Wiseman knew about the earlier note and now knew Wilson was flexible on intervention, even if it involved the Japanese. He could also be confident that Colonel House was an obstacle to convincing Wilson to go along with intervention.[14]

Wisemen steered British arguments in a direction he thought would convince both House and the president. Wiseman's suggestions demonstrated that he had a keen understanding of Wilson and House. The arguments he suggested were those that did actually convince Wilson in the long run. He told London to suggest to Tokyo that they state intervention was to help the Russians and not to gain territory for Japan. Moreover, the British should stop worrying out loud that the Germans could use their gains in Russia to threaten India, as Wilson had little sympathy for the raj. Wiseman argued London should play up the threat of Germany seizing all of the military stores the Allies had sent the Russians. Finally, they should emphasize the liberal humanitarian factors in intervening. The British quickly began pressing the Japanese but were slow to understand how little sympathy the United States had for the British position in South Asia. It was not until well into April that the British stopped mentioning India.[15]

While Wiseman worked on House, the Wilson administration continued to look for ways to deal with the Bolsheviks. The Congress of Soviets met to consider ratifying the treaty with Germany. Wilson issued a statement to the Russian people, in effect hoping to go over the heads of the assembly.[16] The message from Wilson assured the Russian people that the United States would "avail itself of every opportunity that may offer to secure for Russia once more complete sovereignty and independence in her own affairs." While some of the Bolshevik leadership looked to see if the United States would back Russia if it refused to ratify the harsh treaty imposed by the Germans, they were disappointed: "The government of the United States," the note read, "is, unhappily, not now in a position to render the direct and effective aid it would wish to render." The message's tone was disappointing to the Russian leadership, but it also demonstrated the influence of the Sisson documents, suggesting that the Bolshevik government was not representative of the Russian people. Despite Wilson's good intentions, the message flopped. The Congress of Soviets responded with a sarcastic message about those suffering the "horrors of imperialistic war." The United States was still, in Russian eyes, an imperialist power, despite Wilson's protests to the contrary.[17]

ARCHANGEL

Events overtook Wilson in the spring of 1918, however, and Wilson finally agreed to send American troops to join the Allies in northern Russia, landing at Archangel. As with Veracruz in 1914, Wilson persuaded himself that Americans would be welcomed as helping, rather than acting as invaders. A limited intervention would, he convinced himself, be viewed differently than a full-scale invasion. By restoring order and helping Russia resist German pressure, it would actually be consistent with Russian self-determination. Moreover, it would help soothe Britain and France, who had been pressuring him for months. If the Allies could keep the supplies that had been at Archangel out of German hands, that was also a benefit. Wilson had no illusions it would help establish an effective Eastern Front, however. Wilson did not take up the ambassador's suggestions, but the assumptions in David Francis' cable were mirrored in Wilson's eventual policy. First, the ambassador assumed that there were a large majority of Russians who would continue to resist the Germans and their (supposed) agents in Russia. Second, he believed that these "sensible" Russians would welcome foreign intervention. In the meantime, Wilson continued to wait, and hope that the new Bolshevik government would either moderate or be replaced.[18]

The Allies continued to press for the United States to join in a military intervention. It was the Murmansk soviet, ironically, that set events in motion. Taking advantage of the Russian Revolution, Finland had declared its independence, but there were both a Red (pro-Soviet) Finnish government and a White (pro-German) one. By March 1918, the leadership of the Murmansk soviet feared that the White Finns and the Germans threatened the rail line between their city and Petrograd. They were organizing "a socialist armed force" but feared they would need help. The Allied representatives in their city seemed supportive, and the Soviets asked the government what type of "aid may be accepted from the friendly powers. Czech and French detachments, numbering some two thousand men," were available. The cable arrived just as Trotsky believed that the Brest-Litovsk talks had failed and that the Germans would continue their advance further into Russia. Desperate, he sent his reply to the Murmansk soviet, "[Y]ou must accept any and all assistance from the Allied missions."[19] Lt. Hugh Martin, an assistant U.S. military attaché, wired Washington that several hundred British marines landed at Murmansk and that Trotsky had approved the landing. This opening did not last long, but it was enough to crack open the door sufficiently to pull Wilson through.[20]

Wilson still hesitated, convinced that the Russians would reject intervention. In early April, he reluctantly agreed to send a warship to join the Allies. Part of the problem for Wilson was simple logistics. The United States was already struggling to find enough ships to transport men to Europe, even with substantial British help. Warships were also in demand for the war against the U-boats. So in April 1918, when Wilson agreed to send a warship to Murmansk to aid the British, the United States deployed the USS *Olympia*. A cruiser launched in 1892, the *Olympia* was famous as Commo. George Dewey's flagship at the Battle of Manila Bay in 1898. Used as a training ship, the *Olympia* was placed back in active duty for World War I. In other words, Wilson did not send a warship of the first rank, a reflection of both the importance and the threat level posed by the Russians in 1917–18 for Wilson compared to winning the war in France. The aging *Olympia* was sufficient to show the flag, and it did have its complement of Marines.[21]

Wilson's instruction to Secretary of the Navy Daniels noted that he was "anxious to do so if it can be done without sacrificing" more important objects.[22] He was not willing to take "any vessel from the overseas convoy business, but if there is not, that is the end of it." He also instructed Daniels to "caution him [the ship's commander] not to be drawn in further than the present action there without first seeking and obtaining instructions from home."[23] This still left some uncertainty. The arms stores they were supposed to protect originally had already been shipped inland. Was the ship there to protect the Russian Whites from the Bolsheviks, or the Russians from the Finns? One of the bandsmen from the *Olympia* reflected this confusion when he wrote that they played "The Star-Spangled Banner," "God Save the King," and "The Marseillaise" every day, but they did not play "God Protect the Czar" as "we don't yet know which side we are on."[24]

With Wilson having sent a warship, pressure by the Allies increased not only to send forces into Murmansk and Archangel but into Siberia with the Japanese. For Wilson, the sticking point for Siberia was the Japanese, believing that the Russians might support a British-American force, but that they would unify and turn against an Allied force that included the Japanese. "If that were done," he told Wiseman, "he could see Russian soldiers fighting with the Germans on the Western Front." Wilson toyed with the idea of a civilian mission, consisting of American, British, and French experts to aid Russia. However, then they would need armed protection. Wilson's instincts about Russian opposition to foreign intervention were good. However, he clearly did not understand just how war-weary the Russian people were to imagine Russian forces joining the war on the western front, especially on the German side.[25]

The different regions were viewed as separate issues by the Wilson administration. Part of this differentiation was what Lansing in May 1918 called "the racial difficulty which had to be considered in regard to Siberia." The "racial difficult" was the use of Japanese troops. There were other factors as well. Lansing told the British ambassador that "intervention at Murmansk and Archangel would receive far more consideration on our part than intervention in Siberia." Why? "We could understand the military advantage of the former but have been unable, thus far, to find any advantage in sending troops into Siberia." Lansing also noted that it seemed as if Trotsky's "support" for intervention only applied to intervention in the north, not Siberia.

In mid-May 1918, Wilson consulted with Chief of Staff March about sending troops to northern Russia. As Wilson wrote to Lansing, "General March and his staff are clear and decided in their opinion that 1) No strong enough force to amount to anything can be sent to Murmansk without subtracting just that much shipping and manpower from the western front, and 2) that such a subtraction at the present crisis would be most unwise." This came amid the German spring offensives, right between Georgette and Blücher-Yorck. The perilous situation on the western front did not, however, stop the British from asking again. On May 28, Foreign Secretary Arthur James Balfour sent a telegram to ambassador Baron Rufus Isaacs Reading in Washington with a message for Lansing that "on the Murmansk coast assistance from America is badly required and is, in fact, essential." Britain had already sent "such small Marine and military forces as we are able to spare during the present crisis in France." However, "the dispatch of additional French or British reinforcements is impossible." Balfour tried a new argument, one that did seem to strike a chord with Wilson: "Great use has been made already of the divergence of view among the Allied countries with regard to the Russian situation, and for this reason it is of great importance that the United States should show their agreement with us on this matter."[26]

The same day as Balfour's telegram to Reading, the American representative to the Supreme War Council, General Bliss, sent a long message to Secretary of War Baker. Bliss noted that on May 30, the council would discuss Russia and the British, French, and Italians would "probably agree to an occupation of the Ports of Murmansk and Archangel by British Navy and a land force of not more than four or six battalions of British, French, and possibly Americans." Bliss continued, "In view of pressing danger to these ports I propose to agree with my colleagues unless instructed to the contrary." Wilson was still not convinced. He was "heartily in sympathy with any practical military effort which can be made at and from Murmansk or Archangel, but such efforts should proceed, if at all, upon the sure sympathy of the Russian people and should not have as their ultimate object any restoration of the ancient regime or any other interference with the political liberty of the Russian people." The British and French that had already landed would have to do without American help in the north.[27]

SIBERIA AND THE CZECHS

Siberia, however, was another matter. Wilson became much more sympathetic toward intervention there despite having to rely on the Japanese. The cause was the plight of the Czech Legion. The Legion consisted of Czechs and Slovaks who wanted a Czechoslovakia independent from

Austria-Hungary. Many of the members were deserters or POWs from the Austro-Hungarian armies and fought along with the Russian army during the war. With the coming of the Bolsheviks to power in late 1917, the Czech Legion wanted to transfer to the western front to continue the fight. The chair of the Czechoslovak National Council, Tomáš Masaryk, who had arrived in Russia earlier that year, decided that the Legion should travel from Ukraine to Vladivostok. Allied ships could transport them to Western Europe. At first, the Bolsheviks cooperated, happy to have foreign troops leave Russian territory. In February 1918, Bolshevik authorities granted Masaryk and his troops permission to begin the six-thousand-mile trip to Vladivostok. As the Legion made its way east, it continued negotiating with Bolshevik authorities in Moscow and Penza (about four hundred miles southeast of Moscow). On March 25, the two sides signed the Penza Agreement. The Czechs agreed to surrender most of their weapons in exchange for allowing their free passage to Vladivostok. Neither side trusted the other, however, and tensions continued to rise. The Czechs resented the Communists trying to recruit among their members and suspected that the Germans were pressuring the Bolsheviks to stop the Legion's movement east. The Bolsheviks feared that the Czechs would ally themselves with one of the White Russian counterrevolutionary armies.

By May 1918, the Czech Legion was strung out along thousands of miles between Penza to Vladivostok along the Trans-Siberian Railroad. Its evacuation was hampered by the line's poor condition, a lack of sufficient rolling stock, and having to negotiate with each individual soviet along the route, most of which were suspicious of this foreign army on their soil. On May 14, in Chelyabinsk, some Czechs got into a firefight with Austro-Hungarian POWs being repatriated west. The people's commissar for war, Leon Trotsky, ordered the Czechs to be wholly disarmed and arrested. The Legion commanders refused to cooperate and issued ultimatums for their passage to Vladivostok. Fighting between Bolsheviks and the Legion exploded at multiple spots along the Trans-Siberian Railroad. By the end of June, the portion of the Legion under General Mikhail Diterikhs had taken control of Vladivostok, overthrowing the local Bolshevik administration. On July 6, the Legion declared the port to be an Allied protectorate.

Masaryk had arrived in Washington on May 9 and began lobbying for support for the Czechs, including the Legion, and American recognition of their independence. He met with Secretary of State Lansing and Colonel House. Strangely, he did not get to meet Wilson right away. The president had heard of the Czech leader and was favorably disposed toward him. However, Wilson was wary of those who wanted to meet with him to lobby. He preferred written reports and already had read several expressing Masaryk's views. Wilson finally met the Czech leader on June 19.[28] They talked for forty-five minutes and discussed intervention in Siberia and the possible Japanese role. The Czech leader was not in favor of "a so-called intervention." He thought it would take a million Japanese troops to fight the Germans in Russia and agreed with Wilson that the Japanese would demand territory in compensation. Masaryk liked Wilson's idea of a civilian commission to barter goods in Russia for grain and other products to build ties and goodwill. Masaryk opposed using the Czech Legion to control the Trans-Siberian Railroad and told Wilson that he wanted the Legion to be shipped to France. This undoubtedly reassured Wilson, but other Czech leaders in Russia had already agreed with Allied plans to occupy the railway.[29]

The problem with Wilson's idea of a civilian relief force was that given the conditions in Russia, it would, according to House and the British, still require a military component for protection. Wilson had to make a choice; there was no way to sort of intervene. Baker and the War Department opposed intervention in Siberia. So did Bliss. It "seemed impractical because of the vast distances involved and the size of the force necessary to be effective." The expedition would "serve no military purpose," Baker told General Bliss, the U.S. representative to the Supreme War Council. In contrast to the War Department, the State Department was in favor of intervention; in Lansing's view, it had to do something. Colonel House agreed. Wilson vacillated. He agreed with his military about the uselessness of intervention, but the diplomatic and political pressures were only increasing. As George Kennan noted, "The matter had now become the dominant problem of American foreign policy." The Supreme War Council took up the question of Siberia at their June 3 meeting. The sound of "German guns could be heard in the distance. Preparations . . . were under way for the possible evacuation of Paris. Siberia appeared to be the only hope."[30] The council asked Japan that Tokyo promise (1) to respect Russian territorial integrity, (2) to take no side in Russian internal politics, and (3) that Japanese troops advance west "as far as possible" for the purpose of encountering the Germans. Japan refused to agree to the third point and insisted they would not act further without the United States. Finally, however, Wilson agreed to send troops. He latched onto the idea of using the Czechs to keep the Germans out of the region. The Czechs were "cousins" to the Russians, which, Wilson thought, would make their involvement less offensive to the latter.[31]

NORTHERN RUSSIA

Meanwhile, Wilson was also deciding on intervention in northern Russia. The seeming successes of the German spring offensives highlighted the effect of Russia's withdrawal from the war. The offensives had pushed back and, in some places, pierced Allied lines, had threatened Paris, and stretched Allied reserves almost to the breaking point. However, what the Allies could not know at the time was how much they had exhausted German resources. Still, the Allies were desperate to recreate a Russian front to draw German troops away from the western front. The United States took the lesson that the AEF was needed in France, and that any diversion was foolish. Moreover, creating, training, supplying, and shipping American forces to France had already strained American resources. In a talk with Ambassador Reading, Wilson noted that the "productivity capacity of the U.S. was limited and was already very heavily taxed" to meet Allied demands for the AEF in France.[32] However, military logic had to compete with political and diplomatic factors. By the summer of 1918, the pressure to do something in northern Russia had reached the point where it could no longer be ignored. The pressure on Wilson was to do something, somewhere—northern Russia, Siberia, or both.[33]

When Balfour requested an American "brigade to which a few guns should be added" be sent to northern Russia in late May, Wilson asked Lansing to study the issue. On June 3, Wilson replied that he was willing to approve if General Foch gave his consent to the diversion of men and ships. That same day the Supreme War Council met. It issued Joint Note No. 31 on Murmansk and Archangel. In hindsight, the note was unrealistic. It overstated the threat to the region by Germany and Finland and suggested using part of the Czech Legion there, even though it was thousands of miles away. The council asked the Czechs to send forces to the region, and for the four major Allies, including the United States, to send four to six battalions with supplies to Archangel. The force would be under British command. General Bliss, the American representative, approved the note along with the others, but he had been put into an awkward situation. Wilson insisted that the United States not participate in the political meetings but approved what was decided later on his own. He trusted Bliss to handle the purely military questions, but this was both military and political/diplomatic. After Note No. 31 was issued, Baker, March, and Lansing discussed what to do. They asked Bliss to approach General Foch and explain that any American forces sent to northern Russia would come at the expense of those being sent to France. Foch considered and approved "one or two" American battalions to be sent to northern Russia. This still did not settle the matter for Wilson. He asked Bliss, again, to query Foch. Finally, in mid-July Wilson agreed. Baker and March still opposed it, but Wilson made the final decision. He agreed to three battalions, going along with a British request for more troops than Foch had mentioned. Along with three companies of engineers, they would deploy to northern Russia.[34]

The choice of which units to assign was left to General Pershing. On July 30 he approved three battalions of the 339th Infantry Regiment—the 1st Battalion, 310th Engineers; the 337th Field Hospital; and the 337th Ambulance Company. They were placed under the command of Col. George E. Stewart and would become the American Expeditionary Force, North Russia.[35] Mostly draftees from Michigan and Wisconsin, Pershing hoped that soldiers from northern states would better handle the Russian cold than men from the South. Moreover, Colonel Stewart was an experienced veteran who had been awarded the Medal of Honor while serving in the Philippine-American War. The 339th was already encamped in Britain undergoing training when they received their orders to go to Russia rather than the western front. Accordingly, they were issued rifles that were intended for the czar's Russian army, but which had not yet been delivered. That would allow them to use the ammunition that they would supposedly be protecting once they reached Archangel. They set sail from Britain on August 27.[36]

At the same time Wilson was making his decision on northern Russia, he was deciding to intervene in Siberia. He discussed both in his July 17 message to the Allies. He still denounced military intervention, distinguishing what he was planning on doing and what he feared were the counterrevolutionary motives, particularly Britain's.[37] "Military intervention," he claimed, "would add to the present sad confusion in Russia rather than cure it, injure her rather than help her, and that it would be no advantage in the prosecution of our main design, to win the war against Germany." "Military action" was "admissible in Russia" only, Wilson contended, "to help the Czecho-Slovaks consolidate their forces and get into successful cooperation with their Slavic kinsmen and to steady any efforts at self-government or self-defense in which the Russians themselves may be willing to accept assistance." American or Allied forces could only legitimately "guard military stores which may subsequently be needed by Russian forces and to render such aid acceptable to the Russians in the organization of their own self-defense." In effect, Wilson had argued himself into the same situation in which he found himself in Veracruz, Mexico. He understood how foreign intervention would be viewed—with hostility—by the nation being invaded. Nevertheless, he still excused his agreeing to intervene by casting it as protecting the right to self-determination and humanitarian reasons.[38]

American servicemen were also involved, both deliberately and inadvertently, in the internal politics of the area. On August 1 and 2, 1918, an Allied force entered Archangel's harbor and drove off the Soviet government, allowing anti-Bolshevik forces to take control. U.S. Marines from the *Olympia* joined in. They seized a railway engine and a few cars and took off after the retreating Bolsheviks. They went seventy-five miles into Russia before the Bolsheviks could burn a bridge to stop their pursuit.[39]

A month later, just as the first American troops were officially arriving in Archangel, some Russian officers staged a coup. They arrested the members of the civilian anti-Bolshevik government, imprisoning them. When the population launched a general strike in protest, some of the newly arrived American soldiers acted as strike-breakers and operated the streetcars. Since the coup was launched just as American troops arrived, according to the American ambassador, the locals assumed that the United States supported it.[40] A military government was set up in Archangel, with a French colonel as governor. Due to a food shortage, rationing for the civilian population was established. Anyone caught distributing "Bolshevik propaganda" was subject to arrest. When local political leaders complained, the American ambassador replied that this was also true in the United States, and there was "nothing objectionable therein."[41]

Thus, by mid-summer Allied forces were propping up anti-Bolshevik forces in both Murmansk and Vladivostok. The Czech Legion controlled much of the Trans-Siberian Railroad, and the Japanese and British had troops in Vladivostok. American troops were dispatched to join the other Allies. Wilson had left their instructions vague, perhaps purposefully so. In a letter to March written in 1927, Secretary of War Baker claimed that "the president's ambiguity was apparently deliberate and stemmed from his plan to limit the American contribution [to intervention] as much as possible but still play the game with our allies."[42] Unfortunately for Colonel Stewart, he had somehow not been given a copy of Wilson's directive and was under the command of a very aggressive British general, Frederick Poole. Poole had visions of leading a mass military campaign against the Bolsheviks, marching hundreds of miles, picking up 100,000 Russian volunteers, linking with the Czechs, and eventually reestablishing the Eastern Front.[43] There was nothing realistic about the British plan, which was pure fantasy. Even worse for Colonel Stewart, U.S. ambassador David Francis was in Archangel and was stridently supportive of intervention. He did have a copy of Wilson's directive, at least a paraphrase of it, but somehow decided it only applied to Siberia. So when Stewart and his men arrived in Archangel on September 4, Poole immediately began ordering American troops down the railroad lines moving hundreds of miles into Russian territory. By the time Stewart received a copy of Wilson's memorandum outlining his mission, on October 5, it was far too late. The colonel remained in Archangel as American troops ended up fighting for months with insufficient supplies or reinforcements through a nightmarish Russian winter.[44]

At the Supreme War Council, the British passed along General Poole's requests for five thousand men for Murmansk and sufficient reinforcements for Archangel. Bliss was outraged and told March that the British "possibly feel that they may have 'bitten off more than they can chew' and want to throw the responsibility elsewhere." Bliss said, "It is absurd to suppose that General Poole would have made such a demand." He made it "without giving the slightest analysis of the situation or showing why he asks for 5,000 rather than 50,000 men." Bliss noted, "The Allies think that having made a beginning in Russia and having put a foot in the crack of the door the whole body must follow." He was aware that the British and French wanted to push beyond Archangel and Murmansk but thought their desire "grows out of their belief that nothing of material value will result from the movement in Siberia from Vladivostok." President Wilson backed Bliss, and at the September 14 Supreme War Council meeting, Bliss insisted that Poole be ordered to stick to his original instructions. The other military representatives agreed. Poole would not get his reinforcements. Unfortunately for the men under his command, he did not pull them back to more defensible positions and continued to dream of successful marches into the Russian countryside. Despite this, on September 15 the French requested the United States send five additional battalions. Interestingly, the request came from Premier Clemenceau, not from Foch. The British government also asked the Supreme War Council to consider sending more. It was the political leaders at this point who were reluctant to let it go.[45]

Wilson was frustrated by the Allies' actions, particularly those of General Poole. He complained to Lansing of the "utter disregard of General Poole and of all the Allied governments (at any rate of all who are acting for them) of the policy to which we expressly confined ourselves." Wilson fumed, "Is there no way, no form of expression by which we can get this comprehended?" In this instance, he was talking about Poole's efforts to advance the Siberian Czechs far enough to link up with the Allies from Archangel.[46] However, Wilson was angry enough at Poole's "high handed attitude" in setting up a military government that he told the British "the U.S.G. would have to seriously consider the withdrawal of the U.S. contingent from General Poole's command."[47]

London was aware of American irritation with General Poole. In mid-September Wiseman sent a message regarding Wilson's seeming threat to withdraw American forces from northern Russia. He was sure Lansing had spoken "quite sharply" to a British representative about Poole, it was "a good example of how real trouble can be manufactured out of nothing." He continued, "Undoubtedly the U.S.G. rather resent the way in which Poole is running things at Archangel and I should imagine that he is not getting on particularly well with the American representatives there—probably he is rather impatient with them. It is only necessary, however, to explain to the administration the necessity of the action which Poole has taken and promise to do everything possible to respect Russian independence and the authority of the Local Board."[48]

Wiseman's comment indicates that the British were concerned that the United States would withdraw its troops. The sticking point was the Allied-imposed military government, and not Poole's extension of fighting well beyond protecting the ports and the supplies still stored there.

General Poole's reputation in Washington was already low soon after American troops arrived. On September 18, Wilson wrote to Lansing, noting that the British commander's "predictions of what would happen in Northern Russia . . . have been verified, so far as I can see, in no particular." Wilson said,

> [Poole] predicted, you will remember, that large forces of Russians would gather and that the only function of the Allied forces would be to hold Murmansk and Archangel in their rear and see that they were accessible for the shipment of supplies. Not only has this not happened, but you will notice from [Ambassador] Francis' most recent dispatches that they are finding it difficult even by persuasion to make

the local authorities function in any independent way, and that the situation is not at all what it was anticipated it would develop into.[49]

On October 1, General Edmund Ironside replaced Poole. Washington's complaints seemed to have had some effect in London, and Poole left Archangel for a "short leave" back in England. He did not return to Russia. The new commander attempted to spur greater recruitment of Russians for the anti-Bolshevik Russian army. It did not go well, and he had little success. Neither did he pull Allied forces back to Archangel.[50]

Besides reinforcements, the other issue for northern Russia was food. The military government imposed rationing for the civilian population. The British proposed that the United States contribute five million dollars toward supplies. Wilson agreed but hoped the British would take the lead. There was no time to delay. Archangel would be inaccessible from October until the next summer due to ice. This would also prevent reinforcements from arriving. Supplies did arrive, but even if Wilson had wanted to pull American troops out, it was too late. Until the harbor ice thawed in the spring, American troops were there to stay. Wilson was right to fear it would be easier to get in than to get out.[51]

SIBERIA AND JAPAN

In Siberia, by June 1918, the Japanese were backing anti-Bolshevik Lieutenant General Grigory Mikhaylovich Semenov. A reactionary Cossack (he passed out copies of the *Protocols of the Elders of Zion*), Semenov had fled the Bolshevik coup, ending up in the northern Chinese city of Harbin. That city was crucial because it was along the Chinese Eastern Railway, which connected the Russian cities of Krymskaya and Vladivostok. As such, it was a critical part of the Trans-Siberian Railroad system the Allies wanted the Czech Legion to occupy. With aid from the Japanese and Czechs, Semenov established an anti-Bolshevik regime, one of several in eastern Russia competing for Allied support. He was recognized as a local military commander by Admiral Alexander Kolchak's White Siberian government based in Omsk.

Supporting Semenov was only part of Tokyo's efforts to expand its influence over the region. Japan proposed a joint Chinese-Japanese control over the route into Russia, supposedly to keep it out of Bolsheviks' hands. These efforts worried the United States, including Paul Reinsch, the American minister to China. Reinsch worried over Japanese expansion, believing they were as bad as the Germans in expanding militarism. In mid-June 1918, he sent a cable to Washington outlining a series of steps for intervention in Siberia and northeast China to check Japanese expansion. Wilson was impressed enough by the diplomat's message to forward it to Lansing with the note there may "emerge from this suggestion the shadow of a plan that might be worked, with Japanese and other insistence."[52]

Wilson decided to allow the use of American troops at Archangel in mid-July and, at the same time, agreed to landing American forces at Vladivostok. The Supreme War Council on July 3 yet again asked the United States to send its forces to Vladivostok along with Japan to aid the Czech Legion and reopen an eastern front. On July 6, Wilson met with Baker; Daniels; Lansing; General March; and Rear Adm. W. S. Benson, the Chief of Naval Operations. They decided to support the Czechs by sending seven thousand American troops to be matched by an equal number of Japanese. The latter would supply the Czechs with guns and ammunition. The idea of a new eastern front was "physically impossible" because "any advance [of the Czechs] westward of Irkutsk does not seem possible and needs no further consideration." They also discussed the supposed threat by German and Austro-Hungarian POWs whom the Bolsheviks had supposedly armed and thought to be threatening the Czech Legion. The landing was not to interfere in "the internal affairs of Russia" and would not "impair the political or territorial sovereignty of Russia." The civilian leaders agreed. March did not. He thought the Japanese would not limit themselves to seven thousand men and would use the landing to "further her schemes for territorial aggrandizement." He told Wilson so, but the president replied, "We will just have to take that chance."[53]

While the forces of the Allied powers in the northeast were under British command, Wilson did not want the British or the French to participate in Siberia. Only forces sent by the United States and Japan would work with the Czech Legion already there. The decision to limit London and Paris's involvement was also a blunt rejection of the Supreme

War Council's request. Unfortunately, Wilson handled the exclusion of the other allies in an exceptionally clumsy fashion. He met with the Japanese ambassador on Monday morning, July 8. The ambassador was receptive to the American proposal. Wilson met the British ambassador on another matter a few hours later and made no mention of the decision. Later Lansing realized that the Japanese ambassador would likely mention Wilson's plan to his fellow ambassadors. The next day Lansing met separately with the British, French, and Italian representatives and told them Wilson's decision. The meetings did not go smoothly. When the Allies complained, Lansing replied that the United States only did what the others had done in the past, decided and then told the others. That only made the meeting even tenser. Neither Lansing nor Wilson seems to have considered how the Allies might react to the decision. Britain and France especially had been pleading with the United States to intervene with troops. Now Washington agreed, but did not bother to inform the others except as an afterthought, and then did not want the others to participate. It should not be surprising then that the next day, July 10, Britain ordered its garrison in Hong Kong to head north to Vladivostok. Instead of shutting the others out, Wilson and Lansing managed to guarantee that the British at least would participate. So did, in limited numbers, the French, Canadians, Italians, and Chinese.[54]

Wilson's decision went against March's advice, but it was based upon diplomatic and political rather than military reasoning. Indeed, Wilson's plan expressly rejected the Allied military rationale of recreating a new eastern front. However, the rationale Wilson used was no more realistic. While fighting had broken out between the Czech Legion and Austro-Hungarian POWs heading back home, it was not an organized effort by the Bolsheviks or Germans. Instead, it was what one might expect from the two groups coming into contact and getting in each other's way. The Austro-Hungarians (there were few German POWs in Siberia) saw the Czechs as traitors trying to split apart their empire. The Czechs saw the Austro-Hungarians as their oppressors against whom they were fighting for independence. When the groups collided on the Trans-Siberian Railroad, conflict was inevitable. Moreover, although Wilson denounced any effort to interfere with Russian internal affairs, he was picking a side in the Russian civil war by backing the Czechs. The Czechs were mostly fighting the Bolsheviks, not released POWs, and they were allied with the White anti-Bolshevik Russians.

The United States sent two infantry regiments, the 29th and the 30th, from the Philippines and the 8th Division from the American Pacific coast. The new organization was designated American Expeditionary Force, Siberia. Command of the Siberian forces was given to Maj. Gen. William Sidney Graves.[55] His orders were explicit: the western front (the orders specifically included the Italian front in this) took precedence. Graves was not to use his troops to interfere in Russian internal affairs. Even using them to establish a new front to attack in the east would be "making use of Russia, not a method of serving her." He was there to help the Czechs and cooperate with the Russians by acting to "steady any efforts at self-government or self-defense in which the Russians were willing to accept assistance." He was also to guard the military supplies, "which may subsequently be needed by Russian forces and to render such aid as may be acceptable to the Russians in the organization of their own self-defense." Finally, Graves was to feel "obliged to withdraw" his forces, "in order to add them to the forces at the Western front" if it turns out they found themselves in the position to act "inconsistent with the policy to which the government of the United States feels constrained to restrict itself." In other words, he was not to allow his troops to be used as the British were using American troops in northern Russia.[56]

The American Siberian commander kept a rigorous reading of his instructions not to interfere in Russian political affairs. There was a White Russian government in Omsk led by Admiral Alexander Kolchak. Although it was not recognized as the legitimate Russian government by any of the Allies, Kolchak's regime received a great deal of British support. He had very poor relations with the Czech Legion and with the Japanese. Major General Graves disliked Kolchak, thought him a reactionary, and balked at sending aid. This led to multiple attempts to undermine Grave's position, not only by the British but also by the U.S. State Department. In Siberia, the American consul general, Ernest Lloyd Harris, complained that "no one can get along with" Major General Graves. Harris sent reports to Washington newspapers attacking Graves for not backing the fight against the Bolsheviks, as well as any that made Graves look incompetent.[57] Graves found himself in a prolonged political battle over support for Kolchak with the American State Department and even with the intelligence division in the War Department in Washington. He kept the backing of Secretary Baker and Chief of Staff March. Otherwise, his position as commander in Siberia would have likely been very short-lived.

The State Department sent the American ambassador to Japan, Roland S. Morris, to Russia to check out Kolchak's government in Omsk. Morris was apparently more impressed with Kolchak than was Graves, but then the Russian admiral was making all the right comments about democracy to win American support. Graves thought them superficial lip service to win support. Indeed, he was disgusted with how the White Russian troops preyed on the ordinary Russians. However, Morris told Graves that the State Department was running policy in Siberia, to which the general replied, "The State Department is not running me."[58] Wilson was distracted by the ongoing peace conference in Paris during this political battle, although he received disturbing reports. Wilson apparently agreed with Grave's low estimation of Kolchak. This, despite the United States and the other members of the Supreme War Council forcing the Russian admiral to promise to hold free elections if he took power, to recognize political and religious liberties, and to recognize the independence of Poland and Finland. In the end, the United States did send the White Russians food and clothing and allowed the provisional government in exile to send money to Kolchak to buy arms and ammunition.[59]

Wilson was hampered by Congress as he could not give what anti-interventionists in Congress considered a satisfactory answer to why the United States had troops in Siberia. In the summer of 1919, Congress pressed Wilson for reasons beyond protecting the Trans-Siberian Railroad. Ironically, Wilson's half measures, intervention at a limited level, won support from neither the anti-interventionists nor those who wished to drive the Bolsheviks from power. When Wilson went on his 1919 cross-country tour to support ratifying the Versailles Treaty and defend the League of

Nations, his congressional opponents gave speeches attacking Wilson's interventionism using the Siberian mission as an example. On October 2, 1919, Wilson's massive stroke paralyzed the executive branch, and Kolchak's supporters in the State Department found themselves unable to aid the White Russian leader. The Omsk government collapsed, and the Bolsheviks executed Kolchak in early 1920. The AEF-Siberia operated and defended much of the Trans-Siberian Railroad in the east in 1919 and into 1920. They withdrew in early 1920.[60]

WITHDRAWAL FROM NORTH RUSSIA

Wilson decided to pull the American forces out of north Russia in early 1919. In March, he met Brig. Gen. Wilds P. Richardson and ordered him to control "all American forces in North Russia." Richardson met with Wilson in Paris, and the president complained about how the British had misused American forces in Russia. Richardson's mission, the president said, was to get U.S. forces out of Russia "as early as practicable after the opening of navigation." Richardson arrived in Archangel on April 8 and found that one company of the 339th Infantry Regiment had supposedly mutinied. Tired of the fighting, they had refused to load supplies onto sleds to return to the front to fight the Bolsheviks. Colonel Stewart convinced them to continue their work, and the men followed their orders to return to the front. The press exaggerated the extent of the "mutiny," and Chief of Staff March did not help matters by telling reporters that the unit had been infected with Bolshevik propaganda. Richardson investigated, decided that the matter was overblown, and let the matter drop.[61]

The British agreed to pull troops out of north Russia, and that American forces would leave first. However, General Ironside wanted to keep the U.S. Army engineers based there until September 1. To the frustration of Bliss and Wilson, Richardson agreed. Bliss grumbled to Wilson that "Richardson appears to have fallen under the influence of the local British officers and in his telegrams, he repeats the arguments which had been often submitted and considered before he went there." Bliss recommended that Wilson turn down the request. In the future, Bliss suggested, if the United States wanted troops in northern Russia, it should send regular troops, not volunteers. Bliss did suggest that the engineers be withdrawn last among the American troops, which would keep them in Archangel for another few weeks. Wilson agreed.[62]

CONCLUSION

American intervention in northern Russia and Siberia remains two of Wilson's most controversial interventions as president. In the end, about 200 American troops died in combat or from disease in the north Russian campaign and 170 in Siberia from all causes, including disease.[63] They accomplished little. The Czech Legion was never under a real threat from German or Austro-Hungarian prisoners. The White Russian forces were too disorganized and had too little support to defeat the Bolsheviks. The presence of American troops did nothing to stop Japan from sending 70,000 occupiers into Siberia and did nothing to encourage them to leave. The Allied supplies held in the port cities did not reach the Germans because the Russians, including the Bolsheviks, used them first. Russian resources did little to help Germany mainly because the war ended so soon. Wilson was correct that there was little realistic hope of reestablishing an eastern front, but the forces he sent into Russia did nothing to affect that. In short, the Russian interventions did little but help sour future American–Soviet relations.

Why, then, did Wilson do it? There is no single reason, but his decision was based on several factors, some of which were applicable to only the Siberian intervention:

- Wilson did want to protect Russian supplies sent from the Allies from getting into German hands. This was true of both interventions. It was not realistic in the end, but that was clear only in hindsight. The Bolsheviks took the supplies in Archangel before the Allies arrived. The Germans had enough trouble getting material from western Russia into Germany, let alone trying to ship supplies from Russia's Pacific coast.
- He wanted to protect the Czech Legion, which applied to Siberia.
- Wilson wanted to stop the Japanese from territorial expansion in eastern Siberia.

- In both cases he wanted to strengthen the American negotiating position with the idea that it was easier to say "We should leave" and "You should leave."
- Finally, in both interventions, Wilson felt he had to answer Allied diplomatic pressure to intervene. Simply put, the more Wilson said "no" to the Allies on Russia, the less political capital he would have to refuse them on other issues later.

The continual intense lobbying from the British and French played a role as well. For months, starting in early 1918, both Allies had badgered the United States to send troops to Russia. Wilson, Bliss, Lansing, House, Baker—they all heard from the Allies repeatedly. In June, Bliss complained to Baker that the "British and French general staff bureaus and their ministries of foreign affairs give out nothing but that which is favorable to the idea of [Russian] intervention." When he played devil's advocate, they got irritated. "I do not believe," Bliss told his chief, "that the question [of Russian intervention] can be considered in this unbiased light anywhere except in Washington."[64] While Bliss was blind to his own biases, he was correct about the British and the French. The idea of linking the northern Russian front rooted at Archangel with the Siberian front via Irkutsk was frankly nonsense. When Baker told British ambassador Reading that Irkutsk was too many thousands of miles east to help with the eastern front, Reading replied, "It is nearer than Vladivostok." The secretary of war replied that a man standing on his roof was nearer the moon, but he still was not going to reach it.[65] It is not, however, that the Allies convinced Wilson of the rightness of intervention. Instead, it eventually cost too much political capital for Wilson to continue refusing, capital he would instead reserve for the peace talks.

What about other rational reasons for sending U.S. forces? While Wilson would not have been sorry to see the Bolsheviks overthrown, he was not willing to openly intervene to oust them from power. He had no sympathy for the late czar's regime nor for those who would recreate it. British diplomat Sir William Wiseman noted that Wilson "gives every excuse [not opposing intervention] except the real one, which is that he believes the interventionists are reactionaries under another name."[66] Wilson also understood that foreign intervention would strengthen Bolshevik's hold on Russian sentiment, even if he was inconsistent in recognizing what type of American action the Russians would view as an intervention. Likewise, there was little motivation for Wilson to intervene to protect American business interests in Russia, although he was happy to promote business opportunities overseas on other occasions. The contention that Wilson acted in Siberia to promote an "open door to the world" places too much emphasis on economic factors as motivating Wilson's opposition to Japanese expansion. Wilson was an anti-imperialist, even if his understanding of what actions made up "imperialism" was far too limited by the later understanding of the term. Indeed, his support for "the white man's burden" was imperialistic, even if Wilson saw it as educational. Seizing foreign territory for financial advantage was imperialism. Taking a colony to keep indefinitely was imperialism. Seizing a colony, then helping it develop, "inducting them into the rudiments of justice and freedom" was, in Wilson's mind, not.[67] Despite Wilson's idealistic blind spot, seizing another nation's territory by force of arms to annex it—such as the United States feared Japan would do to Russia—met even Wilson's limited understanding of "imperialism."

Wilson followed more of a hands-on approach in his Russian policy than he did elsewhere largely because it touched so closely on his diplomatic objectives. When Major General Graves took command in Siberia, he received explicit orders not to use his troops to interfere in Russian internal affairs, ignoring that to some extent they were interfering just by being there. His instructions to the American forces in north Russia were more ambiguous, but still included instructions to not be drawn further into interfering in Russian affairs, and Wilson was angry that the British commander there expanded their role, and their presence, further into Russia. Wilson, moreover, relied on his military commanders for their judgment regarding Russia. He listened to Bliss, who was hesitant about the idea of a new Russian front, trusted Graves in Siberia despite the State Department's campaign against him, and let Pershing choose which units to send into north Russia. The ineffectiveness of Wilson's Russian policies was due to other factors, such as Allied pressure, rather than from his relations with his own military commanders.

CHAPTER 8

———◆•◆———

Occupation Duty and Smaller Interventions

B esides the significant interventions already discussed, there were multiple other occasions in which the Wilson administration used American armed forces overseas. These varied in scale from an entire army used in the occupation duty in Germany starting in late 1918, to small groups of sailors or Marines sent ashore in a port city during unrest. The degree to which Wilson involved himself in each varied by time and place. From 1917 to 1919 he was distracted by World War I and then the peace talks. His attention to these smaller interventions decreased the further the matter lay from the war and Paris. Events that had direct relationship to the war and the peace talks, however, earned his full attention. After his major stroke in October 1919, his own health issues prevented him from maintaining much attention, only getting involved in Mexico, for example, to prevent a wider war.

This chapter will discuss actions grouped by region:

- Germany, occupation and demobilization
- The Balkans during the unrest after World War I
- Latin America and the Caribbean
- East Asia, including Russia

German Occupation

After the armistice was signed on November 11, 1918, American soldiers would be part of the victorious Allies' occupation of part of western Germany. This deployment of American troops along the Rhine after November 11, 1918, was more peaceful than either Archangel or Vladivostok and so has received little scholarly attention.[1] As part of the armistice agreement, the Allies posted troops along the Rhine, creating bridgeheads at major crossing points. Because the river forms a natural and formidable obstacle to invaders moving east into Germany, setting up bridgeheads for the Allies prevented the Germans from restarting the war behind a natural fortification line. Indeed, General Foch declared in a January 1919 memo that the river was "the *common* barrier of security necessary to the League of Democratic Nations."[2] There were zones for Britain, Belgium, France, and the United States. The American zone initially included Luxembourg and in Germany ran along the Mosel River and the Koblenz bridgehead. To occupy the area, Pershing created the Third U.S. Army under the command of Maj. Gen. Joseph T. Dickman.

The occupation's authority came in Paragraph V of the November 11 armistice: "The [portion of Germany on] the left bank of the Rhine shall be administered by the local authorities under control of the troops of occupation of the Allies and the United States." Both "local authorities" and "under control" were left unclear. However, both U.S. and German authorities interpreted "local authorities" to mean the German officials of the existing German government rather than the assorted local soviets and other revolutionary agencies that arose in cities throughout Germany. The United States also favored a looser form of supervision than the other Allies, preferring to keep interference with locals more to a minimum.[3]

There were other aspects to the occupation, including an initial turnover of weapons from Germany to the Allies as "military reparations."

Belgium received one-tenth, the United States two-tenths, Britain three-tenths, and France four-tenths. For the AEF, that translated to more than 1,200 artillery pieces, almost 600 trench mortars, 10,000 machine guns, and 340 aircraft of various types. The Allied bridgeheads were substantial, being thirty kilometers (about nineteen miles) in radius. A ten-kilometer "demilitarized zone" restricted German military movements near Allied forces. Costs of the occupation were to be paid by the Germans.[4] The American occupation force initially consisted of eight divisions: four regular Army, two National Guard, and two from the National Army (mostly draftees). Two additional divisions guarded the supply line through France and Luxembourg. Additionally, there were support units, truck companies, and aviation units, including aircraft and observation balloons. The total number of personnel was approximately 225,000, and they were responsible for 2,500 square miles with about one million inhabitants.[5]

The March to the Rhine began on November 18, 1918, just one week after the armistice. The German troops were to withdraw to the east side of the river, keeping twenty-five kilometers between themselves and the following Allied armies. This was an easier standard to declare than to maintain. Road conditions were often poor and the routes were clogged with civilian refugees and Allied POWs who, rather than wait for their comrades to arrive, often began walking out of their camps moving westward. Adding to the chaos, some German soldiers began forming soviets, or equivalent organizations, attacking their officers. The Germans were not supposed to sabotage supplies or local resources while retreating, although they sometimes did so. Morale among the Germans was often low, and to keep themselves supplied with food on many occasions took the local livestock and drove the animals before them, although other German units maintained their morale and cohesion and retreated in good order.[6]

The Third Army arrived at its assigned occupation zone on December 13 and was established on December 18. Troops were billeted, as in France, in farms, homes, and in the towns close to their unit's assembly areas. Pershing had retained control of the military government, and the American occupation was less harsh than that of the other Allies.

Several French officers assigned with the Americans were reassigned after treating German civilians too harshly. Major General Dickman answered a complaint from a French officer about German civilians' treatment by noting that the United States was experienced in governing occupied territory, using the examples of Cuba, the Philippines, and China. He might also have included Veracruz, Haiti, and the Dominican Republic. There were rules against fraternization with German civilians. However, Americans met and often fell in love with German girls, and the Army would eventually have to provide transportation for German as well as French wives of servicemen.[7] On July 2, 1919, just days after the Versailles Treaty was signed, the War Department disbanded the Third Army. The U.S. occupying forces became the American Forces in Germany (AFG). The number of troops also decreased as the original 225,000 was reduced to about 87,000 by early July. The number continued to fluctuate from 1919 to 1922 until there were only about 1,000 enlisted men and a little over 100 officers by the end of 1922. In January 1923, the AFG was recalled to the United States and its area of responsibility turned over to the French.[8]

Wilson was involved in setting the occupation policy, relying on advice from Bliss and Pershing. Obviously, it was a military matter, and as noted earlier, Wilson trusted his commanders with purely military matters. However, the occupation of western Germany was also very political and so it crossed over into areas Wilson considered his purview as president. Wilson came to approve the creation of the different occupation zones, including the requirement for bridgeheads, eventually understanding the desire to prevent the Germans from restarting the war. The president also needed an American force among the occupiers to keep an eye on the French. Meanwhile, Paris wanted to deploy their forces in the other Allies' zones, which Pershing vehemently rejected. It would cause problems for supply and command to have such mixed forces in the bridgeheads. He probably also worried about the presence of French African colonial troops in the American zone. Foch responded by reducing the American zone, splitting Koblenz so half the city fell into the French zone. That angered

Pershing and made him even more supportive of sending American troops back home sooner. He even ignored Secretary Baker's willingness to increase the size of the occupation force, to do more than the Americans' "strictly numerical share." This, in turn led to even more tensions with the French, who wanted more troops in Germany, not fewer.[9]

The size of the occupation force and the length of time it would be deployed were questions that overlapped the military and the diplomatic. Foch wanted forty divisions, which would be reduced to thirty, and then to ten, of which one or two would be American. Neither Bliss nor Pershing were enthused about the possibility of a full two divisions of American troops in the Rhineland. Bliss told President Wilson that he thought Foch's desire to have even ten divisions, approximately 150,000 men, could be safely cut in half. For his part, Wilson thought the French supreme commander was obsessed with the Rhine. To come to some sort of arrangement, however, Wilson agreed with French premier Clemenceau to a fifteen-year staged occupation, with a reduction in the number of troops every five years. In the meantime, the United States continued sending troops home and replacing the occupation force with new recruits rather than those who had served in the war. Wilson wanted no more than 5,000 total, but Bliss and Pershing convinced him a few more were needed to include support functions. The result was still fewer than 10,000 Americans, and by the summer of 1919 American troops made up less than 5 percent of the Allied troops on the left bank of the Rhine. They would, Wilson thought, be there for the entire fifteen years.[10]

Once the American zone and the size of the occupation force was established, the occupation became, in Wilson's mind, a military matter. It did not require creating a democratic German government. While Germany suffered from revolutionary violence during the era, including numerous communist revolts, Germany was not like Mexico or Russia with no recognized de facto government. Hence, while important, the political repercussions could be dealt with at the Paris Peace Conference as part of the broader matter of hampering Germany's military abilities enough to guarantee future French safety.

GERMAN DEMOBILIZATION

As soon as the armistice went into effect, American servicemen began asking when they could go home. Technically the war was not yet over and Germany could restart fighting, but the idea of sticking around in France in case the war began again held little appeal for most doughboys. Demobilization raised several issues. The first was the general principle: who went home first? Sending men home in the order they deployed, those with the longest service first, was problematic because the war had not lasted very long for most Americans, six months or less. Another issue was where they would be discharged. There was processing to do and paperwork to be completed before sending the men on their way. Then there was the issue of transportation. The United States was not the only country trying to send its soldiers home. For the British, it was a simple trip across the Channel, but for the Americans, Canadians, Australians, etc., there was an ocean or two to cross, and shipping was still in short supply from the war; there was more demand than there were ships. Finally, how could the United States deal with unemployment? With the end of the war, factories would be retooling for civilian production, so a quick demobilization meant dumping millions of men into a contracting job market.[11]

After considering several ways to demobilize, March decided to send the men home by unit rather than as individuals. One suggestion had been to send home men by occupation, those with vital jobs going first. March determined that this would be so complicated it would slow down demobilization. Instead, each unit was classified as surplus or not, depending on if it was needed in the immediate postwar period. Units judged as surplus would go home first. What about the draft and the men training in camps? Calling up men for the draft ended on November 11, and those in training camps were sent home first. All men to be demobilized were discharged from whichever camp was closest to their home. Those taking training, such as officer classes, were allowed to finish, but no new classes were enrolled. Within units not judged to be surplus, men could file for discharge for hardship or necessity. Finally, every man was asked if they wanted to continue their career in the regular Army or join the reserves. Many did. Conscientious objectors being detained (in case they changed their minds) were also immediately released. By May 1, 1919, the United States had discharged almost two million men. By January 1920, the AEF had effectively been sent home, except for those men serving in occupied Germany. The entire process was overseen by Chief of Staff March, with input from Pershing and Baker.[12]

THE BALKANS

The end of World War I heralded the collapse of the Austro-Hungarian and Ottoman empires. Several new nations arose out of their wreckage, including the Kingdom of Serbs, Croats, and Slovenes (Yugoslavia[13]) which combined Serbia, Montenegro, and parts of what had been Austro-Hungary including Croatia, Slovenia, and Bosnia. However, Yugoslav land claims conflicted with demands made by Italy. The border between Italy and Yugoslavia was one of the most contentious issues of the Paris talks, with the Italian premier at one point walking out of the conference. Rome had joined the Allies in 1915 after the Treaty of London, which promised several sections of Austro-Hungary and much of the Adriatic's eastern coast, including the port city of Fiume, to the Italians. When fighting broke out between Slavs and Italians in the port, British and French troops entered the city to keep the peace, while the British, French, Italians, and Americans stationed warships in ports along the coast while negotiations continued.[14]

Wilson leaned heavily toward the Yugoslavs over Italy, and the United States was the first world power to recognize the new Yugoslav government in February 1919. In part this was due to the American president's frustration with the Italians. Wilson was angry at Italy's Prime Minister Vittorio Orlando for pushing expansionist claims on neighboring territory based on the Treaty of London, which Wilson considered violating the principal of self-determination. Wilson compromised and gave in to Italy's demands in the Tyrol, which awarded Rome territory well beyond the region inhabited by Italian speakers. However, Wilson refused to accede to Rome's demands to the detriment of Belgrade. Wilson found only limited support from the British and French, although they were also exasperated with Italian demands. He tried to find some compromise that would keep both sides happy, asking, for example, if the port city of Split (Spalato) would suffice for Yugoslav access to the Adriatic in place of Fiume. The Yugoslavs assured Wilson it was not satisfactory. Wilson continued to refuse Italian claims to the latter port, suggesting it be a free city, but in Belgrade's economic sphere. Italian irredentists decided to push matters so as to remove the decision from the leaders in Paris.[15]

On September 12 Italian poet Gabriele d'Annunzio entered Fiume and began a fifteen-month period of occupation. Using over a thousand Italian war veterans, the filibusters forced the Allied occupying troops to withdraw. Two weeks later, on September 23, 1919, a small number of Italian soldiers, some three or four truckloads—fewer than one hundred men—crossed the armistice line between Yugoslavia and Italy along the Dalmatian coast near Split. At about 2:00 a.m., they drove into Traù (Trogir) and seized the small Yugoslav garrison. A local Italian nobleman proclaimed himself dictator, and Italian soldiers began patrolling the streets. This could quickly have begun a war between Italy and Yugoslavia; tensions were already so high. The Supreme Council in Paris had assigned this region of the Dalmatian coast to the U.S. Navy for peacekeeping operations. When informed of the coup, the local American commander, Rear Adm. Philip Andrews, ordered the captains of the USS *Olympia* and the USS *Cowell* to intervene. The old cruiser *Olympia* traveled from Split, about sixteen miles east of Traù, arriving about noon. The Americans convinced the local Serbian forces outside the city to not intervene until the Italians had left, preserving the peace. Approximately one hundred sailors and Marines landed to retake the city and the Italians quickly withdrew. The small Yugoslav garrison was freed, and the Americans arrested the local would-be dictator. One vehicle with an Italian officer and three of his men had to be rescued when their transportation broke down. They were turned over to an Italian warship in the harbor. In the end, there were no casualties, besides some Italian pride.[16]

The Republican-controlled Senate was soon in an uproar. Was the United States going to war with Italy? When the incident occurred, Wilson had just abruptly stopped his western tour to convince the American people to back the Versailles Treaty. Not surprisingly, treaty opponent Massachusetts senator Henry Cabot Lodge was one of the leaders of the uproar over the landing. Here was an example of American forces used overseas to keep the peace in a dispute in which no American property or lives were threatened, nor was the area critical to U.S. national security. Was this the type of action the United States would find itself in as a member of the League of Nations? However, the political attack lacked much effect as the incident ended peacefully, and even the Italian government denounced the coup. Moreover, Wilson was out of the battle. On October 2, as the Senate was arguing, he had suffered a massive stroke, leaving him partially blind and partially paralyzed. He may not have even known of the Senate resolution calling on the administration to inform the Senate about the details of the incident. Secretary of the Navy Daniels discussed the matter on the phone with Wilson's wife, Edith. She said that Wilson's physician, Dr. Cary Grayson, "did not wish any business brought before him [Wilson]." Satisfied with the details, and probably realizing there was little political capital to be gained by debating the issue further, the Senate let the matter drop.[17]

Turkey and the Former Ottoman Empire

While Italy and Yugoslavia squabbled over the Dalmatian coast, multiple other European powers argued and maneuvered to gain control over the carcass of the Ottoman Empire in Anatolia. The Turks had signed an armistice with the British on October 30, 1918. On November 13, British troops began landing in Constantinople, the only Central Powers capital city to be so-occupied. A half-dozen of the Allies sent ships to the city and set up an administrative center to oversee the stricken empire's fate. Britain and France took the lead, followed by Italy, Greece, the United States, and Japan. All the maneuvering, secret treaties and wars that were fought over the Ottoman Empire's remains are beyond the boundaries of this study, as the United States (and Japan) were generally just observers. They were present as members of the Allied forces, not because they made claims on Ottoman territory. The Allies offered President Wilson a large piece of what is now Turkey as a mandate. Although tempted, he refused, fearing it would never get past Congress, nor did he believe American public opinion would accept such a responsibility. Wilson also considered, briefly, whether American troops could be used in former Ottoman territories, especially Armenia, as a "garrison" to preserve order. Baker answered that while he had no doubt it would be legal, American public opinion was too strongly in favor of bringing home the troops quickly to support such an action. As a result, American military actions in the former Ottoman Empire were small-scale peacekeeping actions carried out by the Navy.[18]

The United States and the Ottoman Empire had not officially gone to war, although under pressure from Berlin, Constantinople had broken diplomatic relations in 1917. One American warship, the armed American yacht USS *Scorpion* (a veteran of the Spanish-American War), was interned in the capital's harbor. On November 9, 1918, it was allowed to re-hoist the American flag and military equipment removed earlier was returned. A relief crew arrived in December. For a time, it became the flagship of Rear Adm. Mark Lambert Bristol, the American high commissioner to Turkey as part of the Allied command structure in Constantinople. He set up a small naval base in the city that consisted of a few buildings and some warships, more of a token force than anything else. Bristol's position was both diplomatic and military. As a high commissioner, he was responsible to the State Department. However, he was the senior American naval officer on site, so he reported to the Secretary of the Navy through the force commander of U.S. Naval Forces Operating in European Waters.[19]

The United States would need someone with both diplomatic and military authority in the former empire. Both Greece and Italy laid claim to some of the same Turkish territory. When Italy began moving warships to harbors in areas it claimed, the Greeks appealed to the other members of the Big Four at Paris. Wilson was furious at the Italian's pushing so hard for Fiume and so supported Greek claims in other areas as a way to hinder Italian expansion. On May 2, 1919, an inter-Allied fleet was dispatched to the port of Smyrna as Britain, France, and the United States approved Greek occupation of the city. On May 15, Greek troops begin landing in what would later be clear was an enormous error by the Allies. There was a large Greek population in Smyrna, but it was not the majority. By approving the Greek occupation Wilson had ignored his own experts' opinion—not to mention his commitment to avoid turning territory dominated by one ethnic group over to control of another. Greek troops and civilians alike engaged in looting and attacking Turkish residents. The American warship in the harbor, the battleship USS *Arizona*, landed a small force of twenty men to protect the American legation, and the ship provided shelter for Americans and others seeking shelter from the violence. The Allies were so shocked by the violence that they held an official inquiry, chaired by Bristol. The report held the Greeks responsible, and recommended that Allied troops replace them. The Supreme Council, however, could not agree on what to do, so the recommendation was set aside.[20]

In late 1920 several American vessels based at Constantinople were sent to south Russia to watch as the last of the White armies fought the Bolsheviks in the region. When the White forces collapsed in November 1920, the American Navy sent a force of destroyers, a cruiser, and several steamships to rescue Americans from Odessa, Sevastopol, and Novorossiysk. There were civilians and businessmen and workers from the YMCA and Red Cross aboard, as well as Russians fleeing the Bolsheviks. All told at its height, the U.S. fleet in Turkish waters consisted of a dozen destroyers, several small subchasers, two cruisers, and a handful of other ships such as the *Scorpion*. They rescued refugees, kept an eye on the Allies expanding in the area, delivered food to areas in need, and maintained radio communication between American diplomats and Washington.[21]

Latin America
Cuba

During the second Wilson administration, the United States intervened in areas that were not part of the defeated Central Powers as well. There were numerous armed interventions in Central America and the Caribbean, ranging from the very small to fights involving a few thousand men. For the most part they have been forgotten, overshadowed by World War I and even by the American intervention in Russia. They do, however, illustrate some common threads into how Wilson's administration viewed intervention. They should be considered in light of the entire administration including the State Department and the War Department, rather than actions by Wilson alone, even more so than earlier efforts. Wilson's focus was, understandably, on World War I and then on the peace treaty. Wilson's stroke in early October 1919 prevented him from active policy-making for at least six months as well. By 1918 however, he had set enough of a precedent that his cabinet secretaries could follow Wilsonian policies even when the president was at arm's length from events. This was especially true of Secretary of War Baker and Secretary of the Navy Daniels. They were in sympathy with Wilson's goals and motivation. However, Secretary of State Lansing was much more of an interventionist than Wilson and far more skeptical of Wilson's desire to promote democratic governments. Lansing was replaced in early 1920 by Progressive lawyer Bainbridge Colby. The new secretary of state was interested in promoting Wilson's early Pan-American initiatives and was much less likely to intervene, although he still sometimes agreed to do so.[22]

The United States had already intervened in Cuba during the Roosevelt and Taft administrations under the Platt Amendment. Wilson had his opportunity in 1917. Cuba held its presidential election in 1916, and the incumbent Conservative party had to cheat to win. Incumbent president Mario García Menocal "won" by resorting to open fraud. Of the almost 500,000 eligible voters, 800,000 cast their votes. This was the second time in independent Cuba's short history that the Conservative candidate won via fraud. The Liberals were ready to rise in revolt, but they knew Menocal had support in Washington. Moreover, in January 1917 the United States was quickly moving toward war with Germany, and a revolt in Cuba would only anger the Americans. Nonetheless, the Liberals began their revolt in several cities, joined by some of Menocal's military commanders. They sent a letter to Wilson asking for intervention to ensure a free and fair redo of the election in provinces where the fraud was most blatant.23

The United States did not intervene at first, but on February 12, 1917, the USS *Paducah* landed men following a request for protection from

American sugarcane plantation owners in eastern Cuba. They did not interfere in the revolution, but it was a clear sign to the revolutionaries not to threaten American property.[24] The same day, however, one of the revolutionary generals convinced the American naval commander at Santiago to prevent the government from landing troops when rebels seized the city. Neither Wilson nor Lansing approved the American commander's actions.[25]

The American administration began issuing statements that they backed "the Constitutional government of Cuba" by which they meant the Menocal regime. Wilson refused to even communicate with the rebels while the rebellion was ongoing and noted that they would back only "constitutional methods for the settlement of disputes."[26] In the February 27 cabinet meeting, Wilson and his advisers discussed landing troops in Cuba to protect American lives and property. The United States was so close to war with Germany that rumors about German involvement were discussed at the meeting, as well as German and Japanese intrigue in Mexico. Daniels noted that Wilson thought it would be strange if the Japanese and Germans cooperated in Mexico given that they were at war. As for Germans in Cuba, Wilson was, according to Daniels, "free from G[erman] suspicions, but so many things are happening, we cannot afford to let Cuba be involved by G[erman] plots."[27]

The Wilson administration agreed to sell 10,000 rifles and 2,000,000 cartridges to Menocal's military to put down the rebellions. Moreover, the United States landed Marines and bluejackets multiple times between March and May. Naval reports from 1917 indicate that Marine detachments from eleven different ships, including the *Olympia* and the *Maine* landed men in Cuba.[28] The Marines did not directly involve themselves in the fighting, limiting themselves to protecting lives and property. However, their presence was a clear, deliberate reminder that the United States favored quick restoration of order. As the rebels were hoping for American intervention to aid their cause, an ostensibly neutral intervention ended up favoring the existing conservative government. The problem for the Liberals was twofold. First, their reputation in Washington was that they were as corrupt as the Conservatives, perhaps more so. As a result, although their accusations of a stolen election were true, they could not portray themselves as supporting an alternative for constitutional government. Contrast their standing to that of the Constitutionalists in 1913 Mexico, who presented themselves to Wilson as a return to legitimacy. The Cuban Liberal's second problem was one of timing. Wilson had learned of the Zimmermann Telegram on February 24, so German intrigue in Cuba was well within the realm of imagined possibility. Even though there was no sign of the Germans behind the Liberal revolt, Cuba's instability would have looked to Washington as an invitation for Berlin to commit mischief.

At least part of the Liberals' demand was met. New elections were held in two provinces, but they were again subject to blatant ballot-box stuffing by the Conservatives, where, once again, more people voted than were registered. Meanwhile, Cuba declared war on Germany the day after the United States did.[29] Selling sugar was the island nation's most significant contribution to the war effort. Cuban sugar was crucial for Allied war supplies, so anything that threatened the sugar crop was hampering the war effort. American Marines and soldiers remained in Cuba at "training camps." In reality, they were there to protect the sugar. This pseudo-occupation left bitter feelings among much of the Cuban population, and there were anti-American demonstrations in 1918 and 1919. By 1920 however, most of the American forces left in Cuba were confined to Guantanamo Bay.[30]

Cuba held its next presidential election in 1920. Once again, the Conservative incumbent Menocal faced Liberal Alfredo de Zayas. Upon a suggestion by the Americans, the Cuban government invited the United States to send Maj. Gen. Enoch H. Crowder to develop an electoral reform plan. Menocal accepted the general's reforms, however, he rejected direct American supervision of the election. In the meantime, the Conservative-controlled Cuban Congress began passing laws to gut Crowder's reforms. Liberals then argued that the United States had a responsibility to intervene as Washington had closed off the means to effect change through a revolution in 1917. The new American secretary of state, Bainbridge

Colby, demanded that the United States supervise the election, meeting a critical Liberal demand. Menocal refused, although some Americans did end up observing. Unfortunately, there was no clear immediate result due to fraud and confusion.[31]

Major General Crowder arrived in Havana on January 6, 1920, on the battleship USS *Minnesota*, an unsubtle warning to the Cubans. When Menocal complained about the nature of the general's arrival, the State Department replied, "It has not been customary, nor is it considered necessary, for the President of the United States to obtain the prior consent of the President of Cuba to send a special representative to confer with him." Just to make it even plainer that Cuba was expected to cooperate, the message continued, "You may state to President Menocal that it is the earnest desire of this Government to avoid the necessity of taking any measures which could be construed as intervention in Cuba or as supervision of the domestic affairs of that Republic, which we still feel confident can be avoided, provided President Menocal assumes a receptive attitude in respect to the advice and just recommendations which the President has instructed General Crowder to convey to him."[32]

Menocal agreed to accept the American general, who at this point might accurately be described as a proconsul. The decision to send Crowder was Secretary of State Lansing's, apparently from worry about what financial damage would be done to American interests in Cuba. Adding to the uncertainty, sugar prices dramatically fell, dropping from twenty-two cents to a little over a penny a pound, collapsing the economy. The general stayed onboard the warship, issuing "suggestions" that could not be understood as anything but commands. On February 26, the three most powerful politicians in Cuba, Menocal, Zayas, and Miguel Mariano Gómez[33] met with Crowder and agreed to his terms, including new elections in a fifth of Cuba's provinces. When fighting broke out between Liberals and Conservatives, the former boycotted the elections and Zayas became the new president. The United States, however, was satisfied. Electoral procedures were followed, if imperfectly, and there was still an American battleship hovering nearby to maintain order.[34]

Haiti

The U.S. also had to deal with a revolt against American military occupation in Haiti between 1919 and 1920. As discussed in chapter 4, the United States had installed Philippe Sudré Dartiguenave as president of Haiti in 1915. Dartiguenave was willing to make several crucial concessions to Washington, including recognizing a right to intervene (copying to some extent Cuba), American control of customs, and management of Haitian finances. However, Secretary of State Lansing pushed the Haitians to accept a far more comprehensive new treaty, including an indefinite American military occupation and more U.S. control over internal Haitian matters. It would turn Haiti into a vassal state of the United States more than the newly installed pro-American president was willing to tolerate. The State Department pressed for the Haitian government to accept the treaty with no discussions or revisions. Understandably, the Haitians balked. Meanwhile, Rear Admiral Caperton was authorized to collect customs duties and allocate them to organize public works projects and a local native police force, the Gendarmerie. The treaty's provisions, the United States explained, would be carried out whether Haiti agreed or not.[35]

For President Wilson, neither Haiti nor the Dominican Republic was worthy of much attention, so actual policy-making came from several departments. The result was not only a lack of coordination, but policy-making dependent upon the personalities of individual officials not only below the presidential level but often below the level of cabinet secretary. Rear Admiral Caperton's decision to install martial law, for example, was his decision, not that of Secretary of the Navy Daniels, let alone from Wilson. This is not to say Wilson was unaware of what was happening, but that he agreed with the policies and left their formation to others. Rear Admiral Caperton established a military government in both Haiti and the Dominican Republic, the latter openly, the former in effect. Some civilian authorities remained in Haiti, but they were subordinate to the American military. Moreover, because the American admiral tended to stay in the Dominican Republic, Haiti's actual authority devolved to the Marine commander, Col. Littleton T. Waller, and to Maj. Smedley Butler.

Caperton proclaimed martial law as established for occupied enemy territory. The fact that President Dartiguenave had at one point requested martial law, to keep his political opponents at bay, was a convenient excuse but had no real effect besides providing a fig leaf to cover the violation of Haitian sovereignty.[36]

In December 1915, Maj. Smedley Butler formed the Gendarmerie d'Haiti. Intended to be a national force to overcome the existing regional and ethnic-racial divisions, it was also supposed to be politically neutral to negate the revolutionary militias and the scheming by generals in the old Haitian army. The army, and the existing police, were disbanded. In testimony before Congress, Colonel Waller bragged, "We have taken arms from the people [under martial law], and we have disarmed the leaders who led them in revolt, taken their positions from them, and given them no control over the people in any way."[37] Colonel Waller and Major Butler clashed with Rear Admiral Caperton over which organization was responsible for what parts of the Haitian administration. Along with the Gendarmerie, the Marines took over the mail and telegraph systems and public works, repairing, improving, and building new roads. Lacking the available personnel, the State Department delegated much of the financial business to the War Department's Bureau of Insular Affairs. The Navy took responsibility for non-financial matters.[38]

Unable to resist the proposed treaty outright, Dartiguenave and Haitian foreign secretary Louis Borno found ways to stall the process. The foreign secretary asked the United States to reword critical passages to be less offensive to Haitian nationalism. Lansing complied but missed that Borno asked for more substantive changes than Lansing was willing to concede. However, the new treaty text was ambiguous enough that both sides could interpret it differently, giving the Haitians some room to argue in the future. It remained for the Haitian Senate (and that in the United States) to ratify, and the Haitian legislature was not in a hurry. However, Caperton let it be known that the United States was going to act as if Haiti ratified the treaty, even if it did not. The American Senate ratified it on February 28, 1916. The Haitian Senate took a bit longer after trying unsuccessfully, to add "interpretative commentary" to the text.[39]

The treaty having been ratified, the next step for the United States was to redo the Haitian constitution. Washington was especially interested in ending the long-standing prohibition on non-Haitians owning land in Haiti, as well as weakening the power of the troublesome legislature. Dartiguenave also favored the latter, which would strengthen his standing. In April 1916, he tried to dissolve the Senate and asked the deputies to write a new constitution. Colonel Waller was opposed to dismissing the Senate, and the deputies refused to act. Stalemated, Dartiguenave submitted his proposed new constitution to the American State Department for comments. Elections, supervised by American Marines, were held in January, and a new assembly session began in April 1917. The assembly was immediately hostile to American meddling in Haitian affairs. President Dartiguenave quietly encouraged them, hoping the U.S. military would step in to dissolve the legislature. Colonel Waller's successor, however, was willing, but also wanted to get rid of Dartiguenave. The Haitian president hurried to send the assembly home while he still had an office and Marine Major Butler, the commandant of the Gendarmerie, dismissed the deputies in June. Wilson was no doubt too distracted by the United States entering the war with Germany in spring 1917 to worry much about how the American military pulled the strings in Haitian politics.[40]

Haiti was not ignored entirely by the civilian leadership in Washington. In January 1917, Assistant Secretary of the Navy Franklin Roosevelt visited the island nation on an official state trip. The visit demonstrated the high position Major Butler occupied. He escorted Roosevelt. Once, when President Dartiguenave started to get into the official limousine ahead of the white assistant secretary, the Marine officer grabbed him by the collar and yanked him back. Roosevelt graciously allowed the client-state president to get in first. At the official reception, Mrs. Butler acted as hostess for the bachelor Dartiguenave and at the evening ball while white men would dance with Haitian women, white women would not dance with Haitian men. The color line could only be crossed at certain points in particular circumstances.[41]

Unfortunately for Haitian stability, the Marines and the Gendarmerie overstepped the demands they made on the Haitian population and provoked a full-scale revolt, the Second Caco War. The effective military rule of Haiti required an adequate road system that did not exist. Butler used an 1864 Haitian corvée law to gather a labor force. Peasants were required to either pay a road tax or work for three days to build and maintain roads. Since few could afford the tax, Butler had his legal, if unpopular, labor force. At first, it worked well. The workers were fed and paid a small amount. They were not, theoretically at least, abused by their supervisors. By early 1918, when Butler left Haiti, there were 15,000 in the labor force and roads were being built, but his successor was not as capable. Labor conditions were poor, and Haitians were too proud of their history to subject themselves to what seemed like a slave system reborn. Workers were being roped together, kept beyond their required time, beaten, and even killed. Secretary Daniels was shocked when he got reports of the abuses. By then, it was too late. When the corvée was ended in October 1918, its "reign of terror" had already provoked the Haitians' violent reaction.[42]

The rebel leader was Charlemagne Péralte. A commander in the Haitian army in 1915, he retired to his farm rather than surrender to American forces. Convicted of trying to steal a Gendarmerie payroll, in September 1918, he escaped from captivity (along with his guard whom he convinced to join him) and began to gather supporters for armed resistance to the United States and the Gendarmerie. He soon had up to five thousand men under his leadership, with three times that amount in sympathetic local groups. Poorly armed at first, they avoided confronting the Gendarmerie, let alone the U.S. Marines, until they had enough modern weapons. Péralte began leading raids on small, isolated Gendarmerie outposts in October 1918. Unsuccessful at defeating the Gendarmerie, the *cacos* did nonetheless inflict casualties and continued their attacks into 1919. When a new Marine commander in 1919 discovered the hated corvée was still used, he stopped it and ended Gendarmerie patrols into the countryside, which he blamed for sparking attacks through their brutality. Marine reinforcements arrived in Haiti from Guantanamo Bay in March 1919. By then, *cacos* attacks were more frequent on the Gendarmerie and the rebels were even getting financial support from wealthy Haitians among the elite. On October 8, 1919, Péralte and three hundred men attacked Marines and Gendarmerie at Port-au-Prince. They were driven off, but the *cacos* were no longer just attacking small, isolated outposts in the hinterlands.[43]

Péralte was killed on October 31, 1919. A Gendarmerie officer, Jean-Baptiste Conzé, established himself as a defector and a rebel chief to ally himself with Péralte. He then lured the revolutionary into a trap where Marines killed him. To spread knowledge of Péralte's death, the Marines tied his body to a wooden door, propped it up with a Haitian flag and a cross, took photos, and distributed them around the country. Apparently, no one considered how the photo would look as it bore more than a small resemblance to a picture of a crucified Jesus Christ, and Péralte became a martyr for Haitian independence. The war continued. In January 1920, Péralte's successor, Benoit Batraville, led another attack on Port-au-Prince. The offensive failed, suffering heavy casualties, but it demonstrated the rebellion had not died with Péralte. When Batraville was shot in May 1920, the *cacos* fell apart as an organized group, although small-scale attacks continued. The revolution failed, but it did remind President Dartiguenave that he was dependent upon the Marines to maintain his position. About twenty-eight American Marines died in the fighting versus approximately eighty Gendarmerie and more than two thousand *cacos*.[44]

Wilson was absent from policy-making for Haiti in 1919–20. He was distracted by the Paris peace talks and the battle for the treaty in the U.S. Senate, and then his October 1919 stroke removed him from policy-making for several months. Embarrassingly, in August 1920, in a note to Secretary of State Colby, Wilson admitted he had forgotten who the American minister in Haiti was—"I did not know that we were represented by [Arthur] Bailly-Blanchard." The minister was a career diplomat and had been the American representative in Haiti since May 1914.[45] Colby followed with a memo explaining what had been happening in Haiti with respect to the Haitian government's attitude to the treaty with the United States. He did not mention the uprising. He proposed appointing Rear Adm. Harry S. Knapp as military representative to Haiti. That position was held by Rear Admiral Snowden, who was already military governor of

Santo Domingo. Wilson agreed and Knapp left for Haiti as the president left the military in charge of day-to-day Haitian policy.[46]

Central America

In Central America, Wilson's administration used the Marines on a small scale. At times he avoided using them, preferring diplomatic methods. In these cases, the Wilson administration's actions were designed not to foster regime change. Instead, Wilson's motivation (and that of his staff) to use military means were driven by security factors, notably securing the Panama Canal and the desire to preserve or reestablish political order.

There were already American Marines stationed in Central America when Wilson took office. In Nicaragua, for example, he continued the presence of Marines from Taft's administration. There were one hundred Marines in the legation guard based in Managua. They kept the existing pro-American regime in power and guarded American property.[47] With Wilson's knowledge and approval, Secretary of State Bryan tried to find a way around Taft's "Dollar Diplomacy" without using the military. When Wilson took office in March 1913, he found an agreement with Nicaragua awaiting approval. American banks would grant the Nicaraguan president, Adolfo Díaz, a sizable loan in exchange for a major interest in the Nicaraguan National Bank and the National Railroad. Bryan was horrified, especially with the condition requiring Nicaragua to turn over a majority of stock in both the National Bank and the Pacific Railway. Bryan's idea was for the U.S. government to make the loan at a lower interest rate. This would save the Latin nation from predatory American bankers and give Washington extra leverage with Managua. Wilson rejected the idea as too radical. Bryan was forced to turn to the bankers he so disliked to find the money. The secretary of state included an amendment giving the United States the right to intervene in the proposed treaty. It copied the legal arrangement America had with Cuba. However, the treaty immediately ran into problems in the Senate, which objected to the United States taking on more responsibility, and from Nicaragua's neighbors, who feared they would be next. In contrast, the Díaz regime supported the arrangement. The vulnerable president needed the money, not to mention one hundred

U.S. Marines in the capital, to stay in power. When Bryan left to be replaced by Lansing in mid-1915, American policy changed but little. Lansing was far less idealistic than Bryan and much less convinced the United States could teach the Latin American states "to elect good men." Lansing was also more concerned about foreign rivalries, such as British or German competition with the United States in the region. The new secretary was also much more amiable to American business interests. Despite the different emphasis, the end policy looked much the same. Lansing pushed for the treaty, which passed once the right to intervention clause was deleted.[48]

In the 1916 Nicaraguan presidential election, the United States backed conservative candidate Emiliano Chamorro. It was not an automatic decision as both the Liberal and Conservative parties courted Wilson's support. The State Department took the lead on American policy, and it wanted both an honest election and a Conservative victory. However, incumbent president Díaz, although he was a Conservative, was bitter rivals with Chamorro, so he allied with the Liberals. When the United States suggested supervising the election, Díaz refused, then changed his mind, suggesting American Marines act as polling place observers. Wilson had no strong opinions on the candidates, telling Lansing that had only vague recollections based on "desultory conversations" with Bryan. The Latin American division of the State Department decided that Chamorro was the best choice. Nicaragua's minister to the United States returned to his country on an American warship, a clear indication of the American preference. However, when the Liberal Party candidate arrived in Nicaragua from exile, it was clear he had made a deal with Díaz. Fearing disorder, the United States sent two more warships. The American minister met with Díaz and warned him that if the Liberals won, they would have to respect the existing agreements made with Díaz on the debt, and no member of a Liberal government could have participated in any revolutionary movement since 1910. Irías withdrew and told his supporters to neither register nor vote. General Chamorro won easily in the one-sided contest.[49]

Wilson took little role in the decisions, which he left to the State Department, particularly the Latin American Division, which preferred candidates that kept order while promising democratic "reforms." They briefly considered replacing the Marines with a domestic force, similar to Haiti's Gendarmerie, but abandoned the idea. Likewise, they rejected the idea of pulling the Marine legation guard out of Nicaragua. Keeping the Marines in the capital, and sending the occasional warship, seemed to be sufficient to maintain order and allow for elections to be held. The Liberal Party was unhappy, but General Chamorro kept order, backed by one hundred American Marines.

When the 1920 Nicaraguan presidential election came around, Wilson was ill, so the Latin American Division made the decisions, along with Secretary Lansing and then, once he resigned, Secretary of State Colby. Chamorro kept suggesting he would run again, but the United States held that this violated the Nicaraguan constitution and refused to back him. The State Department suggested to Díaz that they send Crowder, who had rewritten Cuba's election laws, to look at how Nicaragua conducted its elections. Chamorro refused. The American representative in Managua, Benjamin Jefferson, suggested they use Marines in civilian clothes as monitors. The State Department refused but worried that an openly unfair election would spark a revolution that would require American intervention. They sent Maj. Jessie I. Miller as a military attaché to oversee the election. Miller had been part of General Crowder's staff, so he knew what he was doing with elections, but sending an attaché rather than a State Department official is a clear sign of how American diplomats relied on the threat of military intervention in unsubtle ways in their Nicaraguan policy. When the election was held there was fraud on both sides, so Miller cabled Washington that both Liberals and Conservatives were waiting on what the State Department would do. The State Department decided to recognize the Conservative candidate, Diego Manuel Chamorro Bolaños, the uncle of his predecessor, General Chamorro. The Marines remained to keep the peace, and the Customs Office, the Central Bank, and the Pacific Railroad of Nicaragua, remained, despite Bryan's efforts, in the hands of the American bankers Brown and Seligman.[50]

This is not to suggest that there was no disorder. Several men were killed in street fights between Liberals and Conservatives during the 1920 election. In one notable incident, a group of U.S. Marines attacked the opposition newspaper *La Tribuna* on February 9, 1921. Angry that the Liberal paper, which opposed American military support of the government, had "libeled" the Marines, they raided its offices and wrecked the presses. Daniels was furious and ordered Rear Adm. Henry F. Bryan to investigate. Daniels and Colby pushed for the military to punish the Marines. Twenty-one received prison sentences of two years, and one received a dishonorable discharge.[51]

Farther south, Panama also held elections in 1916 and 1920 in which the United States got involved. Because of the canal, which opened in August 1914, Panama's strategic importance to the United States was obvious. Conveniently, Article 136 of the Panamanian constitution allowed for intervention by the United States, "in any part of the Republic of Panama to reestablish peace and constitutional order, in the event of their being disturbed, if the said Government, by public treaty, assumes the obligation of guaranteeing the independence and sovereignty of this Republic."[52] It was specific on the right to intervene, but vague on the allowable reasons. Wilson's three different secretaries of state interpreted it differently. Bryan and Colby were less willing to use the American military than Lansing, although they did find ways to intervene. In 1914, for example, for reasons of national security involving the Panama Canal, Bryan demanded that Panama turn over control of its wireless stations to the United States. The Navy had wanted control since 1911. When Panama refused, Secretary of the Navy Daniels pushed Bryan to push Panama for an "immediate monopoly." Panama complied, under protest, a few days after the canal opened in August 1914. The American security concerns were legitimate, even if Washington ran roughshod over Panamanian rights to secure them. Germany had established radio stations throughout South America, which they used early in the war to coordinate German commerce raiders in the Pacific and South Atlantic. In addition, the American Navy was beginning to create a secure multilevel radio communications system of its own that would not depend on undersea cables, which were mostly under British control. Stations in Panama were to be a critical part of this new network.[53] In contrast, Bryan did not intervene when Panama stalled over settling claims resulting from the deaths of American servicemen in anti-American riots in 1912 and 1915. After the third riot, in April 1915, Secretary of War Lindley Garrison pushed Bryan to demand that the United States patrol Panama City and Colón and that the Panamanian police be stripped of their rifles. The matter was still unsettled when Bryan resigned after the sinking of the *Lusitania*. His successor, Lansing, pushed the Panamanians into disarming their police, but not the Presidential Guard.[54]

As the 1916 election approached, the incumbent was Liberal Belisario Porras Barahona. The Liberal Party of incumbent president Porras split, with the anti-Porras faction joining the Conservatives. The pro-Porras faction picked Dr. Ramón M. Valdés as their candidate. The opposition chose Rodolfo Chiari and asked for American supervision to prevent fraud. Lansing agreed, but Porras refused. Wilson wrote Lansing, "It occurs to me it would be wise to make the offer rather insistent." Wilson asked his secretary of state, "Do any rights remain with us"? That is, could the United States justify intervening without Panamanian permission? Lansing found a very thin rationale dating from the Theodore Roosevelt administration but suggested since the United States had just pressed Panama into disarming its police, it was better not to push on election supervision. Besides, he reported, both sides were corrupt but promised to make reforms. When the election was held, the opposition Liberals started a riot hoping to spark American intervention. The United States instead remained aloof, and Porras' candidate won.[55]

As the United States drew closer to entering World War I in early 1917, the Wilson administration began to consider having Panama also declare war, which would make it easier to secure the Panama Canal. Secretary of State Lansing suggested to Wilson that Panama be encouraged to break relations with Germany, which the United States had done just days before. The major concern, regarding both Panama and Cuba, was that Germany would be able to use their territory for "plots and intrigues against [the United States] . . . the possibility of submarine bases, the organization of reservists, the uses of cables, etc."[56] Panama first declared they backed the United States in the war in defending the

Panama Canal, and then in December declared war on Germany without Washington pushing. Panama also interned German nationals on the island of Taboga. This was not quite enough for the Wilson administration, and it transferred the detainees to the United States. Meanwhile, Panama required the remaining German nationals to register with their local government; it also censored the mails and set up an anti-German counterintelligence security network.[57]

President Valdés died in 1918. Former president Porras was eligible again (presidents could serve multiple terms but not in immediate succession), but he was then serving as the Panamanian minister in Washington and needed time to return to Panama to organize political support. Valdés' immediate legitimate successor was Ciro L. Urriola, who issued a decree delaying the National Assembly elections to allow Porras time. It was blatantly unconstitutional and too much for Lansing, who demanded Urriola revoke the decree. Lansing then sent American troops into Panama City and Colón[58] to maintain order. Lansing also demanded multiple reforms including cleaning up the vice districts enjoyed by Americans from the Canal Zone. When Porras' opponents began a rebellion, Lansing sent U.S. forces to crush it and restore order despite Porras' protests that the United States was only supposed to protect against outside invasion, not internal rebellions. When the National Assembly began to deliberate whom to choose to finish the presidential term, the American secretary of state made sure that they chose Porras as well as Washington's preferred candidates for the two *designados* (roughly vice presidents). Porras took office in October 1918, but when the United States asked to keep troops to maintain order in Chiriquí Province, he objected. Washington kept them in the province anyway. Porras stayed in office a little over one year, but he wanted to continue in office past the 1920 election. He resigned at the end of January, six months before the vote, in favor of his third *designado*. Thus, he was eligible to run again. The opposition picked former *designado* Urriola. The opposition asked for American interference claiming that Porras was ineligible. New secretary of state Colby refused to intervene. Urriola's supporters boycotted the election, and Porras won. The election was peaceful, however, and Colby withdrew American troops from Chiriquí Province. For his victory, Porras was rewarded with a state visit to Washington in September. There is no indication he met with President Wilson, who was still ill. However, he did get to sail to Mount Vernon on the presidential yacht *Mayflower* with General Pershing and Secretary of the Navy Daniels and met with Colby.[59]

Farther to the north, in Honduras, the United States intervened multiple times, beginning in 1913, sending warships as warnings to would-be revolutionaries. In March, shortly after Wilson took office, the Honduran president died, and his first designate, Francisco Bertrand, took office. Immediately rumors of coups and revolutions spread. American counsel David Myers requested the Navy send a ship to protect American lives and property. The State Department agreed, and the Navy sent the cruiser USS *Tacoma*. This seemed to calm things briefly, but in August 1913, the American minister to Honduras requested another ship be sent as a warning to would-be revolutionaries. This time the Navy sent the gunboat USS *Nashville*. Thus, only six months into Wilson's first term, a pattern was set. Unrest threatened the Honduran leader, and the United States would send a warship to deter aspiring revolutionaries. A particular problem was the machinations of the United Fruit Company and its fellow banana firms, which financed multiple coup attempts against President Bertrand. The companies preferred someone more pliable to their desires. In the late summer and early autumn of 1915, Secretary of State Lansing had to twice squash plots to ship arms to Honduran revolutionaries. The second time, as the United Fruit Company backed a mercenary named Gen. Lee Christmas, who organized an army to invade Honduras from Guatemala. The U.S. Navy sent the gunboat USS *Machias* and a military attaché to investigate and squelch the plot. President Bertrand won the November election easily, but the plotting continued.[60]

In October 1916, as rumors spread of revolution, the United States sent the warship USS *Sacramento* in anticipation. This support from Washington did not win the Honduran leader much support in his own country. When he tried to declare war on Germany to follow the American lead in 1917, he found little interest. When Honduras *did* declare war on Germany in July 1918, the last Latin American state to do so, it only opened Bertrand to charges he was trying to curry favor with the United States, certainly not an unfair accusation. The Latin American states that declared war on Germany were invited to the Paris talks. Realizing that his position was weakened by following Washington's policies too closely, Bertrand used the opportunity not to support Wilson, but to attack him, attempting to weaken the Monroe Doctrine. In response, Wilson commented that he would apply the doctrine "when I think fit." However, it was clear that neither supporting nor challenging the United States was solidifying Bertrand's position, so he announced he would retire in 1920, but backed the candidacy of his wife's sister's husband. Bertrand followed by having some of his political rivals arrested. There were riots in response, and he had to declare martial law. Once again, the United States sent the USS *Machias* to maintain order.[61]

The Wilson administration was tired of Bertrand by this time and offered to mediate when a real revolution began. The offer went nowhere, and Lansing suggested using force, "it may be necessary for the United States to proceed in a more forceful manner." Wilson balked, but began to consider it as a last measure: "I think the course you here suggest is the only practicable one, and that perhaps there is no escape from it." Before Washington could do more than strongly hint at "more forceful measures," Bertrand fled the country as the revolution against his regime gained strength. An election was held in October 1919, and the different political factions accepted the results. The American use of military intervention was therefore limited to sending warships accompanied by threats of using force. It was nonetheless a form of military intervention, albeit without casualties.[62]

Guatemala was a challenge to Wilson for different reasons. President Estrada Cabrera had been in power since 1898 and had a secure hold on the country. He was careful not only to crush any domestic political opposition, but to support gladly, at least verbally, whatever the American policy happened to be. In 1915, when Mexican troops under Carranza's control, along with Guatemalan exiles, conducted cross-border raids, the United States sent the cruiser USS *Raleigh* to Guatemala and the raids stopped. Showing his gratitude, in 1918 Cabrera made sure Guatemala declared war on Germany. Despite this open support, the Wilson administration was disgusted with Cabrera's dictatorship and was looking for alternatives. The State Department pressed Cabrera to make reforms, particularly in its corrupt and inefficient economy. The Latin American Division was blunt in its advice. The Guatemalan leader should be forced to resign or to change his domestic policies dramatically. By late 1919, however, an effective resistance movement, the Unionists, had begun to gain momentum. In March 1920, Lansing warned Cabrera not to use force to crush the rebellion as open fighting began. The United States sent the USS *Tacoma* and the armed yacht USS *Niagara* and landed armed troops to guard the American legation, but they took no part in the fighting. In the end, Cabrera was arrested and jailed by the successful revolutionaries. Wilson was reluctant to recognize a government that took power via force but did so upon a promise of reforms. Unfortunately, the new government was unable to consolidate its power, and after Wilson had left office it was ousted in a coup.[63]

Mexico

Finally, of course, there was always Mexico. The United States and different Mexican factions fought several times between 1918 and 1919. American troops crossed the border in pursuit of "bandits" at least three times in 1918 and on at least a half-dozen occasions in 1919. However, the most significant danger of a wider war came not from these conflicts but from the U.S. Senate. A bipartisan coalition of legislators pushed an ill Woodrow Wilson toward full-scale armed intervention.[64]

Even as the United States was fighting Germany in Europe, it worried about German activity in Mexico. It was not an unreasonable concern. The Carranza government did have cordial relations with Berlin and allowed German agents to be active in Mexico, including operating a powerful wireless station. In August 1918, the United States fought a day-long pitched battle at the border town of Ambos Nogales in Arizona and Sonora. The border went through the middle of town, cleaving the main street down the center. Sentries from both countries managed the traffic back and forth, and there were several instances where a Mexican civilian was shot. In one case, a deaf and mute man was killed because he did not hear an American soldier's orders to stop. Moreover, the American border agents were notorious for being rude to the Mexicans. Local tensions rose until August 27, 1918, when a Mexican carpenter tried to cross into Mexico while carrying a bundle. An American soldier on guard ordered him to halt while the Mexican soldier on his side of the border ordered the man to continue. Confused at the conflicting orders, the carpenter froze. The Mexican soldier opened fire on the American, who returned fire killing the Mexican soldier. Soon a firefight broke out as both sides sent for reinforcements. American soldiers tried to flank the Mexican side of the town by crossing the border into the neighboring hills but were driven back. Snipers opened fire from rooftops on both sides. The Mexican town's popular mayor was mortally wounded while trying to wave a white flag to stop the fighting. By the end of the day most of the dozens of dead and wounded were civilians, although the civilians also grabbed their weapons and joined the fight. Fortunately, the local military leadership on both sides worked quickly and effectively to enforce the peace. Border guards on both sides were disarmed, issued clubs and pistols rather than the standard rifles. A wall was placed along the main street, dividing the two nations so that their respective citizens could no longer just cross from one to another.[65]

The last major confrontation of the undeclared Mexican-American border war—the Battle of Ciudad Juárez—came in June of 1919. In this instance, the U.S. troops were on the same side as the Mexican government army, fighting against Villistas. The revolutionary was still in the field trying to oust Carranza. On June 14, 1919, Villa attacked Juárez. After a day of hard fighting, he succeeded in driving the Mexican army back, taking over most of the city. Carrancista General Francisco Gonzalez requested help from the American side. Villista snipers had already begun firing on Americans, killing and wounding several. Several American infantry and cavalry brigades attacked the Villistas, while Carranza's forces withdrew to get out of the way. By mid-day June 16, U.S. forces had driven the revolutionaries out of the city. American forces pursued past city limits but then withdrew back across the border, suffering few casualties.[66]

The last battle came as pressure mounted on Wilson to intervene in Mexico. There was a bipartisan coalition in the U.S. Senate that was particularly vocal in pressuring Wilson. The driving factor was not the border fighting, but economic. Carranza's revolutionary government was notably protective of Mexico's economic resources, reflecting the anger many Mexicans felt toward how the Porfiriato (1884–1910) had welcomed foreign investment and exploitation of Mexican economic development. The new Mexican constitution, written in 1917, included Article 27, which stated that "all-natural resources in national territory are property of the nation, and private exploitation may only be carried out through concessions." Foreign oil and mining interests were panicked at the thought that they might suddenly lose the rights to the material they had been extracting. Their most vocal spokesman in the Senate was the Republican senator Albert Fall of New Mexico. One of the new state's first senators, Fall and Woodrow Wilson despised one another. Fall believed Wilson neglected protecting American interests in Mexico, and Wilson thought Fall a liar interested only in promoting big business's financial interests.[67]

Wilson had long relegated Central American policy to the State Department and the Bureau of Latin American Affairs. After the United States entered World War I, he often neglected American policy toward Mexico as well. This left open the possibility for intervention in Mexico as the State Department under Robert Lansing opposed Wilson's "Watchful Waiting." Robert Lansing; Undersecretary Frank Polk; U.S. ambassador to Mexico, Henry P. Fletcher; and chief of the Mexican Division, Boaz Long, all disliked and distrusted Carranza and considered Wilson's policy too weak. Lansing continued sending "legalistic notes to the Carranza government supporting American property rights, demanding that it pay indemnities for losses of American life." Mexico ignored Lansing's prodding. Perhaps they were listening to Wilson, who still insisted he would not interfere with Mexico's revolution.[68]

While Wilson and Lansing were in Paris for the peace talks, Undersecretary Polk and Ambassador Fletcher "unilaterally initiated a harsher policy."[69] They pressed harder for the protection of American lives and property. In March 1919, Fletcher sent a lengthy memo to Wilson suggesting taking a more active role toward Mexico to force them to protect Americans. Wilson did not even read the memo until August. His note to Lansing stated that he was "ashamed" to have been so neglectful and asked if Fletcher would still suggest Mexico be pushed to "do its duty internationally." "Are there any memoranda in your office which would answer his questions?" Wilson asked. Fletcher replied that his analysis had not changed and re-sent his March message suggesting that the United States send a message, a "call," to Mexico, "making therein a last effort to avert intervention." Carranza made the situation worse by initiating an anti-American campaign in Mexico and Latin America, blaming Wilson and the United States for Mexico's troubles. Wilson suggested to Lansing that Fletcher be sent back to Mexico City from Washington, to act as a "restraining influence upon Carranza." Fletcher wrote a letter of resignation but remained until early 1920.[70] Fletcher may have been a restraining influence on Carranza, but Wilson remained the major restraining influence in his administration. Polk warned the Mexican ambassador that the American president was the only ally Mexico had in the U.S. government, and "if they lost him, they lost everything." However, Wilson's patience was not infinite. In July, Wilson approved a message to Carranza's government from the State Department that, if Mexico did not do a better job protecting American lives and property, "this government may be forced to adopt a radical change in its policy with regard to Mexico."[71]

In October 1919, an American businessman and American consul in Puebla, William Jenkins, was supposedly kidnapped by a counterrevolutionary group and held for ransom. Jenkins cooperated with his kidnappers to cast blame on Carranza's government, communicating through the American embassy and Senator Fall inciting as much outrage as he could in the United States. While the Senate considered a resolution instructing Wilson to use force to rescue him, Jenkins paid the ransom himself. In November, a Puebla court indicted Jenkins for giving false information. Jenkins refused to pay his bail and demanded the U.S. government get him out of jail. That same month, Carranza began to seize foreign-owned oil wells that had begun drilling without permits. As tensions rose, Lansing got into an argument with the Mexican ambassador in his office. The now-untrustworthy secretary of state, who had already fallen out with President Wilson over the League of Nations (Lansing was dubious of its usefulness) began to meet with Senator Fall and handed over diplomatic correspondence between the United States and Mexico. Lansing contacted the White House, but told Wilson's secretary, Joseph Tumulty, he would talk to the ill president when the situation became critical, which apparently it was not. "I am right, so I don't care [if Wilson agreed with him]," Lansing wrote in his diary. The secretary of state was not the only member of Wilson's administration to push toward taking harsh measures with Mexico. American ambassador Fletcher was also meeting with Fall, debating how to word a resolution to force American intervention in Mexico. The ambassador mentioned to Third Assistant Secretary of State Breckenridge Long that a war with Mexico might "be a good remedy for domestic difficulties of the United States."[72]

Warned by Tumulty, Wilson rallied to issue a statement saying he had no intention of going to war with Mexico. Lansing promptly denied having anything to do with Fall's resolution. When called before Fall's committee investigating Mexico, Lansing attacked American Mexican policy, starting with Taft, as "supine" and "vacillating." The European situation, he said, had prevented the United States from having a more assertive policy. Fall was furious. Had the secretary of state, he demanded to know, discussed this with Wilson. Lansing claimed he had not discussed anything with Wilson since late September. That immediately raised suspicions that Wilson was too ill to take part in his own administration's policy. In response, the Senate appointed the so-called Smelling Committee to go visit Wilson to determine his health.[73] Fall and Wilson's ally Senator Gilbert Hitchcock visited Wilson at the White House on December 5, 1919. Wilson had all the lights in the room turned on. He was sitting up in bed, his paralyzed left side hidden in the bedcovers. He talked to the senators for forty minutes about Mexico, reaching for papers with his good right hand, and carried himself well, convincing both men that he was able to participate in policy-making. It was enough to make his opposition to war with Mexico stick. In reality, he could not yet walk even with help. Of course, it helped that his doctor came in the room during the meeting to announce that Jenkins had been released.[74]

This was the closest the United States had come to war with Mexico since the Battle of Carrizal in June 1916. Wilson's stroke created the opening for Lansing and the other interventionists, but Wilson's inattention to Mexican policy, indeed to most policy-making in regard to Latin America after early 1917, was the underlying cause. Had Lansing not been an interventionist, or even if he had just been faithful to the policies of the administration to which he belonged, the danger of another Mexican-American war would not have been so acute. As it was, Jenkin's release and Wilson's convincing performance in meeting Fall and Hitchcock made the difference between peace and war, a harrowingly narrow margin of error.

China

Finally, there were several minor instances of troop deployments in Asia aside from the American presence in eastern Russia as part of the intervention in the Russian Revolution discussed in chapter 7. From February 16, 1920, through November 19, 1922, U.S. Marines were stationed on Russian Island in the Bay of Vladivostok to protect an American wireless station and other American property. They remained even after the rest of the American forces in Siberia were withdrawn in early spring 1920.[75] However, the most common place for intervention was in China, where unrest remained widespread after the Revolution of 1911. When Yuan Shikai, whom the United States recognized as the legitimate ruler of China, died in 1916, the country entered into the "Warlord Era" (1916–28), during which the Nationalist government based in Nanjing ruled only parts of the south. With no one central authority existing, the United States and the other world powers kept their ambassadors and ministers in Beijing to deal with whatever faction seemed to be in control at the time. The result was chaos and violence.

There were three different, independent groups of American military forces in China in the 1910s: the Navy's Yangtze Patrol, a Marine guard at the legation in Beijing, and an Army group at Tientsin. They each had their own function and their own chain of command. The latter two groups were permitted on Chinese territory due to the Boxer Protocol of September 7, 1901. Imposed upon a defeated China after the Boxer Rebellion in 1900, the Boxer Protocol included two sections, Articles 7 and 9, that allowed foreign powers to maintain their own military forces. They were to guard their nation's legation in Beijing and occupy points along the railroad from Tientsin to the capital to maintain communications between the diplomats and the rest of the world in case of another anti-foreign outbreak. The Yangtze Patrol was permitted by several "Most-Favored Nation" treaties, which gave the United States the same rights as Britain, France, and the other powers. The Navy presence was also the most active of the three groups during the Wilson administration.[76]

According to the Congressional Research Service, the United States landed forces in China at least three times during the Wilson administration when American lives and property were threatened:

- In 1916 to "quell a riot" taking place on American property in Nanjing
- In 1917 to protect American lives during a political crisis in Chongqing (Chungking)
- In 1920 to protect lives during a disturbance at Jiujiang on March 14

All three cities are on the Yangtze River away from the coast—Chongqing is well over a thousand miles inland.[77] As part of the U.S. Asiatic Fleet, the Yangtze Patrol based multiple warships in Chinese waters, including their rivers, as a warning and a safe harbor for American citizens in China. Though much smaller than the other American fleets, the Asiatic Fleet was responsible for protecting American lives and property in China and the Philippines, a broad mission. Its commander held a powerful position and could be more influential than the American minister to China. While the fleet's headquarters was in Manila, the ships assigned to the Yangtze had more autonomy than many of their compatriots. Often out of radio range, their captains could travel wherever they felt they would be needed, or where they wanted to go. One captain noted in 1914, "We are out of communications . . . and having the time of our young lives." In June 1914, the Asiatic Fleet's flagship, the armored cruiser USS *Saratoga*, traveled six hundred miles inland to Hankow because the fleet's commander wanted to see the middle Yangtze.[78] While such freedom was liberating, the ships themselves were usually old and obsolete. The aforementioned *Saratoga* was launched in 1891. Originally named the USS *New York*, the *Saratoga* was a Spanish-American War veteran; still a capable warship, she was no longer among the first rank of the American fleet. The *Saratoga* was powerful enough for showing the flag and protecting Americans from pirates and warlords raiding river shipping. In August 1914, the European powers and Japan pulled all of their seaworthy warships out of Chinese ports for use elsewhere. That left the United States as the primary power with the largest presence on the Yangtze. The fleet was stretched thin, with eight of the nine ships based at ports from Shanghai to Chongqing and the ninth roving where needed. When bandits threatened a section of the river's vital traffic, an American warship used its artillery to scatter the pirates and clear the way for civilian ships to pass unmolested.[79]

From 1916 until 1928 China had multiple competing governments, many run by local warlords. With no central national government to maintain order, warlords and pirates preyed upon the river traffic. World War I had depleted the other powers' forces, so they often depended upon the United States. In 1916, the Russian consul general in Hankow promised barrack space to the United States to maintain a few dozen armed volunteers. The American naval officer on the scene refused but was overridden by Assistant Secretary of the Navy Franklin Roosevelt. By the end of the year, a small contingent of some thirty U.S. volunteers were drilling on British property, storing their ammunition in a French armory, and sleeping in a Russian barracks.[80]

When the United States entered the war in April 1917, its status as a belligerent prevented it from legally keeping armed forces on the river. However, pulling American warships off the river would remove the last foreign presence to prevent bandits and warlords from preying on river traffic. Moreover, Washington was worried that this would give Japan an excuse to begin patrolling the Yangtze, despite its being a belligerent and not a neutral, thus furthering Japan's efforts to extend its influence over

China. Secretary of the Navy Daniels told the Asiatic Fleet's commander that it was "very desirable" for American warships to remain "active on duty protecting foreigners in interior of China as long as possible." The United States hoped that China would not insist that the Americans deactivate their fleet, placing it in internment. China, however, did take the international rules for belligerent nations seriously, probably keeping an eye toward Japan. Nonetheless, Chinese internment was conducted on relatively lenient terms. American crews remained on board their warships and handed over the breechblocks for their ship's guns to local American consuls rather than surrendering them to Chinese government officials.[81]

The American Navy objected to even this inoffensive style of internment. Daniels asked the State Department if the United States should ask the other powers for a mandate to continue patrolling the Yangtze in the name of "performing an international service." The State Department replied that then the Japanese would probably insist on joining as part of an international patrol, precisely what neither America nor China wanted. Unhappy, the Navy gave in a month after the United States declared war on Germany. Better, the Navy apparently thought, to allow bandits to prey on river traffic than to allow Tokyo an excuse to further its military presence in China. The internment was short-lived. When China entered the war in August 1917, the breechblocks were returned to the American crews, and the fleet resumed its duties. There was little for the United States to do against German ships. The civilian ships that had been interned in Chinese harbors were scuttled or otherwise rendered inoperable by their crews when China entered the war. The closest thing to anti-German activity by the American fleet seems to have been taking over the prime mooring spots for warships in Shanghai that Germany held the rights to use. After the war in Europe was finished, the war against the river pirates and greedy warlords continued, as the other power's fleets rejoined the Americans on the Chinese waters.[82]

The war was just as quiet for the Marine legation guard and the U.S. Army group guarding the railroad in Tientsin. After Japan declared war on Germany in 1914 and took over the German concessions in China, the Japanese asked the Americans to assume the duty of guarding the German section of the railroad between the coast and Beijing. The United States agreed and began patrolling the extra section. The seven hundred or so Marines and doughboys spent the war quietly, enjoying the benefits of the low cost of living in China (even enlisted men could afford a single servant) and fighting boredom. The commands remained divided, with responsibility devolving to the State Department, but the political battles in Washington over that status were left to the Warren G. Harding administration to fight anew. During Wilson's administration, the American troops in China were largely forgotten, at least by Wilson. They were noticeable only when they were required to guard American property during a riot or bandit raids. They were in place in 1913 and would remain so after Wilson left office, a part of the broader American deployment into its areas of interest that Washington took for granted.[83]

CONCLUSION

On the surface, Wilson's actions may seem inconsistent. Sometimes he was directly involved in sending troops, and sometimes he delegated such duties to his cabinet or even to American commanders on the spot. He was consistent, however, in maintaining greater control over events if intervention threatened to expand into a wider war, or intervention threatened to affect a larger diplomatic issue.

In cases where these two conditions did not apply, such as in Central America, Wilson kept informed but generally kept his distance from policy, trusting the State Department and the military. In other cases, such as China, intervention was reacting to events on the ground, and commanders on the spot had greater leeway, within certain limits. But in situations where greater diplomatic issues were involved, such as in the Balkans, Wilson kept a closer eye on events, ready to intercede if local American commanders acted in a way to interfere with Wilson's policies. As always, the military was a tool—and a powerful one—but one among several, for Wilson to employ to achieve his goals. The more important the goal, the more his grip tightened, although he never indulged in micromanaging his commanders.

Conclusion

Woodrow Wilson's record as commander in chief is mixed. In an era when armed interventions by the larger powers in their spheres of influence were common, Wilson nonetheless committed more military forces in more places than all but a handful of his fellow presidents. Respectful of but not obsequious to the military, the twenty-eighth president regarded military force as one important tool available for him to use. He saw the military as a way to protect American national security from immediate threats and as a diplomatic tool to ensure American security in the long term by constructing a more stable and just international system. As such, he used armed force not just to counter armed aggression against the United States, nor just to maintain order within the western hemisphere, but also to construct his new diplomacy in Europe and Asia.

Wilson relied on military expertise for what he thought of as purely military matters, generally tactical decisions, and strategic matters, although he kept a close eye on the latter to see that the War Department and the Navy Department did not cross over unchaperoned into diplomatic or political matters. However, Wilson's field of vision was relatively limited as he did not understand the need for long-term planning, especially when it came to logistics. This may be one of his greatest weaknesses as commander in chief, as his hobbling of war planning added significantly to the delay in getting troops into France in 1917. This was part of his keeping both the Army and Navy on a short rein. Wilson trusted Secretary of War Newton Baker and Secretary of the Navy Daniels, but he still required regular updates from them, more so than he did from most of his other cabinet officials.

Wilson gave the military more leeway when it was called on to respond to disorder, especially in Central America and the Caribbean, although this also applied to China. This greater freedom of action was partly due to Wilson's being distracted by more pressing issues, such as World War I and the peace conference that followed. Wilson also gave the military more latitude in areas where intervention was not likely to spiral into a wider war. In places where a more extensive war was a realistic danger, such as Mexico or Russia, Wilson tended to keep a firmer hand on policy, acting to make sure the situation did not escalate. In contrast, the dispatch of a small number of men, such as landing some Marines to protect American property in a Chinese city, was left to local commanders. In Central America, the State Department stayed informed to monitor the region while in the Caribbean military commanders had more leeway, especially in Haiti and the Dominican Republic.

Wilson did not keep as close an eye as he perhaps should have on the State Department, which often had its own diplomatic goals under Lansing. This varied by time and region. After the United States entered World War I, Wilson paid less attention to Latin America, although he never totally ignored it. After his stroke in early October 1919 Wilson often had little control over policy. This almost led to a war with Mexico over the Jenkins affair, but Wilson was able to intercede in time. Had Secretary of State Robert Lansing been more in line with Wilson's policies, this would not have been as great a problem. As it was, Lansing let his resentment of Wilson and their differing attitudes toward armed intervention steer his judgment in the direction of which Wilson disapproved. Replacing Lansing with Colby in 1920 made a significant difference as the latter was much more in agreement with Wilson's attitude toward the use of American force. In the Colby era, Wilson's military policy was replaced by "the determination to employ nonmilitary methods" in an effort "to thwart hostile powers in traditionally significant areas."[1]

One of Wilson's most critical weaknesses as commander in chief was his lack of understanding of the need for a clear chain of command. This was most apparent during World War I. Neither Wilson nor Secretary of War Baker ever clarified the relationship between Pershing in Europe and March in Washington. They generally treated Pershing as March's equal, but not always. The result was wasted effort and added confusion, which could only hinder the war effort. Fortunately, both generals were capable commanders working toward the same goal: Germany's defeat.

Wilson's use of intelligence vastly improved during World War I. While he still sometimes relied on knowledgeable amateurs, he also received daily reports from the military, which covered events worldwide, not just news from the western front. These reports were generally reliable, and Wilson used them to good effect during the Paris Peace Conference. Along with the Inquiry reporting, Wilson received a solid base from which to formulate policy. Wilson's most notable weakness was that he was sometimes too busy to keep up with all the written reports he received, which must have seemed overwhelming at the time, such as Ambassador Fletcher's report on Mexico in 1919, which Wilson did not read for months.

As president, Wilson showed respect for Congress' role in asking for authorization to send troops. Of course, there were the declarations of war against Germany and then Austria-Hungary in 1917, but he also asked for authorization to use force in Mexico in both 1914 and 1916. Smaller interventions, such as sending a gunboat to a Central American nation, did not require congressional approval. Note, however, that Wilson only asked for two declarations of war. The rest of the time, he asked for an authorization to use force. He carefully differentiated between going to war against an internationally recognized government, such as imperial Germany, versus other actors' interventions. Sticking with the Mexican examples, Wilson did not declare war in 1914 because the United States did not recognize General Huerta's government. In 1916 Pancho Villa was not the head of a recognized government, so a declaration of war was unnecessary once again. Moreover, in both cases, he wanted a limited commitment of American force, not a full-scale war. Wilson gave a great deal of weight to motivation in determining the justness of a policy, including Congress exercising its responsibility for oversight. As a result, he did not always welcome congressional oversight, especially when he believed it was designed by political opponents to be an attack on his policies. The efforts by the Republican-led Senate in 1919 to tie intervention in the Adriatic to the proposed League of Nations, to use just one example, was designed as an attack on the Versailles Treaty. Senate treaty opponents argued that this was an example of American armed forces being used where direct American national security was not threatened. The issue died as American intervention proved to be both small-scale and brief.

Wilson resorted to military force for multiple reasons, and none of the interventions can be attributed to one sole reason. There were always multiple factors; most critically, reasons of national security. Entering World War I is the most obvious example. German submarine warfare, the sabotage campaign against the United States, which included such events as the explosion at Black Tom, and then the attempts to spark a war between the United States and Mexico created a genuine threat to America. Also, the diplomatic factor was of crucial importance to Wilson. Convinced he could negotiate a lasting peace if he had a place of influence at the postwar peace talks, Wilson realized by April 1917 that the only way to secure that spot in negotiations was as a belligerent; there seemed to be no practical or moral alternative. Even then, it took a unanimous vote by Wilson's cabinet to go to war (on top of German provocations) to force Wilson into making the final decision. Afterward, Wilson only belatedly asked Congress to declare war on Germany's ally, Austria-Hungary, in December 1917. The United States never did declare war on Germany's other allies, Bulgaria and the Ottoman Empire. Wilson was not willing to take that final step, even if a symbolic declaration of war against the last two would have in reality required little in the way of the commitment of American forces.[2]

There was also a national security component to Wilson's decision to intervene in the Caribbean and Central America due to the new Panama Canal. Chaos and disorder in Haiti and the Dominican Republic seemed to threaten to leave room for European intervention along with the approaches to the canal. As exaggerated as these fears may have been, they were present. Threats of political violence and revolution in Panama itself, while minor in scale compared to the violence on Santo Domingo, were enough to draw an American response, as was revolution in Cuba, which threatened the sugar fields. Intervention in other areas, such as Russia and China, had national security implications as well, but mostly due either to its relationship to World War I (in Russia's case) and the threat to the existing international order in Asia.

As numerous historians have pointed out over the years, there were also economic factors at play, as the United States intervened to protect American business interests and property. Sometimes the threat was direct, such as the threat to American-owned sugar fields in Cuba in 1917–18. Other times it was more theoretical, such as the possibility of American business opportunities in Haiti. Other than the small-scale direct threats to property during a period of chaos, however, they were never the most crucial reason for intervention. Wilson distrusted those who pushed for intervention for economic reasons, as did Bryan and Colby. Secretary of State Lansing was willing to intervene for American business interests, however, and while he was secretary of state, economic reasons for intervening cannot be wholly ruled out.

Wilson also had an unfortunate tendency to intervene in places where it actually threatened to undermine his policy. He realized that intervention increased nationalistic resentment toward the United States. The Veracruz intervention made that quite clear. Nonetheless, he kept doing it. Why? Partly it was due to his rationalization that he was doing so for the other party's benefit. Wilson judged others' rationale for intervention and set a particular standard for his own, even if it was self-serving.

Moreover, other factors were outweighing Wilson's reluctance. Chaos in the Caribbean or Central America, for example, seemed to require an American response for moral and strategic reasons alike. Haiti provides a useful example. As noted in chapter 4, Haiti was a failed state with a revolving door succession of presidents, ending with the brutal murder of President Jean Vilbrun Guillaume Sam and the slaughter of political prisoners. In this instance, Wilson felt that he had little choice, given the degree of violence. As Wilson noted in another context, sometimes you have to knock someone down to force them to listen, in this case, to force Haiti to accede to American demands to allow U.S. control of Haiti's customs and then of its elections. The broader context of World War I also fed into Wilson's decision to intervene in Haiti, as he feared that France, or even Germany, might intervene to restore order. The fear was not very realistic; both countries were far too engaged in the war in Europe to worry about Port-au-Prince. However, unrealistic fears influence policy-making, just as much as realistic fears.

The Mexican intervention of 1916 was an even more dramatic case of Wilson having no choice but to use troops to invade another country. Pancho Villa's raid on Columbus was a provocation no president could afford to ignore, especially in an election year. The chants of "We didn't go to war" at the 1916 Democratic Convention were ironic, as the United States had gone to war even if it were undeclared. In terms of scale—the number of men involved and the length of time—the Mexican intervention of 1916–17 was second to World War I but was more significant than the other Wilsonian interventions. The other Latin American interventions, from the Dominican Republic in 1916 through Panama in 1920, fit this pattern as well, but not as dramatically as Haiti or Mexico. They all resulted from domestic disorder within the American sphere of influence, which the Wilson administration felt required the interjection of American armed forces in order to quell, restore order, prevent outside intervention by a European power, or stop threats to American lives and property.

Several military interventions were influenced by Wilson's desire to foster international cooperation or as part of an alliance. Entering World

War I offers the most critical example. Joining as an associated power guaranteed Wilson a place at the postwar peace table as an equal. The use of the American military earned the United States that spot. The intervention scale grew beyond what Wilson initially may have considered, but the rationale was present. Intervention in Russia is the second clear example. Wilson was never happy about sending American forces into Russia, but he did not want to spend the political capital to continue saying no to Allied requests for assistance when he would need that capital at the peace talks. The smaller American interventions in the Balkans and Turkey fit this model since the United States acted as one of the major victorious powers. Even in China, the small military interactions there were part of a broader international role. The United States held itself apart as an "associated" power during World War I, but on multiple occasions used its military as if it were a part of more formal military alliances. This proved to be problematic for Wilson during the Senate fight for the League of Nations.

Wilson as commander in chief was fallible but well intentioned. He trusted the military's professionalism, but still observed them to guarantee they stayed within their assigned role. His use of force went well beyond national security concerns to include other factors, but when American national security demanded the use of force, he committed as much of his country's resources as he could. His paternalism toward weaker nations was palpable, but he genuinely wanted to restore order and a democratic system, and not just use force to protect American big business. Wilson would not necessarily make a good role model today—the world system has changed too much. His willingness to use force to teach the Latin American states to "elect good men"[3] would be unacceptable now, alienating friendly and Allied governments. His refusal to specify a clear chain of command during World War I would be difficult to imagine currently; it would lead to chaos were it to reoccur in the twenty-first century. Finally, his discomfort with preexisting military planning while still relying on the use of the American military as a diplomatic tool was a recipe for disaster, and he was lucky that the American military did not run into any large-scale disasters due to ad hoc planning between 1913 and 1921.

That actions such as the quick seizure of Veracruz in 1914 went as well as they did is more of a tribute to the professional soldiers, sailors, and Marines rather than a credit to Wilson's actions as commander in chief.

There are worse models modern presidents could follow than the well-intentioned Wilson. He picked good commanders, even skipping over better politically placed and more senior generals, as in the case of John J. Pershing. His chosen civilian leaders varied in quality, but Newton Baker was an excellent pick for secretary of war, and Josephus Daniels adequate as Navy Secretary. More importantly, Wilson was able to avoid "mission creep" for the most part, as in Mexico where he pulled back on his military's reins multiple times to prevent a wider war. Likewise, he was able—albeit a bit slowly—to appreciate the value of good intelligence, and for the most part trusted the professionals he picked; he did not press his intelligence officers to give him the conclusions he wanted to hear. In the end he kept a vision of where he wanted to go and trusted the professionals to help him realize that vision, while keeping them from heading off on their own direction. That is a model worth copying.

NOTES

INTRODUCTION

1. Jack Sweetman, *The Landing at Veracruz: 1914* (Annapolis, MD: Naval Institute Press, 1968), 47–49.
2. Sweetman, *Landing*, 123.
3. Samuel P. Huntington, *The Soldier and the State: The Theory and Practice of Civil-Military Relations* (Cambridge, MA: Belknap, 1957).
4. The consensus school of historiography emerged after World War II. It deemphasized the idea of conflict, particularly class conflict, as a motivating factor in American history and emphasized factors that unified the nation. The conflicts of the 1960s and '70s forced a reevaluation by younger historians and the consensus school quickly became outmoded.
5. Sarah Burns, *The Politics of War Powers: The Theory & History of Presidential Unilateralism* (Lawrence: University Press of Kansas, 2019). See also Michael W. McConnell, *The President Who Would Not Be King: Executive Power under the Constitution* (Princeton: Princeton University Press, 2020).
6. Each initially published in 1788.
7. Alexander Hamilton, "The Executive Department Further Considered," Federalist No. 70. There are two versions of No. 70. This work uses Version A on Yale University's online Avalon Project, http://avalon.law.yale.edu/subject_menus/fed.asp (accessed January 5, 2019).
8. Alexander Hamilton, "The Command of the Military and Naval Forces, and the Pardoning Power of the Executive," Federalist No. 74.
9. Hamilton, "Command," Federalist No. 74.
10. John Jay, "The Same Subject Continued: Concerning Dangers from Foreign Force and Influence," Federalist No. 4.
11. Jay, "Same Subject," Federalist No. 4.
12. Jay, "Same Subject," Federalist No. 4.
13. He wrote this essay for publication in New York as the state debated ratifying the new federal constitution. On the careful crafting of the president's war

powers by the Constitutional Convention, see McConnell, *President Who Would Not be King*, 201–12.

14. Alexander Hamilton, "The Real Character of the Executive," Federalist No. 69.

15. Henry Wilkinson Bragdon, *Woodrow Wilson: The Academic Years* (Cambridge: Harvard University Press, 1967), 74, 112.

16. On Wilson's marginalia see "Marginal Notes" in Woodrow Wilson, *The Papers of Woodrow Wilson* (Princeton: Princeton University Press, 1966), February 1880, 1:598–601. See also "Notes for Lectures at Johns Hopkins," in Wilson, *Papers* (1969), January 26, 1891, 7:129–42. Henceforth, this series will be referred to as PWW followed by the volume and page number.

17. "Lecture Notes, Politics," March 5, 1898, PWW 10:469 (emphasis in original). This specific quote is dated April 4, 1898, just weeks before the United States declared war on Spain over Cuba, at the height of the war scare. The Sampson Report, which blamed the sinking of the battleship *Maine* on "the explosion of a submarine mine," had come out on March 21, 1898.

CHAPTER 1. WILSON VIEWS THE PRESIDENCY

1. For the first three decades of Johns Hopkins University's existence, there were no academic "departments" as such; similar disciplines were classified together in what was known as the Group System. History, political science, economics, and for a time, philosophy, were collected together in a single group. While Wilson's degree was technically in history, his scholarly focus was aimed squarely at political science. He completed his doctoral requirements in 1885, but for reasons that are not entirely clear, his degree was conferred the following year (however, his alumnus standing is given as 1885 in the authoritative *Johns Hopkins Half-Century Directory* [1926]). Wilson also attended Davidson College in North Carolina for one year and law school at the University of Virginia for a year.

2. Scott Berg, *Wilson* (New York: G. P. Putnam's Sons, 2013), 100. It remains in print, but only because Wilson wrote it; Bragdon, *Academic*, 112–14.

3. Bragdon, *Academic*, 128–33; Woodrow Wilson, *Congressional Government*, 15th ed. (Boston: Houghton Mifflin, 1900), 52.

4. Wilson, *Congressional*, 130.

5. Bragdon, *Academic*, 134–37.

6. Woodrow Wilson, *The State: Elements of Historical and Practical Politics*, rev. ed. (London: Isbister and Company, 1900), 543, 548–49. I refer to Wilson's revised edition, which, even though he reworked it after the Spanish-American War, still spent very little time discussing the president's role in wartime.

7. Wilson, *The State*, 125–27.

8. John Milton Cooper Jr., *Woodrow Wilson: A Biography* (New York: Alfred A. Knopf, 2009), 60–65.

9. Wilson, *The State*, 388.

10. Bragdon's *Woodrow Wilson: The Academic Years* gives the standard account of Wilson's writing *Division*. He notes that Wilson did not have many class notes to fall back on while writing this book, so he had to do much research from scratch, a task made more difficult as Wilson was a slow reader (Bragdon, 234). It is also possible that Wilson may have rushed the last chapters because they covered events that he had lived through and so may have felt that they did not require as much effort; Woodrow Wilson, *Division and Reunion* (New York: Longmans, Greens, 1901), preface.

11. "Civil War in Augusta," Augusta https://www.visitaugusta.com/things-to -do/civil-war/ (accessed 12/23/2018). Ray Stannard Baker, *Woodrow Wilson: Life and Letters: Youth, 1856–1890* (New York: Doubleday, 1927), 50–51.

12. Arthur Link, "The American as Southerner," *The Higher Realism of Woodrow Wilson and Other Essays* (Nashville: Vanderbilt University Press, 1971), 33.

13. Cooper, *Wilson*, 76; Arthur S. Link, *Wilson: The Road to the White House* (Princeton: Princeton University Press, 1947), 30.

14. Bragdon, *Academic*, 246–47, 252. At the same time he was working on *History*, Wilson wrote an extended essay for the *Cambridge Modern History* titled, "States Rights: 1850–1861." In "States Rights," better written than either *Division* or *History*, Wilson advanced the same arguments about the evolving nature of the Constitution and how the North and South came to see the federal government in a different light. "States Rights" was not published until 1907, although Wilson had completed it by 1902. However, because this essay does not discuss the war itself, it is not included in this comparison. "Adolphus William Ward to Woodrow Wilson," August 12, 1899, PWW 11:222.

15. Woodrow Wilson, *A History of the American People* (New York: William H. Wise, 1931), III:148.

16. Wilson, *History*, III:192.

17. Wilson, III:212.

18. Wilson, III:218–23.

19. Wilson, *Division*, 150.

20. Wilson, 227.

21. Fitz W. Woodrow to Arthur C. Walworth, April 12, 1948. Quoted in Arthur C. Walworth, *Woodrow Wilson* (New York: Norton, 1948), 2:101.

22. Wilson, *History*, V:270.

23. Wilson, V:270–73.

24. Wilson, V:280–82.

25. The worst of Wilson's cabinet-level appointments was probably James Clark McReynolds, first as attorney general, and then to the Supreme Court. Wilson did not know McReynolds well and may have promoted him to the court to get him out of the cabinet.

26. Lee A. Craig, *Joseph Daniels: His Life and Times* (Chapel Hill: University of North Carolina Press, 2013), 183–88.

27. For FDR's role as Daniels' assistant secretary, see Alonzo Hamby, *Man of Destiny: FDR and the Making of the American Century* (New York: Basic Books, 2015), 51–84; Warner R. Schilling, "Civil-Naval Politics in World War I," *World Politics* 7 no. 4 (1955): 572–91; U.S. Naval Institute Staff, "A Hundred Years Dry: The U.S. Navy's End of Alcohol at Sea," *USNI.org*, July 1, 2014, https://news.usni.org/2014/07/01/hundred-years-dry-u-s-navys-end-alcohol-sea (accessed May 31, 2019).

28. Douglas B. Craig, *Progressives at War: William G. McAdoo and Newton D. Baker, 1863–1941* (Baltimore: Johns Hopkins, 2013), 21. Besides Princeton, Wilson also taught classes at Johns Hopkins.

29. James P. Tate, *The Army and Its Air Corps: Army Policy toward Aviation 1919–1941* (n.p.: Air University Press, 1998), 3.

30. Arthur S. Link, *Wilson: The New Freedom* (Princeton: Princeton University Press, 1956), 7–8.

31. Link, *Wilson: The New Freedom*, 277–82.

32. Cooper, *Wilson*, 295, 367.

33. For a brief discussion of House and Wilson, see Robert C. Hilderbrand, "Wilson as Chief Executive: Relations with Congress, the Cabinet, and Staff," in *A Companion to Woodrow Wilson*, edited by Ross A. Kennedy (Malden, MA: Wiley-Blackwell, 2013), 100–101. See also Charles E. Neu, *Colonel House: A Biography of Woodrow Wilson's Silent Partner* (New York: Oxford University Press, 2015).

34. Joseph Tumulty, *Woodrow Wilson as I Know Him* (New York: Doubleday, Page, 1921), 158.

35. Link, *Wilson: The Road to the White House*, 2.

36. Cooper, *Wilson*, 18.

37. Edwin A. Weinstein, *Woodrow Wilson: A Medical and Psychological Biography* (Princeton: Princeton University Press, 1981); Baker, *Wilson: Life and Letters: Youth*, 49–55.

38. Wilson, *The State*, 572–73; "An Address in Denver on the Bible," May 7, 1911, PWW 23:15.

39. *New York World*, March 12, 1913; Woodrow Wilson, "Address to National Press Club, May 15, 1916," *Selected Literary and Political Papers and Addresses*

of Woodrow Wilson (New York: Grosset and Dunlap, n.d.), 2:161; "An Address to Spanish War Veterans in Atlantic City," September 10, 1912, PWW 25:129–32.

40. Wilson, *History*, IV: 122; Wilson, "An Address in Chicago on Preparedness," January 31, 1916, PWW 36:70. Notably, Wilson did not consider the wars of conquest against Native Americans, an interesting exception that falls outside the realm of this work. Wilson, *History*, V:122, 297–98.

41. James Turner Johnson, "Historical Roots and Sources of the Just War Tradition in Western Culture," *Just War and Jihad: Historical and Theoretical Perspectives on War and Peace in Western and Islamic Traditions*, edited by John Kelsay and James Turner Johnson (Westport, CT: Greenwood Press, 1991), 16–19; Paul Ramsey, *The Just War: Force and Political Responsibility* (New York: Charles Scribner's Sons, 1968), 42–43, 48, 51.

42. "A Look Back . . . George Washington: America's First Military Intelligence Director," https://www.cia.gov/news-information/featured-story -archive/2007-featured-story-archive/george-washington.html (accessed August 11, 2019).

43. Arthur C. Walworth, *Woodrow Wilson: American Prophet* (New York: Norton, 1948), 1:354–55.

44. G. J. A. O'Toole, *Honorable Treachery: A History of U.S. Intelligence, Espionage, and Covert Action from the American Revolution to the CIA* (New York: Atlantic Monthly Press, 1991), 178–80, 192.

45. Richard Hume Werking, *The Master Architects: Building the United States Foreign Service, 1890–1913* (Lexington: The University Press of Kentucky, 1977), 128–38, 245–47.

46. Rhodri Jeffreys-Jones, *Cloak and Dollar: A History of American Secret Intelligence*, 2nd ed. (New Haven, CT: Yale University Press, 2003), 60–63. Two of Lansing's nephews, John Foster Dulles and Allan Dulles, were President Dwight Eisenhower's secretary of state and head of the CIA, respectively. They were responsible for multiple coups in the developing world during the Cold War, as well as attempted assassinations of foreign leaders believed to be anti-American. His father-in-law, John Watson Foster, was President Benjamin Harrison's secretary of state and was instrumental in the coup that overthrew Hawaii's government in 1893.

47. Wilson also liked the *New York Evening Post*. James D. Startt, *Woodrow Wilson and the Press* (New York: Palgrave-MacMillan, 2004), 17; "Wilson to Walter H. Page," May 18, 1914, PWW 30:42; Jerry W. Knudson, "John Reed: A Reporter in Revolutionary Mexico," *Journalism History* 29, no. 2 (Summer

2003): 60–61. Some of the crank mail can still be found in Wilson's papers with his notes on them, thus providing the best evidence that he had perused some of the letters himself. There were warnings to the president against conspiracies by the Pope, protestants, Masons, or Jews, depending on the writer's prejudices. For the would-be assassin, see "Sidney A. Witherbee to Wilson," November 10, 1913, and "Witherbee to Wilson," November 14, 1913, Wilson Papers, Series 4, Case 95. Witherbee tried, unsuccessfully, to convince Secretary of State William Jennings Bryan to send him to Mexico to kill Huerta.

48. "Wilson to Lansing," August 31, 1915, 812.00/16017–1:2, M274, RG59, National Archives and Records Administration (hereafter NARA).

49. Cooper, *Wilson*, 419–22.

50. Woodrow Wilson, "An Address to the United States Chamber of Commerce," February 3, 1915, PWW 32:180.

51. The most notable exception is Measurement and Signature Intelligence (MASINT). Reliant on technical analysis, it existed in terms of chemical analysis, such as in examining the specifics of an enemy's use of poison gas in combat, but was extremely limited in 1913 and would not have risen to the level that would engage the commander in chief.

52. "Wilson to Mary Allen Hulbert," September 21, 1913, PWW 28:311.

53. "Wilson to Ralph Pulitzer," March 2, 1914. Quoted in Link, *Wilson: The New Freedom*, 83–84.

54. Jonathan Reed Winkler, *Nexus: Strategic Communications and American Security in World War I* (Cambridge, MA: Harvard University Press, 2008).

55. James L. Gilbert, *World War I and the Origins of U.S. Military Intelligence* (Lanham, MD: Scarecrow Press, 2012), 9.

56. Thank you to the Woodrow Wilson House for allowing me to review Wilson's copy. There was a sheet with Wilson's writing stuck between pages from a message to Colonel House for the British sent in January 1916. It used the original page numbering system, so the page reversal was added after that. Given the identities of those for which Wilson gave code names (Bryan, Cox, Glass, etc.) it seems likely they were added when Wilson was following the 1920 Democratic Convention that nominated James Cox as the Democratic nominee for president. Those listed each played an important role at the convention as opposed to pre-1920 diplomatic issues.

57. This interpretation of Wilson and force is taken from Frederick S. Calhoun, *Power and Principle: Armed Intervention in Wilsonian Foreign Policy* (Kent, OH: Kent State University Press, 1986), esp. 3–4, 19–33.

CHAPTER 2. THE WORLD IN 1912

1. Cooper, *Wilson*, 182.
2. For the overall numbers, see table 2–11 from Department of Defense: Selected Manpower Statistics–Fiscal Year 1997; numbers of ships comes from https://www.naval-encyclopedia.com/wwi/US-Navy.php (accessed June 24, 2019).
3. Lester D. Langley, *The Banana Wars: United States Intervention in the Caribbean, 1898–1934* (Lexington: University Press of Kentucky, 1983), 59–70.
4. Peter James Hudson, *Bankers and Empire: How Wall Street Colonized the Caribbean* (Chicago: University of Chicago Press, 2017), 155–59.
5. Hugh Thomas, *Cuba: The Pursuit of Freedom* (New York: Harper & Row, 1971), 481–93.
6. Charles Cumberland, *Mexican Revolution: Genesis under Madero* (Austin: University of Texas Press, 1952), 111–20; Alan Knight, *The Mexican Revolution: Volume I, Porfirians, Liberals and Peasants* (Lincoln: University of Nebraska Press, 1986), 77.
7. Cumberland, *Mexican Revolution*, 188–204, 218.
8. Knight, *Mexican Revolution*, 247–57.
9. Henry Lane Wilson, *Diplomatic Episodes in Mexico, Belgium, and Chile* (New York: Doubleday, Page, 1927), 240; Knight, *Mexican Revolution*, 485; Peter Calvert, *The Mexican Revolution, 1910–1914: The Diplomacy of Anglo-American Conflict* (Cambridge, MA: Cambridge University Press, 1968), 126. *Papers Relating to the Foreign Relations of the United States* (Washington, DC: Government Printing Office, 1918), 1911:519–23. Hereafter this series will be referred to as FRUS followed by the year and page numbers.
10. Wilson, *Diplomatic*, 234–35. Ambassador Wilson quoted Madero's message in his memoirs, huffing that it proved Madero was "unstable" and "ungrateful" for Wilson's "sympathetic attitude." Cole Blasier, *The Hovering Giant: United States Responses to Revolutionary Change in Latin America* (Pittsburgh: University of Pittsburgh Press, 1976), 41.
11. Paul V. N. Henderson, "The Military and the Madero Regime: The Case of General Félix Díaz," *Social Science Journal* 12–13 (1975–76): 139–48; Cumberland, *Mexican Revolution*, 232–35; FRUS: 1913, 704, 708, 711–714; Wilson, *Diplomatic*, 273; Knight, *Mexican Revolution*, 486; Friedrich Katz, *The Secret War in Mexico: Europe, the United States and the Mexican Revolution* (Chicago: University of Chicago Press, 1981), 99–105; *New York World*, March 7, 1913, 1–2.
12. FRUS: 1913, 718; Katz, *Secret War*, 98; Lowell L. Blaisdell, "Henry Lane Wilson and the Overthrow of Madero," *Southwestern Social Science Quarterly* 43 (1962):

132; FRUS: 1913, 720–21; George Jay Rausch, "Victoriano Huerta: A Political Biography," PhD diss. (University of Illinois, 1960), 80; Kenneth Grieb, "The United States and Huerta," PhD diss. (Indiana University, 1966), 64–66.

13. "Secretary of State to Ambassador Wilson," February 21, 1913, William Howard Taft Papers, Series 6, Reel 376, Library of Congress (hereafter LC); "Secretary of State to Secretary of War," February 23, 1913, Taft Papers, Series 6, Reel 376, LC; Walter and Marie Scholes, *The Foreign Policies of the Taft Administration* (Columbia: University of Missouri Press, 1967), 101–4.

14. FRUS: 1913, 735.

15. Louis M. Teitelbaum, *Woodrow Wilson and the Mexican Revolution, 1913–1916* (New York: Exposition Press, 1967), 32.

16. Teitelbaum, *Woodrow Wilson*, 32; "Woodrow Wilson to William Bayard Hale," April 19, 1913, PWW 27:335.

17. "A Report by William Bayard Hale," June 18, 1913, PWW 27:536–52. Hale had written Wilson's official campaign biography.

18. Cabinet Diary, May 20, 1913, Josephus Daniels Papers, LC; Diary of Colonel House, May 2, 1913, PWW 27:383; Tumulty, *Wilson as I Know Him*, 148; Daniels Cabinet Dairy, April 11, April 18, May 21, 1913, Daniels Papers, LC; Henry Breckinridge Diary, April 27, 1914, Container 516, Henry Breckinridge Papers, LC; Josephus Daniels, *The Wilson Era: Years of Peace: 1910–1917* (Chapel Hill: University of North Carolina Press, 1944), 182.

19. Walter LaFeber, *The Panama Canal: The Crisis in Historical Perspective*, updated ed. (New York: Oxford University Press, 1980), 36–39, 48–49, 55.

20. Hans Schmidt, *The United States Occupation of Haiti, 1915–1934* (New Brunswick, NJ: Rutgers University Press, 1995), 31.

21. Langley, *Banana Wars*, 118–19.

22. There were multiple uprisings, some of which were before October 10. However, this is the celebrated date marking the Wuchang Uprising.

23. Tien-yi Li, *Woodrow Wilson's China Policy: 1913–1917* (New York: University of Kansas Press, 1952), 13–15.

24. For a well-written description of the crisis, see the classic George Dangerfield, *The Strange Death of Liberal England: 1910–1914* (New York: G. P. Putnam's Sons, 1961), 333–425.

25. Dominik Geppert, William Mulligan, and Andres Rose, "Introduction" Dominik Geppert, William Mulligan, and Andres Rose, eds., *The Wars before the Great War: Conflict and International Politics before the Outbreak of World War I* (Cambridge, MA: Cambridge University Press, 2015), 7–9.

26. I. F. Clarke, *Future Wars* (Liverpool: Liverpool University Press, 2012).

CHAPTER 3. VERACRUZ

1. See Mark E. Benbow, *Leading Them to the Promised Land: Woodrow Wilson, Covenant Theology, and the Mexican Revolution, 1913–1915* (Kent, OH: Kent State University Press, 2010).

2. John S. D. Eisenhower, *Intervention! The United States and the Mexican Revolution, 1913–1917* (New York: W. W. Norton, 1993), 99–101.

3. Eisenhower, *Intervention!*, 101; "Admiral Henry Mayo to Captain Doughty," April 15, 1913; "Fregattenkapitan Kohler to Mayo," April 15, 1913; "Admiral Christopher Cradock to Mayo," April 15, 1913; Henry T. Mayo Papers, LC, Container 11, Military File-Tampico Incident-Correspondence with Foreign Naval Officials.

4. "Wilson to Bryan," April 10, 1914, PWW 29:421; "O'Shaughnessy to Bryan," April 19, 1914, PWW 29:467; "O'Shaughnessy to Bryan," April 15, 1914, PWW 29:447; "O'Shaughnessy to Bryan," April 17, 1914, PWW 29:459; "Bryan to O'Shaughnessy," April 18, 1914, PWW 29:464–65.

5. Robert Quirk, *An Affair of Honor: Woodrow Wilson and the Occupation of Veracruz* (New York: Norton, 1962), 163–66.

6. "Robert Lansing to Wilson," [c. April 14, 1914], PWW 29:437–39; "Remarks at a Press Conference," April 16, 1914, PWW 29:452; "Memo from Lansing to Wilson, "April 16, 1914, Robert Lansing Papers, LC, 2:268–69.

7. "A Press Statement," April 14, 1914, PWW 29:433–34.

8. "Henry Breckinridge to Desha Breckinridge," April 27, 1914, Henry Breckinridge Papers, Container 518, Letterbook.

9. Ray Stannard Baker, *Woodrow Wilson, Life and Letters: President 1913–1914* (New York: Doubleday, Doran, 1931), 325–28; Link, *Wilson: The New Freedom*, 398–99; *New York World*, April 22, 1914.

10. *New York World*, April 21, 1914.

11. "Canada to Bryan, enclosure, Bryan to Wilson," April 21, 1914, PWW 29:476–77; "Memo for Chief of Staff," April 21, 1914, Henry Breckinridge Papers, Container 517, Letterbook. The *Ypiranga* was also the ship that took Porfirio Díaz into exile. The ship's regular route was between Hamburg and Veracruz.

12. "Daniels to Fletcher," April 21, 1914, Josephus Daniels Papers, LC, Container 536; "Daniels to Ray Stannard Baker," April 12, 1929, Ray Stannard Baker Papers, LC, Daniels file.

13. Lind opposed the Republican stance supporting the gold standard and so ran as the nominee of both the Democrats and of the Republicans who favored a bi-gold-silver standard. George M. Stephenson, *John Lind of Minnesota* (Port

Washington, NY: Kennikat Press, repr. 1971), 105–22; Larry D. Hill, "The Progressive Politician as a Diplomat: The Case of John Lind in Mexico," *The Americas* 27 (1971): 356–57. Lind, a native of Sweden, turned down the post at Stockholm because he believed that the U.S. ambassador should not be somebody born in their assigned country; Felix Frankfurter, *Felix Frankfurter Reminisces* (New York: Reynal, 1960), 67–68.

14. Jack L. Snyder, "Rationality at the Brink: The Role of Cognitive Processes in Failures of Deterrence," *World Politics* 30 (1978): 345–48; Weinstein, *A Medical and Psychological Biography*, 254–57; "John Lind to the Secretary of State," November 4, 1913, John Lind Papers, Reel 2. For more on how revolutions can increase misperception and correspondingly raise the chances of war with other states, see Stephen M. Walt, *Revolution and War* (New York: Cornell University Press, 1996), esp. 287–99.

15. Frederick C. Turner, "Anti-Americanism in Mexico, 1910–1913," *Hispanic American Historical Review* 47 (1967): 505–6; *Mexican Herald*, April 25, 1914.

16. Richard D. Challener, *Admirals, Generals, and American Foreign Policy* (Princeton: Princeton University Press, 1973), 387–89.

17. Challener, *Admirals*, 389–90.

18. Challener, 389.

19. Challener, 385.

20. Challener, 391.

21. Challener, 393–94.

22. Challener, 395.

23. Eisenhower, *Intervention!*, 113–17, 122; Sweetman, *Landing*, 53, 62, 70–72.

24. Quirk, *Affair*, 89–90.

25. Quirk, 90–120; Also see Edith O'Shaughnessy's description of Maass in *A Diplomat's Wife in Mexico* (New York: Harper and Brothers, 1916), 305–6.

26. Sweetman, *Landing*, 77; "Consul Canada to the Secretary of State," April 21, 1914, FRUS: 1914, 480; Huerta's efforts to arm civilians against an American invasion were reported by American consuls in the country. See flyer "Alerta Mexicanos" attached to "Davis to the Secretary of State," August 1913, 812.00/8210, M274, RG59, NARA.

27. Quirk, *Affair*, 53; Ray Stannard Baker, *Woodrow Wilson—Life and Letters: President, 1913–1914* (Garden City, NY: Doubleday, Doran, 1931), 330; "Daniels to Wilson, 'Sailors who fell at Veracruz,'" (n.d.), Ray Stannard Baker Papers, LC, Josephus Daniels file. Thirteen of the nineteen dead were twenty-two years old or younger. Only three were over thirty; Rear Adm. Cary T. Grayson, *Woodrow Wilson: An Intimate Memoir* (Washington, DC: Potomac Books, 1977), 30.

28. Alain Rouqié, *The Military and the State in Latin America*, trans. Paul E. Sigmund (Berkeley: University of California Press, 1987), 34; Charles Cumberland, *The Constitutionalist Years* (Austin: University of Texas Press, 1972), 126; Will B. Davis, *Experiences and Observations of an American Consular Officer during the Recent Mexican Revolutions* (Los Angeles: Wayside Press, 1920), 25–31; "Reminiscences of Hilarion Noel Branch," Columbia University Oral History Project, 1966, 91.

29. Katz, *Secret War*, 197; "Burnside to War College Staff," April 26, 1914, included in Leonard Wood Diary, Leonard Wood Papers, Container 8, LC; William K. Meyers, "Pancho Villa and the Multinationals: United States Mining Interests in Villista Mexico, 1913–1915," *Journal of Latin American Studies* 23 (1991): 148. For examples of how the war scare spread through the border area, see *San Francisco Chronicle*, April 21–26, 1914; New York *Sun*, April 25, 1914; *San Diego Union*, April 22, 1914; *El Paso Herald*, April 23–26, 1914. Gen. John J. Pershing's papers at the Library of Congress contain a scrapbook of clippings covering this issue including the editions just cited.

30. "Remarks at a Press Conference," April 23, 1914, PWW 50:470–71; "Bryan to Carothers," April 24, 1914, 812.00/11654, M274, RG59, NARA.

31. "Carothers to Bryan," May 10, 1914, 812.00/11875, M274, RG59, NARA; Philip H. Lowry, "The Mexican Policy of Woodrow Wilson," PhD diss. (Yale University, 1949), 132–33; Lind's actions were a focal point of the 1920 Fall Hearings on Mexico contained in *United States Senate, Investigation of Mexican Affairs: Hearings before a Subcommittee of the Committee on Foreign Relations* (Washington, DC: GPO, 1920). Hereafter referred to as Fall Committee Report. See the testimony of John Lind, 2:2358–59, William F. Buckley, 1:792–93, Sherburne Hopkins, 2:2411–14; Stephenson, *John Lind*, 275; *New York Commercial*, April 27, 1914.

32. "Mexico: The Record of a Conversation with President Wilson, by Samuel G. Blythe," April 27, 1914, PWW 29:516; Knight, *Mexican Revolution*, 165–67. See, for example, the positive reaction to mediation in Carlo DeFornaro, *Carranza and Mexico* (New York: Mitchell Kennerley, 1915), 209–11; Thomas F. McGann, *Argentina, the United States, and the Inter-American System 1880–1914* (Cambridge, MA: Harvard University Press, 1957), 306–7.

33. "Secretary of State to the Special Commissioners," May 27, 1914, FRUS: 1914, 509–10; "Secretary of State to the Special Commissioners," June 3, 1914, FRUS: 1914, 522–23.

34. Arthur S. Link, *Wilson: The Struggle for Neutrality, 1914–15* (Princeton: Princeton University Press, 1960), 412–13; *New York World*, June 14, 1914, 4; June 29, 1914, 4; June 13, 1914, 2; June 27, 1914, 5; Katz, *Secret War*, 201.

35. Link, *Wilson: The New Freedom*, 401.
36. "Memorandum for the Adjunct General April 26, 1914." Enclosure in "Lindley Miller Garrison to Woodrow Wilson," April 26, 1914, PWW 29: 510.
37. Eisenhower, *Intervention!*, 134–35.
38. *New York American*, December 22, 1913; *San Francisco Examiner*, July 30, 1914; W. A. Swanberg, *Citizen Hearst: A Biography of William Randolph Hearst* (New York: Charles Scribner's Sons, 1961), 296–97.
39. "Wilson to Walter H. Page," May 18, 1914, PWW 30:42. The *New York World* was also reasonably accurate, especially compared to Hearst's papers. While researching Wilson and Mexico for my dissertation in the 1990s I was struck by how the *World*'s coverage matched what historians later found to be happening in Mexico. For example, their reporting on Huerta's 1913 coup prompted Wilson's sending Hale to investigate, and Wilson's agent's reports backed up the *World*'s account.
40. "From the Diary of Colonel House," April 28, 1914, PWW 28:330.
41. Eisenhower, *Intervention!*, 136–37. Examples of the postage stamps may be found in NARA, Records Group 141, Records of the Military Government of Veracruz.
42. "Nation Honors Veracruz Dead in Grieving City," *New York Times*, May 12, 1914; Baker, *Life and Letters*, 342–43.
43. Sweetman, *Landing*, 77.
44. American Mexican Claims Commission, *Report to the Secretary of State* (Washington, DC: GPO, 1948), 165–68; Michael Meyer, "The Arms of the *Ypiranga*," *Hispanic American Historical Review* 50 (1970): 547–50; Thomas Baecker, "The Arms of the *Ypiranga*: The German Side," *The Americas* 30 (1973): 12–15.
45. "State Department to American Embassy Tokyo," May 3, 1914, "Guthrie to American Consul Dairen," May 9, 1914, and "Guthrie to Bryan," May 9, 1914. All are in Confidential U.S. Diplomatic Post Records Japan: I Japan 1914–1918, microfilm in the special collections of Georgetown University.
46. Nancy Mitchell, *The Danger of Dreams: German and American Imperialism in Latin America* (Chapel Hill: University of North Carolina Press, 1999), 195–208.
47. Cumberland, *Constitutionalist Years*, 134–43; *New York World*, July 12, 1914, 1; July 16, 1914, 1; "Carbajal, Huerta's Successor, Seen at Close Range," *New York Times*, July 19, 1914, Section 5; Wilson to Leon Joseph Canova, July 16, 1914, PWW 30:285–86; Wilson to William Charles Adamson, July 20, 1914, PWW 30:289; William Jennings Bryan's newspaper, *The Commoner*, made

sure to take the opportunity to reprint congratulations from the pro-Wilson press, "'Watchful Waiting' Wins in Mexico," *The Commoner*, September 1914, 3–4; Bryan's memoirs noted that Wilson and various cabinet members were having dinner at the secretary of state's house when the news came and that some of the men "danced about like boys." He does not specify which of those present were included in this description. William Jennings Bryan and Mary Baird Bryan, *The Memoirs of William Jennings Bryan*, orig. printed 1925 (New York: Haskell House, 1971), 355–56.

CHAPTER 4. HAITI AND THE DOMINICAN REPUBLIC

1. Former-president Zamor returned to Haiti and was assassinated in prison in July 1915. See David Healy, *Gunboat Diplomacy in the Wilson Era: The U.S. Navy in Haiti, 1915–1916* (Madison: University of Wisconsin Press, 1976), 28–33; Link, *Wilson: The Struggle*, 518–25.
2. Link, *Wilson: The Struggle*, 525–26.
3. United States Congress Senate Selected Committee on Haiti and Santo Domingo (1922), *Inquiry into Occupation and Administration of Haiti and Santo Domingo: Hearings before a Select Committee on Haiti and Santo Domingo*, United States Senate, Sixty-Seventh Congress, First and Second Sessions, Pursuant to S. Res. 112 Authorizing a Special Committee to Inquire into the Occupation and Administration of the Territories of the Republic of Haiti and the Dominican Republic, U.S. Government Printing Office; "The Secretary of State to Minister Blanchard," December 15, 1914, File 838.516/17, FRUS Document 570. Untitled, December 18, 1914, File 838.516/23, FRUS, Document 572.
4. Healy, *Gunboat*, 35–36.
5. Healy, *Gunboat*, 36–37.
6. Langley, *Banana Wars*, 120–21.
7. Healy, *Gunboat*, 44–47.
8. Healy, *Gunboat*, 47–52.
9. Healy, *Gunboat*, 52.
10. Healy, *Gunboat*, 54–55.
11. Langley, *Banana Wars*, 121–22.
12. John F. Schmitt, "Peacetime Landing Operations: Lessons from Haiti, 1915," *Marine Corps Gazette* 78, no. 3 (March 1994): 72–74.
13. "Woodrow Wilson to Robert Lansing," August 4, 1915, PWW 34:78; Cooper, *Wilson*, 248.
14. Link, *Wilson: The Struggle*, 536–37.
15. "From Robert Lansing with Enclosure," August 7, 1915, PWW 34:121–22.

16. "From Robert Lansing," August 9, 1915, PWW 34:142–44; "From Robert Lansing with Enclosure," August 10, 1915, PWW 34:157–58.

17. "From William Banks Caperton," August 11, 1915, PWW 34:164–65.

18. "From Robert Lansing," August 13, 1915, PWW 34:183; "To Edith Bolling Galt," August 13, 1915, PWW 209, emphasis in the original; "Two letters to Edith Bolling Galt," August 19, 1915, PWW 34:256.

19. "To Edith Bolling Galt," August 24, 1915, PWW 34:311.

20. "To Edith Bolling Galt," August 30, 1915, PWW 34:367; "To Edith Bolling Galt, with Enclosure," September 9, 1915, PWW 34:437.

21. J. Fred Rippy, *Haiti and the United States, 1714–1938* (Durham, NC: Duke University Press, 1940), 217–19.

22. Edward S. Kaplan, *U.S. Imperialism in Latin America: Bryan's Challenges and Contributions, 1900–1920* (Westport, CT: Greenwood Press, 1998), 69–70.

23. Link, *Wilson: The Struggle*, 498–99; Cooper, *Wilson*, 247.

24. Link, *Wilson: The Struggle*, 499.

25. Link, 500–501.

26. Link, 501–2.

27. Link, 503–5.

28. Link, 509–10.

29. Link, 510–11.

30. Link, 511–13.

31. Link, 513; Dana G. Munro, *Intervention and Dollar Diplomacy in the Caribbean, 1900–1921* (Princeton: Princeton University Press, 1980), 292.

32. Link, *Wilson: The Struggle*, 543–44; Munro, *Intervention*, 305–6.

33. G. Pope Atkins and Larman Curtis Wilson, *The Dominican Republic and the United States: From Imperialism to Transnationalism* (Athens: University of Georgia Press, 1998), 48–49.

34. Link, *Wilson: The Struggle*, 541; Munro, *Dollar*, 306.

35. Stephen Fuller and Graham A. Cosmas, *Marines in the Dominican Republic 1916–1924* (Honolulu: University Press of the Pacific, 2005), 16.

36. Ivan Musicant, *The Banana Wars: A History of the United States Military Intervention in Latin America from the Spanish-American War to the Invasion of Panama* (New York: MacMillan, 1990), 253–63.

37. "To Robert Lansing with Enclosure, PWW 40:81–82.

38. Fuller and Cosmas, *Marines*, 26; Leo J. Daugherty III, *Counterinsurgency and the United States Marine Corps: Volume 1, the First Counterinsurgency Era, 1899–1945* (Jefferson, NC: MacFarland, 2015), 58–59.

39. Michael Kazin, *A Godly Hero: The Life of William Jennings Bryan* (New York: Alfred A. Knopf, 2006), 229–30.

40. Cooper, *Wilson*, 248.

CHAPTER 5. THE BORDER WAR

1. Charles H. Harris III and Louis R. Sadler, "The Plan of San Diego and the Mexican-United States War Crisis of 1916: A Reexamination," *Hispanic American Historical Review* 58 (1978): 381. See also Harris and Sadler, *The Plan de San Diego: Tejano Rebellion, Mexican Intrigue* (Lincoln: University of Nebraska Press, 2013).

2. Harris and Sadler, "Plan of San Diego," 383–85.

3. James A. Sandos, *Rebellion in the Borderlands: Anarchism and the Plan of San Diego, 1904–1923* (Norman: University of Oklahoma Press, 1992), 119; *New York World*, August 12, 1915; August 30, 1915; Garrett to the Secretary of State, August 28, 1915, 812.00/15946, M274, RG59, NARA.

4. The State Department records for 1915 in the National Archives contain weekly reports of conditions along the border, including details of these raids. See M274, RG59, NARA.

5. Allen Gerlach, "Conditions along the Border–1915: The Plan de San Diego," *New Mexico Historical Review* 43 (1968): 200–203; Douglas W. Richmond, "La Guerra de Texas se Renova: Mexican Insurrection and Carrancista Ambitions, 1900–1920," *Aztlán* 11 (1980): 17.

6. George J. Rausch Jr., "The Exile and Death of Victoriano Huerta," *Hispanic American Historical Review* 42 (1962): 134–35; Captain Von Rintelen, *The Dark Invader: Wartime Reminiscences of a German Naval Intelligence Officer* (New York: MacMillan, 1933), 175–77.

7. Barbara W. Tuchman, *The Zimmermann Telegram* (New York: Macmillan, 1966), 78–80. Richard B. Spence, "K. A. Jahnke and the German Sabotage Campaign in the United States and Mexico, 1914–1918," *Historian* 59 (1996): 92–93.

8. Rausch, "Exile," 138–39.

9. *New York World*, June 28, 1915, 1; Henry Thayer Mahoney and Marjorie Locke Mahoney, *Espionage in Mexico: The Twentieth Century* (San Francisco: Austin & Winfield, 1997), 96–99; Newman, Texas, is next to El Paso.

10. "Wilson to House," July 7, 1915, Ray Stannard Baker Papers, LC; Lansing Desk Diary, 1915, Robert Lansing Papers, LC; *New York World*, August 10, 1915.

11. Wilson referred to the Latin Powers as "A.B.C. and B.U.G." in a letter to his future wife Edith Galt, August 12, 1915, PWW 34:179.

12. "Woodrow Wilson to Colonel House," July 7, 1915, PWW 33:479–80.

13. "Two Telegrams from Robert Lansing to Woodrow Wilson," July 29, 1915, PWW 34:43; Chandler Anderson Diary, July 30, 1915, Container 1, Chandler Anderson Papers, LC.

14. *New York World*, August 6, 1915, 9; "Robert Lansing to Woodrow Wilson with enclosures," August 6, 1915, PWW 34:111–12.

15. "Continuation of the Conference on Mexican Affairs," August 11, 1915, 812/15754½, M274, RG59, NARA. At this same time Villa's lobbyists, who used to meet with Lansing in person, were only getting polite form letters from Lansing's secretary in response to their messages.

16. Copies of the responses of the A.B.C.-B.U.G. countries are in the State Department files. See 812.00/15964–5, M274, RG59, NARA; Kahle, "Recognition," 364; *New York World*, August 16, 1915; August 29, 1915; *New York Times*, September 9, 1915; September 10, 1915; September 11, 1915.

17. "Woodrow Wilson to Edith Bolling Galt," August 18, 1915, PWW 34:241.

18. "Woodrow Wilson to Robert Lansing," September 8, 1915, 812.00/16041, M274, RG59, NARA.

19. "Woodrow Wilson to Edith Bolling Galt," August 18, 1915, PWW 34:241.

20. Weinstein, *Medical and Psychological Biography*, 291–93; "Woodrow Wilson to Robert Lansing," September 13, 1915, PWW 34:460; Diary of Colonel House, September 23, 1915, PWW 34:509–10.

21. Necah Furman, "Vida Nueva: A Reflection of Villista Diplomacy, 1914–1915," *New Mexico Historical Review* 53 (1978): 185; Paul Fuller to Lansing, September 10, 1915, 812.00/16102, M274, RG59, NARA.

22. *New York Times*, September 19, 1915; September 21, 1915; October 10, 1915; October 11, 1915; October 12, 1915.

23. Louis G. Kahle, "Robert Lansing and the Recognition of Venustiano Carranza," *Hispanic American Historical Review* 38, no. 3 (August 1958): 364–66; McAdoo to Lansing, August 18, 1915, Robert Lansing Papers, LC 12/2047–48; FRUS: 1915, 735, 737, 746, 767–69, 771–72. Despite the announcement, Guatemala delayed recognition and gave shelter to some Villistas in the futile hope Carranza would be overthrown.

24. *El Paso Morning Times*, October 8, 1915, quoted in Friedrich Katz, *The Life and Times of Pancho Villa* (Stanford, CA: Stanford University Press, 1998), 524.

25. *Los Angeles Examiner*, January 14, 1916, quoted in Arthur Link, *Wilson: Confusions and Crises, 1915–1916* (Princeton: Princeton University Press, 1964), 202. Emphasis in original.

26. Link, *Wilson: Confusions*, 203–4; "From Cleveland Henry Dodge," January 14, 1916, PWW: 35, n1; Ray Stannard Baker, *Woodrow Wilson Life and Letters: Facing War, 1915–1917* (New York: Charles Scribner's Sons, 1937), 68.

27. Frank Tompkins, *Chasing Villa: The Last Campaign of the U.S. Cavalry* (Silver City, NM: High-Lonesome Books, 1996), 41–44; Charles H. Harris III and Louis R. Sadler, *The Secret War in El Paso: Mexican Revolutionary Intrigue, 1906–1920* (Albuquerque: University of New Mexico Press, 2009), 250–51.

28. Harris and Sadler, *Secret War*, 250.

29. Tompkins, *Chasing*, 55–57.

30. Tompkins, 1.

31. Memorandum by the Secretary of State of a Conversations with Mr. Arredondo, March 9, 1916, *FRUS, The Lansing Papers, 1914–1920*, 2:554–55.

32. Link, *Wilson: Confusions*, 207–8.

33. Craig, *Progressives*, 143.

34. Link, *Wilson: Confusions*, 208–9; Craig, *Progressives*, 143; Frederick Palmer, *Newton D. Baker: America at War*, 2 vols. (New York: Dodd, Mean & Company, 1931), I:12–14.

35. Link, *Wilson: Confusions*, 209–11.

36. Steven T. Ross, *American War Plans 1890–1939* (London: Frank Cass, 2002), 54, 67–74.

37. Link, *Wilson: Confusions*, 215–16. Link quotes the full text.

38. Link, 217; Brian G. Shellum, *Black Officer in a Buffalo Soldier Regiment: The Military Career of Charles Young* (Lincoln: University of Nebraska Press, 2010), 235.

39. Katherine Bjork, *Prairie Imperialists: The Indian Country Origins of American Empire* (Philadelphia: University of Pennsylvania Press, 2019), 237.

40. Bjork, *Prairie Imperialists*, 239–40.

41. Link, *Wilson: Confusions*, 216.

42. Link, 218–19.

43. Shellum, *Black Officer*, 236–37; Frank E. Vandiver, *Black Jack: The Life and Times of John J. Pershing*, 2 vols. (College Station: Texas A&M University Press, 1977), II:634; Tompkins, *Chasing*, 135–44.

44. Vandiver, *Black Jack*, II:632.

45. Vandiver, II:633.

46. Link, *Wilson: Confusions*, 284–84.

47. Link, 284–86.

48. Link, 288. The quote is Link, paraphrasing Carranza.

49. The latter part of the phrase quotes Carranza. Link, *Wilson: Confusions*, 288.

50. Link, *Wilson: Confusions*, 288.

51. Link, 288–89.

52. Link, 288–89.

53. Charles H. Harris III and Louis R. Sadler, *The Great Call-Up: The Guard, the Border, and the Mexican Revolution* (Norman: University of Oklahoma Press, 2015), 18–19; Link, *Wilson: Confusions*, 289–91.

54. Harris and Sadler, *Great Call-Up*, 19–21; "From Amos Richards Eno Pinchot," June 28, 1916, *PWW* 37:321, n1.

55. Harris and Sadler, *Great Call-Up*, 22–40.

56. "A Memorandum by Ray Stannard Baker of a Conversation at the White House," May 12, 1916, PWW 37:36.

57. Link, *Wilson: Confusions*, 297.

58. Link, 297–98.

59. Link, 299–300; Harris and Sadler, *Plan de San Diego*, 172–73.

60. Link, 300–301; Harris and Sadler, *Great Call-Up*, 61.

61. Link, *Wilson: Confusions*, 302–3.

62. Link, 303–6; Joseph A. Stout Jr., *Border Conflict: Villistas, Carrancistas, and the Punitive Expedition, 1915–1920* (Fort Worth: Texas Christian University Press, 1999), 84–87; Vandiver, *Black Jack*, I:653.

63. "A Draft of an Address to a Joint Session of Congress," June 26, 1916, PWW 37:298–304.

64. Stout, *Border*, 89–90; Katz, *Secret War*, 311.

65. Quoted in Stout, *Border*, 91.

66. "Robert Lansing to Woodrow Wilson," July 3, 1916, PWW 37:348–50; Stout, *Border*, 93–102; Katz, *Secret War*, 311–13.

67. Eileen Welsome, *The General and the Jaguar: Pershing's Hunt for Pancho Villa* (New York: Little, Brown, 2006), 223.

68. Katz, *Secret War*, 308–9.

69. Harris and Sadler, *Plan de San Diego*, 262.

70. Keren Yarhi-Milo, *Who Fights for Reputation: The Psychology of Leaders in International Conflict* (Princeton: Princeton University Press, 2018), esp. 20–22, 68–71, 265–77.

71. See, for example, Kenneth A. Schultz, *Democracy and Coercive Diplomacy* (New York: Cambridge University Press), 2001.

72. E. Neal Claussen, "He Kept U.S. Out of War: Martin H. Glynn's Keynote," *Quarterly Journal of Speech* 52, no. 1 (1966): 23–32. For the full approved text of the speech, see Democratic National Committee, *Official Report of the Proceedings of the Democratic National Convention and Committee* (Washington, DC: 1916), 14–41.

73. *Official Report*, 31–32.

CHAPTER 6. WORLD WAR I

1. This was not a linear progression. American–British relations, for example, were strained for much of 1916 due to the British blacklist of companies they believed were trading with Germany and other sundry violations of American neutrality.

2. See, for example, Stephen Badsey, *The German Corpse Factory: A Study in First World War Propaganda* (Warwick, UK: Helion, 2019).

3. See Jules Witcover, *Sabotage at Black Tom: Imperial Germany's Secret War in America* (Chapel Hill, NC: Algonquin Books, 1989).

4. Wilson's efforts came closer than many historians realize in starting peace talks; see Philip Zelikow, *The Road Less Traveled: The Secret Battle to End the Great War, 1916–1917* (New York: Public Affairs, 2021).

5. My classrooms at Marymount University overlook this same golf course, and I point out to students that this is where the president went to steady himself before his speech.

6. Quoted in Harvey DeWeerd, *President Wilson Fights His War: World War I and American Intervention* (New York: Macmillan, 1968), 201.

7. Arthur C. Walworth, *Woodrow Wilson: American Prophet* (New York: Norton, 1948), 2:101.

8. Craig, *Progressives*, 154–55; "Woodrow Wilson an Unpublished Statement," May 28, 1918, PWW 48:173–74; "Woodrow Wilson to Richard Hooker," June 5, 1918, PWW 48:242.

9. DeWeerd, *Wilson*, 203; Vandiver, *Black Jack*, I:678.

10. Vandiver, *Black Jack*, I:678.

11. Vandiver, I:678–81; John J. Pershing, *My Experiences in the World War* (New York: Harper & Row, 1931), I:14.

12. Vandiver, *Black Jack*, I:683–84.

13. Pershing, *Experiences*, I:15–16; Vandiver, *Black Jack*, I:685–86.

14. Pershing, *Experiences*, I:17–18.

15. "From Theodore Roosevelt," May 18, 1917, PWW 42:324; "A Statement," May 18, 1917, PWW, 42:324–26.

16. Vandiver, *Black Jack*, I:93–94.

17. "From Newton Diehl Baker to John Joseph Pershing," May 26, 1917, PWW 42:404–5.

18. David R. Woodward, *The American Army, and World War I* (New York: Cambridge University Press, 2014), 89–90.

19. Pershing, *Experiences*, I:40–41.

20. Included in Pershing, *Experiences*, I:39–40.

21. Andrew Carroll, *My Fellow Soldiers: General John Pershing and the Americans Who Helped Win the Great War* (New York: Penguin Press, 2017), 114–15.

22. Carroll, *My Fellow Soldiers*, 116–17; Pershing, *Experiences*, I:41–56.

23. Carroll, *My Fellow Soldiers*, 117–18.

24. Carroll, 119; Vandiver, *Black Jack*, I:717–24.

25. "Walter Hines Page to Frank Lyon Polk," July 18, 1917, PWW 43:208–9; "Frank Lyon Polk to Walter Hines Page," July 20, 1917, PWW 43:236–37.

26. William N. Still Jr., *Crisis at Sea: The United States Navy in European Waters in World War I* (Gainesville: University Press of Florida, 2006), 22–23, 281.

27. Elting E. Morison, *Admiral Sims and the Modern American Navy* (Boston: Houghton Mifflin, 1942), 339–40.

28. Edison actually did act as an adviser to the Wilson administration. His statistical report on U-boat sinkings of merchant ships was so thorough that Wilson and Daniels had it sent to Britain. Josephus Daniels, *The Cabinet Diaries of Josephus Daniels: 1913–1921*, edited by E. David Cronon (Lincoln: University of Nebraska Press, 1963), 222n21.

29. Still, *Crisis*, 5–6.

30. Daniels, *Cabinet Diaries*, see entries for May 4, 1917; May 8, 1917; June 9, 1917; July 15, 1917.

31. For a mostly critical view on the state of the fleet, see Still, *Crisis*, 6–7.

32. Craig, *Josephus Daniels*, 325–27.

33. Still, *Crisis*, 8.

34. William S. Sims, *The Victory at Sea* (New York: Doubleday, Page, 1920), 8–11.

35. "From Josephus Daniels with Enclosure," April 23, 1917, PWW 42:121–22; Sims, *Victory*, 50–51.

36. Still, *Crisis*, 341–42, 345; Morison, *Sims*, 361–63.

37. "An Address to the Officers of the Atlantic Fleet," August 11, 1917, PWW 43:428.

38. Still, *Crisis*, 344–46.

39. Carroll, *My Fellow Soldiers*, 147–48.

40. Carroll, 147–53.

41. Carroll, 158–61.

42. "From Newton Diehl Baker," December 26, 1917, PWW 45:364.

43. Meighen McCrae, *Coalition Strategy and the End of World War I: The Supreme War Council and War Planning, 1917–1918* (New York: Cambridge University Press, 2019), 13–20; David F. Trask, *The United States in the Supreme War Council: American War Aim and Inter-Allied Strategy, 1917–1918* (Middletown, CT: Wesleyan University Press, 1963), 24–29.

44. Palmer, *Newton D. Baker*, II:106–7.

45. "From Newton Diehl Baker, with Enclosures," January 3, 1918, PWW 45:438–40.

46. George B. Clark, *The American Expeditionary Force in World War I: A Statistical History, 1917–1919* (Jefferson, NC: MacFarland, 2013), 17–19.

47. Robert B. Bruce, *A Fraternity of Arms: America and France in the Great War* (Lawrence: University Press of Kansas, 2003), 160.

48. Richard Slotkin, *Lost Battalions: The Great War and the Crisis of American Neutrality* (New York: Henry Holt, 2005), 174, 176.

49. Vandiver, *Black Jack*, I:863–67; Ray Stannard Baker, *Woodrow Wilson Life and Letters: War Leader, April 6, 1917–February 28, 1918* (New York: Doubleday, Doran, 1939), 333. For Baker and Wilson discussing the tour, see "From Newton Diehl Baker," February 20, 1918, PWW 46:400–401; and Woodrow Wilson, "Two Letters to Newton Diehl Baker," February 22, 1918, PWW 46:414.

50. Palmer, *Baker*, II: 97–103.

51. Palmer, II:103–5.

52. Palmer, II:141.

53. Palmer, II:144–46.

54. David T. Zabecki, *The General's War: Operational Level Command on the Western Front in 1918* (Bloomington: University of Indiana Press, 2018), 138, 153–54. Pershing later claimed that he recognized that the Germans were limited by their need to transport supplies over the damaged rail system for their offensives so the need was not as desperate as it may have seemed.

55. Palmer, *Baker*, II:151, 312; Pershing, *Experiences*, II:94.

56. Zabecki, *General's War*, 172; Pershing, *Experiences*, II:120–24; Palmer, *Baker*, II:260–64; For the size of divisions, see Brian Neumann, "A Question of Authority: Reassessing the March-Pershing 'Feud' in World War I," *Journal of Military History* 73, no. 1135 (October 2009): n75. The 40,000 figure comes from Zabecki which includes noncombatant troops.

57. Zabecki, *General's War*, 186–87; Pershing, *Experiences*, II:145.

58. Woodward, *American*, 185–86; Neumann, "Question," 1119.

59. Woodward, *American*, 185–88.

60. Woodward, *American*, 189–90.

61. Baker's comments were made in 1934. Quoted in Edward M. Coffman, *The Hilt of the Sword: The Career of Peyton C. March* (Madison: University of Wisconsin Press, 1966), 116.

62. Pershing, *Experiences*, II:319. Quoted in Neumann, "Question," 1120n7.

63. Neumann, "Question," 1125–26.

64. Rory McGovern, *George W. Goethals and the Army: Change and Continuity in the Gilded Age and Progressive Era* (Lawrence: University of Kansas Press, 2019), 190–93.

65. Palmer, *Baker*, II:345–49.

66. Woodward, *American*, 346; James J. Cooke, *Pershing and His Generals: Command and Staff in the A.E.F.* (Westport, CT: Praeger, 1997), 132–33; Pershing, *Experiences*, II:335–36; Carroll, *My Fellow Soldiers*, 305.

67. Pershing, *Experiences*, II:359–65; Bullitt Lowry, *Armistice 1918* (Kent, OH: Kent State University Press, 1996), 67–71.

68. Lowry, *Armistice*, 95–96.
69. Pershing, *Experiences*, II:366–67; Lowry, *Armistice*, 96.
70. Lowry, *Armistice*, 97–98; "From Edward Mandell House," October 31, 1918, PWW 51:523–525.
71. Lowry, *Armistice*, 98–99; "From Newton Diehl Baker, with Enclosures," November 1, 1918, PWW 51:544–45; "From Newton Diehl Baker, with Enclosure," November 5, 1918, PWW 51:596–98; "To Newton Diehl Baker," November 7, 1918, PWW 51:617–18.

CHAPTER 7. RUSSIAN INTERVENTION

1. Cooper, *Wilson*, 439.
2. Supply figures come from Frederick Palmer, *Bliss, Peacemaker: The Life and Letters of General Tasker Howard Bliss* (New York: Dodd, Mead, 1934), 290.
3. Palmer, *Bliss*, 290.
4. Woodrow Wilson, "An Address to the United States Chamber of Commerce," February 3, 1915, PWW 32:180.
5. Committee for Public Information, George Creel, Chairman, "The German-Bolshevik Conspiracy," War Information Series, no. 20 (October 1918), 3.
6. Christopher Lasch, *The American Liberals and the Russian Revolution* (New York: McGraw-Hill, 1972), 113; Donald Davis and Eugene P. Trani, *The First Cold War: The Legacy of Woodrow Wilson in U.S.-Soviet Relations* (Columbia, MO: University of Missouri Press, 2002), 48, 75–76; Carl J. Richard, *When the United States Invaded Russia* (New York: Rowman & Littlefield, 2013), 23. On Robins providing the documents, see George F. Kennan, *Russia Leaves the War: Soviet-American Relations, 1917–1920* (Princeton: Princeton University Press, 1956), 413.
7. Lasch, *American Liberals*, 113–14; W. B. Fowler, *British-American Relations, 1917–1918: The Role of Sir William Wiseman* (Princeton: Princeton University Press, 1969), 177; Kennan, *Russia Leaves*, 446–49.
8. Fowler, *British-American Relations*, 177.
9. David S. Foglesong, *America's Secret War against Bolshevism: U.S. Intervention in the Russian Civil War, 1917–1920* (Chapel Hill: University of North Carolina Press, 1995), 191.
10. Arno J. Mayer, *Wilson vs. Lenin: Political Origins of the New Diplomacy, 1917–1918* (Cleveland, OH: Meridian, 1959), 287–88; Trask, *War Council*, 101; Joint Notes #5 December 23, 1917, M923, RG120, NARA.
11. Trask, *War Council*, 103; Fowler, *British-American Relations*, 167.
12. From 1912 until mid-January 1918, the British ambassador to the United States was Sir Cecil Arthur Spring-Rice. While a capable diplomat, he was

a close friend to Theodore Roosevelt and even served as the best man for Roosevelt's second wedding. While this hampered his effectiveness somewhat, given Roosevelt and Wilson's mutual disdain, both he and Wilson treated each other with courtesy. Still, London sent Wiseman as a second channel to the White House, bypassing Spring-Rice. London replaced the ambassador in early 1918 due to a conflict with other British diplomats, rather than because of his relationship with Wilson.

13. Fowler, *British-American Relations*, 170–71.

14. Fowler, 170–71; Ray Stannard Baker, *Woodrow Wilson: Life and Letters: Armistice* (New York: Doubleday, Doran, 1939), 4–5.

15. Fowler, *British-American Relations*, 172–73. The chief of the Imperial General Staff, Sir Henry Wilson, was especially focused on the supposed threat to India.

16. Not unlike his speaking tour in the United States in the late summer of 1919, trying to bypass the U.S. Senate by going directly to the people.

17. Lasch, *American Liberals*, 94–95; Foglesong, *Secret War*, 191–92; Baker, *Life and Letters: Armistice*, 283–84.

18. Foglesong, *Secret War*, 189–90; Fowler, *British-American Relations*, 166.

19. George F. Kennan, *The Decision to Intervene: Soviet-American Relations, 1917–1920* (Princeton: Princeton University Press, 1958), 45–46; Foglesong, *Secret War*, 193.

20. Foglesong, *Secret War*, 193.

21. Kennan, *Decision*, 56–57.

22. "To Josephus Daniels," April 8, 1918, PWW 47:290.

23. Wilson quoted in Kennan, *Decision*, 57.

24. Still, *Crisis at Sea*, 87–88.

25. Wilson quoted in Fowler, *British-American Relations*, 180.

26. Kennan, *Decision*, 268–69; Fowler, *British-American Relations*, 181.

27. "From Newton Diehl Baker, with Enclosures," Mary 28, 1918, PWW 48:179–82.

28. Kennan, *Decision*, 359–61.

29. Betty Miller Unterberger, *The United States, Revolutionary Russia, and the Rise of Czechoslovakia* (Chapel Hill: University of North Carolina Press, 1989), 223–24.

30. Kennan, *Decision*, 381–84.

31. Kennan, 384–90; "To Robert Lansing, with Enclosure" June 17, 1918, PWW 48:335–36.

32. Fowler, *British-American Relations*, 188n62.

33. Kennan, *Decision*, 357–58.

34. Kennan, 365–79; Trask, *War Council*, 118–19; Unterberger, *Czechoslovakia*, 248–49; Baker, *Wilson: Armistice*, 283–84; for March's opinion, see "Peyton Conway March to Newton Diehl Baker, with Enclosure," June 24, 1918, PWW 48:418–21.

35. John W. Long, "American Intervention in Russia: The North Russian Expedition, 1918–19," *Diplomatic History* 6, no. 1 (Winter 1982): 56.

36. James Carl Nelson, *The Polar Bear Expedition: The Heroes of America's Forgotten Invasion of Russia, 1918–1919* (New York: William Morrow, 2019), 28–29.

37. Fowler, *British-American Relations*, 188.

38. "To Frank Lyon Polk, with Enclosure," July 17, 1918, PWW 48:639–43.

39. Kennan, *Decision*, 264, 424–25.

40. Long, "American Intervention," 59–60.

41. "From Robert Lansing, with Enclosures," September 9, 1918, PWW 49:492, 496.

42. Long, "American Intervention," 56n38.

43. Nelson, *Polar Bear*, 35; Foglesong, *Secret War*, 208.

44. Long, "American Intervention," 57–58.

45. Long, 59–60; "From Peyton Conway March, with Enclosure," September 12, 1918, PWW 49:531–32; "From Robert Lansing, with Enclosure," September 16, 1918, PWW 51:17; "From Benedict Crowell, with Enclosure," September 17, 1918, PWW 51:33.

46. "To Robert Lansing, with Enclosure," September 5, 1918, PWW 49:448; Long, 60, n60.

47. "Colville Adrian de Rune Barclay to the Foreign Office," September 9, 1919, PWW 49:508. See also "From Robert Lansing, with Enclosure," September 11, 1918, PWW 49:516–17.

48. "Sir William Wiseman to Arthur Cecil Murray," September 14, 1918, PWW 51:8–9.

49. "To Robert Lansing," September 18, 1918, PWW 51:50.

50. Nelson, *Polar Bear*, 89–93.

51. "From Robert Lansing," September 17, 1918, PWW 51:31; "To Robert Lansing," September 19, 1918, PWW 51:75.

52. "To Robert Lansing, with Enclosure," June 17, 1918, PWW 48:335. This is the same message in which Wilson remarked that the Czechs were "cousins" to the Russians.

53. Kennan, *Decision*, 394–98; "A Memorandum by Robert Lansing," July 6, 1918, PWW 48:542–43; "Josephus Daniels to Austin Melvin Knight," July 6, 1918, PWW 48:543; "From the Diary of Josephus Daniels," July 6, 1918, PWW 48:544.

54. Kennan, *Decision*, 405–8.
55. William Graves, *America's Siberian Adventure, 1918–1920* (n.p.: Carousel, 2019), 10–11; Palmer, *Bliss*, 321.
56. Graves, *Adventure*, 10–11.
57. Graves, 74, 120–23, 141.
58. Graves, 103, 122–23, 131–36.
59. Foglesong, *Secret War*, 180–82.
60. Foglesong, 182–84.
61. Nelson, *Polar Bear*, 228–30; Leonid I. Strakhovsky, *Intervention at Archangel: The Story of Allied Intervention and Russian Counter-Revolution in North Russia, 1918–1920* (Princeton: Princeton University Press, 1944), 175; Capt. Joel R. Moore, Lt. Harry H. Meade, and Lt. Lewis E. Jahns, *History of the American Expedition Fighting the Bolsheviks: U.S. Military Intervention in Soviet Russia, 1918–1919* (Detroit: Polar Bear, 1920), 279–80.
62. "From Tasker Howard Bliss," May 29, 1919, PWW 59:599–601; "From Gilbert Fairchild Close," June 6, 1919, PWW 60:241; "To Tasker Howard Bliss," June 10, 1919, PWW 60:359.
63. The number of casualties varies from source to source. For Siberia, I am using Richard, *When the United States Invaded Russia*, 171. For the northern expedition, I am using Nelson, *Polar Bear*, 270.
64. Palmer, *Bliss*, 295.
65. Palmer, 302, 318.
66. Fowler, *British-American Relations*, 192.
67. Cooper, *Wilson*, 76. Wilson was, for example, proud of the Jones Act of 1916, which granted the Philippines its own elected legislature. After leaving the White House in 1921 Wilson kept a statue given to him by a Filipino artist on the mantel in his bedroom. It featured an adult woman, representing the United States, leading a child (the Philippines) over broken chains and a crushed crown.

CHAPTER 8. OCCUPATION DUTY AND SMALLER INTERVENTIONS

1. The best scholarly study is Keith L. Nelson, *Victors Divided: American and the Allies in Germany, 1918–1923* (Berkeley: University of California Press, 1975).
2. "A Translation of a Letter from Ferdinand Foch, with Enclosure," March 14, 1919, PWW 55:508. Written in January, the document was sent to Wilson in March. Emphasis in original.
3. Alexander Barnes, *In a Strange Land: The American Occupation of Germany, 1918–1923* (Atglen, PA: Schiffer Military History, 2011), 11–12.
4. Barnes, *Strange Land*, 15–16.
5. Barnes, 19–20, 40.

6. Barnes, 42. For details on the German retreat, including POWs on the roads, see the operational report, "Conditions Encountered in Advance," Center of Military History, U.S. Army, *United States Army in the World War, 1917–1919: American Occupation of Germany* (Honolulu: University Press of the Pacific, 1991, 2005 reprint), 15–44; R. Scott Walker, "The U.S. Third Army and the Advance to Koblenz, 7 December–17 December 1918," *Army History* (Fall 1994): 32, 29.

7. Walker, "U.S. Third Army," 30–31; Paul Herbert, "Watch on the Rhine: The 1st Division in the Occupation of Germany, 1918–1919," *On Point* 15, no. 2 (Fall 2009): 37; Susan Zeiger, *Entangling Alliances: Foreign War Brides and American Soldiers in the Twentieth Century* (New York: New York University Press, 2010), 48–50.

8. Douglas F. Habib, "Chastity, Masculinity, and Military Efficiency: The United States Army in Germany, 1918–1923," *International History Review* 28, no. 4 (December 2006): 738–40.

9. Nelson, *Victors*, 40–41.

10. Nelson, 87, 95, 109, 119, 124, 139, 145–46.

11. E. Jay Howenstine Jr., "Demobilization after World War I," *Quarterly Journal of Economics*, November 1943, 92; "Demobilization after World War I," *Social Science Review*, June 1944, 249; Peyton C. March, *The Nation at War* (Garden City, NJ: Doubleday, Doran, 1932), 310–12.

12. Howenstine, "Demobilization," 94–97; March, *Nation at War*, 315–29.

13. It became the Kingdom of Yugoslavia in 1929. I will use the later, more well-known name here.

14. Stephen Bonsal, *Suitors and Suppliants: The Little Nations at Versailles* (New York: Prentice Hall, 1946), 113–40; Cooper, *Wilson*, 492–94.

15. Dejan Djokić, *Nikola Pašić and Ante Trumbić: The Kingdom of Serbs, Croats, and Slovenes* (London: Haas Histories, 2010), 114–21; Spencer M. DiScala, *Vittorio Emanuele Orlando: Italy* (London: Haas Histories, 2010), 152–60; Margaret MacMillan, *Paris 1919* (New York: Random House, 2001), 298.

16. "Traù Recovered without a Fight by Olympia's Men," *New York Times*, September 28, 1919; "Andrews Keeping Order," *New York Times*, October 1, 1919; MacMillian, *Paris*, 302.

17. "Landing at Traù Hotly Condemned in Senate Debate," *New York Times*, September 30, 1919; "Senate Gets Facts of Traù Incident," *New York Times*, October 3, 1919; "From the Diary of Josephus Daniels," October 7, 1919, PWW 63:557; "Josephus Daniels to Edith Bolling Galt Wilson," October 7, 1919, PWW 63:557–58.

18. Andrew Mango, *From the Sultan to Atatürk: Turkey* (London: Haus, 2009), 56–57; MacMillian, *Paris*, 379, 435; "To Newton Diehl Baker," February 8,

1919, PWW 55:27–28; "From Newton Diehl Baker," February 11, 1919, PWW 55:81–82.

19. Henry P. Beers, "United States Naval Detachment in Turkish Waters, 1919–1924," *Military Affairs* 7, no. 4 (Winter 1943): 209–13.

20. Beers, "Turkish Waters," 214–15; Peter M. Buzanski, "The InterAllied Investigation of the Greek Invasion of Smyrna, 1919," *The Historian* 25, no. 3 (May 1963): 325–327; Ray Stannard Baker, *Woodrow Wilson and World Settlement* (New York: Doubleday, Page, 1922), II:191–93; Mango, *Sultan to Atatürk*, 63; MacMillian, *Paris*, 431–33.

21. Beers, "Turkish Waters," 214–16.

22. On Colby, see Daniel M. Smith, "Bainbridge Colby and the Good Neighbor Policy, 1920–1921," *Mississippi Valley Historical Review* 50, no. 1 (June 1963): 56–78.

23. Thomas, *Cuba*, 526–29.

24. Musicant, *Banana Wars*, 74.

25. Thomas, *Cuba*, 529; "From Robert Lansing, with Enclosure," February 21, 1917, PWW 41:269n1; "Cuban Troops Take Two Rebel Cities," *New York Times*, February 18, 1917.

26. "Robert Lansing to Pearl Merrill Griffith," February 23, 1917, PWW 41:279.

27. "From the Diary of Josephus Daniels," February 27, 1917, PWW 41:298.

28. This USS *Maine* was the successor ship to the *Maine* destroyed in Havana harbor in 1898. Commissioned in 1902 she was scrapped in 1923. For the list of ships involved see "From the Diary of Josephus Daniels," February 27, 1917, PWW 41:299, n1. Figures are from *Annual Reports of the Navy Department for the Fiscal Year 1917* (Washington, DC: U.S. Government Printing Office, 1918), 840.

29. When the United States declared war on Austro-Hungary in December 1917, Cuba did as well.

30. Musicant, *Banana Wars*, 78.

31. Jeffrey W. Meiser, *Power and Restraint: The Rise of the United States, 1898–1941* (Washington, DC: Georgetown University Press, 2015), 178–79.

32. Louis A. Perez Jr., *Cuba under the Platt Amendment, 1902–1934* (Pittsburgh: University of Pittsburgh Press, 1986), 193.

33. Menocal was the incumbent Conservative president. The Liberal candidate was Miguel Mariano Gómez. The latter defeated Zayas for the Liberal Party nomination, so Zayas formed his own party and formed an alliance with Menocal in exchange for supporting Menocal in 1924 running for another term. Louis A. Perez Jr., "The Military and Electoral Politics: The Cuban Election of 1920," *Military Affairs* 37, no. 1 (February 1973): 5.

34. Meiser, *Power*, 179–80; Lars Schoultz, *In Their Own Best Interest: A History of the U.S. Effort to Improve Latin America* (Cambridge, MA: Harvard University Press, 2018), 65–68.

35. Ludwell Lee Montague, *Haiti and the United States, 1714–1938* (Durham: University of North Carolina Press, 1940), 214–17.

36. Montague, *Haiti*, 219–20; Magdaline W. Shannon, *Jean Price-Mars, the Haitian Elite, and the American Occupation, 1915–35* (New York: St. Martin's, 1996), 36–37.

37. Hans Schmidt, *Maverick Marine: General Smedley D. Butler and the Contradictions of American Military History* (Lexington: University Press of Kentucky, 1987), 83.

38. Schmidt, *Maverick Marine*, 84–85; Shannon, *Jean Price-Mars*, 36–37.

39. Montague, *Haiti*, 221–23.

40. Montague, 224–28.

41. Schmidt, *Maverick Marine*, 89–90.

42. Schmidt, *Maverick Marine*, 93; Montague, *Haiti*, 232–33; George B. Clark, *The United States Military in Latin America: A History of Interventions through 1934* (Jefferson, NC: McFarland, 2014), 76–78.

43. Clark, *Military in Latin America*, 81–84; Montague, *Haiti*, 233; Munro, *Intervention and Dollar Diplomacy in the Caribbean, 1900–1921* (Princeton: Princeton University Press, 1980), 373; Daugherty, *Counterinsurgency*, 90.

44. Clark, *Military in Latin America*, 85–93; Munro, *Intervention*, 73; Daugherty, *Counterinsurgency*, 91–92.

45. "To Bainbridge Colby, with Enclosure," August 25, 1920, PWW 66:63.

46. "From Bainbridge Colby," August 28, 1920, PWW 66:72–73; "To Bainbridge Colby," August 30, 1920, PWW 66:78; "Two Letters from Bainbridge Colby," September 6, 1920, PWW 66:99–100.

47. Musicant, *Banana Wars*, 70.

48. Benjamin T. Harrison, "Woodrow Wilson and Nicaragua," *Caribbean Quarterly* 51, no. 1 (March 2005): 25–27, 41; Kaplan, *U.S. Imperialism*, 41.

49. Kaplan, *U.S. Imperialism*, 408–13.

50. Kaplan, 417–24.

51. "U.S. Marines Raid Newspaper in Nicaragua, Wreck Presses," *New York Times*, February 10, 1921; "Marines Who Wrecked Newspaper Arrested," *New York Times*, February 11, 1921; "Admiral Bryan at Corinto," *New York Times*, February 20, 2920; George W. Baker, "The Wilson Administration and Nicaragua, 1913–1921," *The Americas* 22, no. 4 (April 1966): 373–74.

52. Jose Ignacio Rodrigues, *American Constitutions: A Compilation of the Political Constitutions of the Independent Nations of the New World with Short Historical*

Notes and Various Appendixes, 2 vols. (Washington, DC: U.S. Government Printing Office, 1906), 1:420.

53. Winkler, *Nexus*, 64–69, 82; George W. Baker Jr., "The Wilson Administration and Panama, 1913–1921," *Journal of Inter-American Studies* 8, no. 2 (April 1966): 281–82.

54. Baker, "Panama," 281–82.

55. Baker, 287–88; "See Revolt in Panama if Wilson Doesn't Act," *New York Times*, June 14, 1916; "Panamans [sic] Request U.S. to Run Their Election," *New York Times*, March 5, 1916, 3.

56. "Two Letters to Robert Lansing," February 6, 1917, PWW 41:131–32; "From Robert Lansing," March 26, 1917, PWW 41:472–73; "Three Letters to Robert Lansing" March 26, 1917, PWW 41:475–76; "Robert Lansing to William Jennings Price," April 12, 1917, PWW 42:51.

57. Baker, "Panama," 289; Michael Streeter, *Central America and the Treaty of Versailles* (London: Haas, 2011), 61–62.

58. The two cities were within the Canal Zone but were supposed to be governed by local jurisdiction.

59. Baker, "Panama," 289–93; "America Assumes Control in Panama," *New York Times*, June 29, 1918; "Porras New Panama Chief," *New York Times*, October 14, 1918; "Lefevre Now Panama's President," *Washington Post*, February 2, 1920; "Panama Election Puzzle," *New York Times*, July 22, 1920; "Panama Elects Porras," *New York Times*, August 3, 1920; "Porras to Visit Washington," *Washington Post*, August 31, 1920; "President-Elect Porras of Panama, Guest of Nation, on *Mayflower* with Officials, Visits Mount Vernon," *Washington Post*, September 19, 1920.

60. George W. Baker, "Ideas and Realities in the Wilson Administration's Relations with Honduras," *The Americas* 21, no. 1 (July 1964): 4–8.

61. Baker, "Honduras," 9–14; Stefan Rinke, *Latin American and World War I* (New York: Cambridge University Press, 2017), 168; Michael Streeter, *South America and the Treaty of Versailles* (London: Haas, 2010), 133.

62. Baker, "Honduras," 14–15.

63. George W. Baker, "The Woodrow Wilson Administration and Guatemalan Relations," *The Historian* 27, no. 2 (February 1965): 156–68.

64. Congressional Research Service, "Instances of Use of United States Armed Forces Abroad, 1798–2020" (Washington, DC: CRS, 2020), 9.

65. Carlos Francisco Parra, "Valientes Nogalenses: The 1918 Battle between the U.S. and Mexico That Transformed Ambos Nogales," *Journal of Arizona History* 51, no. 1 (Spring 2010): 11–21.

66. John A. Hamilton, " 'Upon No Account Were They to Undertake an Invasion of Mexico': American Troops and the Third Battle of Ciudad Juárez, June 1919," *Southwestern Historical Quarterly* 122, no. 4 (2019): 424–36.

67. Wilson's instincts were essentially correct. Fall was the first U.S. cabinet official sentenced to federal prison for his Teapot Dome role in the 1920s.

68. Link, *Wilson: Confusions*, 282n5; Clifford W. Trow, "Woodrow Wilson and the Mexican Interventionist Movement of 1919," *Journal of American History* 58, no. 1 (June 1971): 57.

69. As a neutral, especially one that leaned toward Berlin, Mexico was not invited to the peace talks.

70. "Two Letters from Robert Lansing," August 4, 1919, PWW 62: 142; "From Robert Lansing, with Enclosure," August 18, 1919, PWW 62:332–33; "From Robert Lansing with Enclosure," August 21, 1919, PWW 62:449–51; "To Robert Lansing," August 22, 1919, PWW 62:459; Trow, "Woodrow Wilson," 59.

71. Trow, "Woodrow Wilson," 58–59.

72. Trow, 61–64, 67n76.

73. Trow, 66–67.

74. Cooper, *Wilson*, 547–48.

75. Congressional Research Service, "Instances of Use," 9.

76. Evans F. Carlson, "Legal Bases for Use of Foreign Armed Forces in China," *Proceedings of the U.S. Naval Institute* 62, no. 405 (November 1936): 1547–48.

77. Robert Nield, *China's Foreign Places: The Foreign Presence in China in the Treaty Port Era, 1840–1943* (Hong Kong: Hong Kong University Press, 2015), 75–80, 162–64, 291.

78. Kemp Tolley, *Yangtze Patrol: The U.S. Navy in China* (Annapolis, MD: Naval Institute Press, 1971), 71–72.

79. The "bandits" might also be interpreted as resistance to the foreign powers' influence over China, but that discussion belongs elsewhere. See Eric J. Hobsbawm, *Bandits* (New York: Dell, 1969); Benjamin R. Beede, ed., *The War of 1898 and U.S. Interventions, 1898–1934: An Encyclopedia* (New York: Garland, 1994), 606; Tolley, *Yangtze Patrol*, 74.

80. Tolley, *Yangtze Patrol*, 76.

81. William R. Braisted, *The United States Navy in the Pacific, 1909–1922* (Annapolis, MD: Naval Institute Press, 1971), 313–14.

82. Tolley, *Yangtze Patrol*, 76–81; Braisted, *United States Navy*, 314–15.

83. Louis Morton, "Army and Marines on the China Station: A Study in Military and Political Rivalry," *Pacific Historical Review* 29, no. 1 (February 1960): 51–53.

CONCLUSION

1. Errol MacGregor Clauss, "'Pink in Appearance, but Red at Heart': The United States and the Far Eastern Republic, 1920–1922," *Journal of American-East Asian Relations* 1, no. 3 (1992): 328.

2. Indeed, Britain was uninterested in having the other Allies, outside of Dominion forces, join them in the Middle East campaigns, which would have introduced other powers as rivals into the region Britain was so interested in dominating.

3. Eisenhower, *Intervention!*, 32.

BIBLIOGRAPHY

PRIMARY SOURCES

Selected Books and Articles by Woodrow Wilson

Wilson, Woodrow. *Cabinet Government in the United States*. Stamford, CT: Overbrook, 1947.

———. *Congressional Government*. 15th ed. Boston: Houghton Mifflin, 1900.

———. *Constitutional Government in the United States*. New York: Columbia University Press, 1908.

———. *Division and Reunion, 1829–1889*. New York: Longmans Green, 1901.

———. *A History of the American People*. Vols. 1–5. New York: William H. Wise, 1931.

———. *The Papers of Woodrow Wilson*. Edited by Arthur S. Link, et al. 69 vols. Princeton, NJ: Princeton University Press, 1966–96.

———. *Selected Literary and Political Papers and Addresses of Woodrow Wilson*. New York: Grosset and Dunlap, n.d.

———. *The State: Elements of Historical and Practical Politics*. London: Isbister, 1900.

Published Government Documents

Annual Reports of the Navy Department: 1917. Washington, DC: Government Printing Office, 1918.

Inquiry into Occupation and Administration of Haiti and Santo Domingo: Hearings before a Select Committee on Haiti and Santo Domingo. United States Senate. Government Printing Office, 1922.

Investigation of Mexican Affairs. Preliminary Report and Hearings of the Committee on Foreign Relations, United States Senate. 2 vols. Washington, DC: Government Printing Office, 1920.

Papers Relating to the Foreign Relations of the United States: The Lansing Papers, 1914–1920. Vols. 1–2. Washington, DC: Government Printing Office, 1939–40.

Papers Relating to the Foreign Relations of the United States: 1911. Washington, DC: Government Printing Office, 1918.

Papers Relating to the Foreign Relations of the United States: 1912. Washington, DC: Government Printing Office, 1919.

Papers Relating to the Foreign Relations of the United States: 1913. Washington, DC: Government Printing Office, 1920.

Papers Relating to the Foreign Relations of the United States: 1914. Washington, DC: Government Printing Office, 1922.

Papers Relating to the Foreign Relations of the United States: 1915. Washington, DC: Government Printing Office, 1924.

Library of Congress Manuscript Collections

Anderson, Chandler P.

Baker, Newton D.

Baker, Ray Stannard

Breckinridge, Henry (Breckinridge Family)

Bryan, William Jennings

Daniels, Josephus

Fletcher, Henry P.

Garfield, James R.

Lansing, Robert

Mayo, Admiral Henry T.

McAdoo, William

Pershing, General John J.

Scott, General Hugh

Taft, William Howard

Wilson, Woodrow

Wood, General Leonard

National Archives and Records Administration

Records Group 59. Correspondence between President Woodrow Wilson and Secretary of State William Jennings Bryan.

Records Group 59. Records of the Department of State: Purport Lists for the Decimal File, M973.

Records Group 59. Records of the Department of State Relating to Internal Affairs of Mexico, 1910–1929, M274.

Records Group 59. Records of the Department of State Relating to Mexican Relations with the United States, 1910–1929, M314.

Newspapers

New York Times. New York. 1913–20.

New York World, The. New York. 1912–15.

Washington Post. Washington, DC. 1913–20.

Books, Articles, and Miscellaneous Papers

American Mexican Claims Commission. *Report to the Secretary of State.* Washington, DC: GPO, 1948.

Bryan, William Jennings, and Mary Baird Bryan. *The Memoirs of William Jennings Bryan.* New York: Haskell House, 1971.

Butler, Smedley D. *Old Gimlet Eye: The Adventures of Smedley D. Butler as Told to Lowell Thomas.* New York: Farrar and Rinehart, 1933.

Committee for Public Information. George Creel, Chairman. "The German-Bolshevik Conspiracy." War Information Series, no. 20. October 1918.

Congressional Research Service. "Instances of Use of United States Armed Forces Abroad, 1798–2020." Washington, DC: CRS, 2020.

Curtis, Roy Emerson. "The Law of Hostile Military Expeditions as Applied by the United States." *American Journal of International Law* 8, no. 1 (January 1914): 1–37.

———. "The Law of Hostile Military Expeditions as Applied by the United States." *American Journal of International Law* 8, no. 2 (April 1914): 224–52.

Daniels, Josephus. *The Cabinet Diaries of Josephus Daniels, 1913–1921.* Edited by E. David Cronon. Lincoln: University of Nebraska Press, 1963.

Davis, Will B. *Experiences and Observations of an American Consular Officer during the Recent Mexican Revolutions.* Los Angeles: Wayside Press, 1920.

DeFornaro, Carlo. *Carranza and Mexico.* New York: Mitchell Kennerley, 1915.

Democratic National Committee. *Official Report of the Proceedings of the Democratic National Convention and Committee.* Washington, DC: 1916.

Graves, William. *America's Siberian Adventure, 1918–1920.* N.p.: Carousel Books, 2019.

Grayson, Rear Admiral Cary T. *Woodrow Wilson: An Intimate Memoir.* Washington, DC: Potomac Books, 1977.

Landau, Captain Henry. *The Enemy Within: The Inside Story of German Sabotage in America.* New York: G. P. Putnam's Sons, 1937.

Lawrence, David. *The True Story of Woodrow Wilson.* New York: George H. Doran, 1924.

Lind, John, Papers. Zimmerman Library, University of New Mexico. Albuquerque, NM.

March, Peyton C. *The Nation at War.* Garden City, NJ: Doubleday, Doran, 1932.

Moore, Capt. Joel R., Lt. Harry H. Meade, and Lt. Lewis E. Jahns. *History of the American Expedition Fighting the Bolsheviks: U.S. Military Intervention in Soviet Russia, 1918–1919.* Detroit: Polar Bear, 1920.

O'Shaughnessy, Edith. *A Diplomat's Wife in Mexico.* New York: Harper and Brothers, 1916.

Palmer, Frederick. *Bliss, Peacemaker: The Life and Letters of General Tasker Howard Bliss*. New York: Dodd, Mead, 1934.

———. *Newton D. Baker: America at War*. 2 vols. New York: Dodd, Mead & Co., 1931.

Pershing, John J. *My Experiences in the World War*. 2 vols. New York: Harper & Row, 1931.

Pray, Eleanor L. "Wars, Revolutions, and Foreign Intervention." In *Letters from Vladivostok, 1894–1930*, edited by Birgitta Ingemanson, 160–93. Seattle: University of Washington Press, 2013.

Seymour, Charles. *The Intimate Papers of Colonel House Arranged as a Narrative*. Vol. 1–4. Boston: Houghton Mifflin, 1926–28.

Sims, William S. *The Victory at Sea*. New York: Doubleday, Page, 1920.

Tompkins, Frank. *Chasing Villa: The Last Campaign of the U.S. Cavalry*. Silver City, NM: High-Lonesome Books, 1996.

Tumulty, Joseph P. *Woodrow Wilson as I Know Him*. Garden City, NY: Doubleday, Page, 1921.

United States Navy. *Yangtze River Patrol and Other U.S. Navy Asiatic Fleets Activities in China, 1920–1942*. N.p., n.d.

Von Rintelen, Captain. *The Dark Invader: Wartime Reminiscences of a German Naval Intelligence Officer*. New York: MacMillan, 1933.

Wilson, Henry Lane. *Diplomatic Episodes in Mexico, Belgium, and Chile*. New York: Doubleday, Page, 1927.

SECONDARY SOURCES

Books, Articles, and Dissertations

Ambrosius, Lloyd E. *Wilson Statecraft: Theory and Practice of Liberal Internationalism during World War I*. Wilmington, DE: Scholarly Resources, 1984.

———. *Wilsonianism: Woodrow Wilson and His Legacy in American Foreign Relations*. London: Palgrave Macmillan, 2002

Anderson, Mark C. *Revolution by Headlines: Mass Media in the Foreign Policy of Francisco "Pancho" Villa*. Norman: University of Oklahoma Press, 2001.

Atkins, G. Pope, and Larman Curtis Wilson. *The Dominican Republic and the United States: From Imperialism to Transnationalism*. Athens: University of Georgia Press, 1998.

Baecker, Thomas. "The Arms of the 'Ypiranga': The German Side." *The Americas* 30, no. 1 (July 1973): 1–17.

Baker, George W., Jr. "Ideas and Realities in the Wilson Administration's Relations with Honduras." *The Americas* 21, no. 1 (July 1964): 3–19.

———. "The Wilson Administration and Nicaragua, 1913–1921." *The Americas* 22, no. 4 (April 1966): 339–76.

———. "The Wilson Administration and Panama, 1913–1921." *Journal of Inter-American Studies* 8, no 2 (April 1966): 279–93.

———. "The Woodrow Wilson Administration and Guatemalan Relations.'" *The Historian* 27, no. 2 (February 1965): 155–69.

Baker, Ray Stannard. *Woodrow Wilson: Life and Letters.* 8 vols. New York: Double-day, Doran, 1927–39.

———. *Woodrow Wilson and World Settlement.* 3 vols. New York: Doubleday, Pages, 1922.

Barnes, Alexandria. *In A Strange Land: The American Occupation of Germany, 1918–1923.* Atglen, PA: Schiffer Military Publishing, 2011.

Beede, Benjamin R., ed. *The War of 1898 and U.S. Interventions, 1898–1934: An Encyclopedia.* New York: Garland, 1994.

Beers, Henry P. "United States Naval Detachment in Turkish Waters, 1919–1924." *Military Affairs* 7, no. 4 (Winter 1943): 209–20.

Benbow, Mark. "'All the Brains I Can Borrow': Woodrow Wilson and Intelligence Gathering in Mexico, 1913–1915." *Studies in Intelligence* 51, no. 4 (December 2007), 1–15.

———. *Leading Them to the Promised Land: Woodrow Wilson, Covenant Theology, and the Mexican Revolution, 1913–1915.* Kent, OH: Kent University Press, 2010.

Berg, A. Scott. *Wilson.* New York: G. P. Putnam's Sons, 2013.

Berman, Eli, and David A. Lake *Proxy Wars: Suppressing Violence through Local Agents.* Ithaca, NY: Cornell University Press, 2019.

Bjork, Katherine. *Prairie Imperialists: The Indian Country Origins of American Empire.* Philadelphia: University of Pennsylvania Press, 2019.

Blaisdell, Lowell L. "Henry Lane Wilson and the Overthrow of Madero." *Southwestern Social Science Quarterly* 43, no. 2 (September 1962): 126–35.

Blasier, Cole. *The Hovering Giant: United States Responses to Revolutionary Change in Latin America.* Pittsburgh: University of Pittsburgh Press, 1976.

Bonsal, Stephen. *Suitors and Suppliants: The Little Nations at Versailles.* New York: Prentice Hall, 1946.

Bragdon, Henry Wilkinson. *Woodrow Wilson: The Academic Years.* Cambridge, MA: Harvard University Press, 1967.

Braisted, William R. *The United States Navy in the Pacific, 1909–1922.* Annapolis, MD: Naval Institute Press, 1971.

Brinkley, George A. *The Volunteer Army and Allied Intervention in South Russia, 1917–1921.* Notre Dame, IN: Notre Dame Press, 1966.

Bruce, Robert B. *A Fraternity of Arms: America and France in the Great War.* Lawrence: University Press of Kansas, 2003.

Burns, Sarah. *The Politics of War Powers: The Theory and History of Presidential Unilateralism.* Lawrence: University Press of Kansas, 2019.

Buzanski, Peter M. "The Interallied Investigation of the Greek Invasion of Smyrna, 1919." *The Historian* 25, no. 3 (May 1963): 325–43.

Calder, Bruce J. "Caudillos and Gavilleros versus the United States Marines: Guerrilla Insurgency during the Dominican Intervention, 1916–1924." *Hispanic American Historical Review* 58, no. 4 (1978): 649–75.

Calhoun, Frederick S. *Power and Principle: Armed Intervention in Wilsonian Foreign Policy.* Kent, OH: Kent State University Press, 1986.

———. *Uses of Force and Wilsonian Foreign Policy.* Kent, OH: Kent State University Press, 1993.

Calvert, Peter. *The Mexican Revolution, 1910–1914: The Diplomacy of Anglo-American Conflict.* Cambridge, MA: Cambridge University Press, 1968.

Carlson, Evans F. "Legal Bases for Use of Foreign Armed Forces in China." *Proceedings of the U.S. Naval Institute* 62, no. 405 (November 1936): 1544–56.

Carroll, Andrew. *My Fellow Soldiers: General John Pershing and the Americans Who Helped Win the Great War.* New York: Penguin Press, 2017.

Carson, Austin. *Secret Wars: Covert Conflict in International Politics.* Princeton, NJ: Princeton University Press, 2018.

Center of Military History, U.S. Army. *United States Army in the World War, 1917–1919: American Occupation of Germany.* Honolulu: University Press of the Pacific, 1991; 2005 reprint.

Challener, Richard D. *Admirals, Generals, and American Foreign Policy, 1898–1914.* Princeton, NJ: Princeton University Press, 1973.

Clark, George B. *The American Expeditionary Force in World War I: A Statistical History.* Jefferson, NC: McFarland, 2013.

———. *The United States Military in Latin America: A History of Interventions through 1934.* Jefferson, NC: McFarland, 2014.

Clarke, I. F. *Future Wars.* Liverpool: Liverpool University Press, 2012.

Clauss, Errol MacGregor. "'Pink in Appearance, but Red at Heart': The United States and the Far Eastern Republic, 1920–1922." *Journal of American-East Asian Relations* 1, no. 3 (1992): 327–57.

Claussen, E. Neal. "'He Kept Us Out of War': Martin H. Glynn's Keynote." *Quarterly Journal of Speech* 52, no. 1 (1966): 23–32.

Clements, Kendrick A. *William Jennings Bryan: Missionary Isolationist.* Knoxville: University of Tennessee Press, 1982.

———. *Woodrow Wilson: World Statesman.* Boston: Twayne, 1987.

————. "Woodrow Wilson's Mexican Policy, 1913–1915." *Diplomatic History* 4, no. 1 (Spring 1980): 113–36.

Clendenen, Clarence C. *Blood on the Border: The United States Army and the Mexican Irregulars.* London: MacMillan, 1969.

————. *The United States and Pancho Villa: A Study in Unconventional Diplomacy.* Ithaca, NY: Cornell University Press, 1961.

Coerver, Don M., and Linda B. Hall. *Texas and the Mexican Revolution: A Study in State and National Border Policy, 1910–1920.* San Antonio: Trinity University Press, 1984.

Coffman, Edward M. *The Hilt of the Sword: The Career of Peyton C. March.* Madison: University of Wisconsin Press, 1966.

Cooke, James J. *Pershing and His General: Command and Staff in the AEF.* Westport, CT: Praeger, 1997.

Cooper, John Milton, Jr. *Woodrow Wilson: A Biography.* New York: Alfred A. Knopf, 2009.

Craig, Douglas B. Craig. *Progressives at War: William G. McAdoo and Newton D. Baker, 1863–1941.* Baltimore: Johns Hopkins University Press, 2013.

Craig, Lee A. *Josephus Daniels: His Life and Times.* Chapel Hill: University of North Carolina Press, 2013.

Cumberland, Charles. *Mexican Revolution: The Constitutionalist Years.* Austin: University of Texas Press, 1972.

————. *Mexican Revolution: Genesis under Madero.* Austin: University of Texas Press, 1952.

Dangerfield, George. *The Strange Death of Liberal England: 1910–1914.* New York: G. P. Putnam's Sons, 1961.

Daniels, Josephus. *The Wilson Era: Years of Peace: 1910–1917.* Chapel Hill: University of North Carolina Press, 1944.

Daugherty, Leo J., III. *Counterinsurgency and the United States Marine Corps: Volume 1, The First Counterinsurgency Era, 1899–1945.* Jefferson, NC: McFarland, 2015.

Davis, Donald E., and Eugene P. Trani. *The First Cold War: The Legacy of Woodrow Wilson in U.S.-Soviet Relations.* Columbia, MO: University of Missouri Press, 2002.

"Demobilization after World War I." *Social Service Review* 18, no. 2 (June 1944): 248–50.

DeWeerd, Harvey. *President Wilson Fights His War: World War I and American Intervention.* New York: Macmillan, 1968.

DiScala, Spencer M. *Vittorio Emanuele Orlando: Italy.* London: Haus Histories, 2010.

Djokić, Dejan. *Nikola Pašić and Ante Trumbić: The Kingdom of Serbs, Croats, and Slovenes.* London: Haas Histories, 2010.

Doerries, Reinhard R. *Imperial Challenge: Ambassador Count Bernstorff and German-American Relations, 1908–1917.* Translated by Christa D. Shannon. Chapel Hill: University of North Carolina Press, 1989.

Eisenhower, John S. D. *Intervention! The United States and the Mexican Revolution, 1913–1917.* New York: W. W. Norton, 1993.

Esposito, David. "Political and Institutional Constraints on Wilson's Defense Policy." *Presidential Studies Quarterly* 26, no. 4 (Fall 1996): 1114–25.

Ferrell, Robert H. *Woodrow Wilson & World War I, 1917–1921.* New York: Harper & Row, 1985.

Foglesong, Davis S. *America's Secret War against Bolshevism: United States Intervention in the Russian Civil War, 1917–1920.* Chapel Hill: University of North Carolina Press, 1995.

Fowler, W. B. *British-American Relations, 1917–1918: The Role of Sir William Wiseman.* Princeton, NJ: Princeton University Press, 1969.

Fox, John F., Jr. "Bureaucratic Wrangling over Counterintelligence, 1917–1918." *Studies in Intelligence* 49, no. 1 (2005): 9–17.

Fuller, Stephen, and Graham A. Cosmas. *Marines in the Dominican Republic 1916–1924.* Honolulu: University Press of the Pacific, 2005.

Furman, Necah. "Vida Nueva: A Reflection of Villista Diplomacy, 1914–1915." *New Mexico Historical Review* 53, no. 2 (April 1978): 171–92.

Gardner, Lloyd C. *Safe for Democracy: The Anglo-American Response to Revolution: 1913–1923.* New York: Oxford University Press, 1984.

———. *Wilson and Revolutions: 1913–1921.* Washington, DC: University Press of America, 1934.

Gaughan, Anthony. "Woodrow Wilson and the Legacy of the Civil War." *Civil War History* 43, no. 2 (June 1997): 225–42.

Gelfand, Lawrence E. *The Inquiry: American Preparations for Peace, 1917–1919.* New Haven, CT: Yale University Press, 1963.

George, Alexander, and Juliette L. George. "The 'Operational Code': A Neglected Approach to the Study of Political Leaders and Decision-Making." *International Studies Quarterly* 13, no. 2 (June 1969): 190–222.

Geppert, Dominik, William Mulligan, and Andres Rose, eds. *The Wars before the Great War: Conflict and International Politics before the Outbreak of World War I.* Cambridge: Cambridge University Press, 2015.

Gerlach, Allen. "Conditions along the Border–1915: The Plan de San Diego." *New Mexico Historical Review* 43, no. 3 (July 1968): 195–212.

Gilbert, James L. *World War I and the Origins of U.S. Military Intelligence.* Lanham, MD: Scarecrow Press, 2012.

Gilderhus, Mark T. *Diplomacy and Revolution: US-Mexican Relations under Wilson and Carranza*. Tucson: University of Arizona Press, 1977.

Grieb, Kenneth. "The United States and Huerta." PhD diss., Indiana University, 1966.

Habib, Douglas F. "Chastity, Masculinity, and Military Efficiency: The United States Army in Germany, 1918–1923." *International History Review* 28, no. 4 (December 2006): 737–57.

Haley, P. Edward. *Revolution and Intervention: The Diplomacy of Taft and Wilson with Mexico, 1910–1917*. Cambridge, MA: MIT Press, 1970.

Hamby, Alonzo. *Man of Destiny: FDR and the Making of the American Century*. New York: Basic Books, 2015.

Hamilton, John A. "'Upon No Account Were They to Undertake an Invasion of Mexico': American Troops and the Third Battle of Ciudad Juárez, June 1919." *Southwestern Historical Quarterly* 122, no. 4 (2019): 418–442.

Harris, Charles H., III, and Louis R. Sadler. *The Border and the Revolution: Clandestine Activities of the Mexican Revolution: 1910–1920*. Silver City, NM: High-Lonesome Books, 1988.

———. *Border Revolution*. Las Cruces: New Mexico State University Press, 1989.

———. *The Great Call-Up: The Guard, the Border, and the Mexican Revolution*. Norman: University of Oklahoma Press, 2015.

———. *The Plan de San Diego: Tejano Rebellion, Mexican Intrigue*. Lincoln: University of Nebraska Press, 2013.

———. "The Plan of San Diego and the Mexican-United States War Crisis of 1916: A Re-Examination." *Hispanic American Historical Review* 58, no. 3 (August 1978): 381–408.

———. *The Texas Rangers and the Mexican Revolution: The Bloodiest Decade, 1910–1920*. Albuquerque: University of New Mexico Press, 2004.

Harrison, Benjamin T. "Woodrow Wilson and Nicaragua." *Caribbean Quarterly* 51, no. 1 (March 2005): 25–36.

Healy, David. *Gunboat Diplomacy in the Wilson Era: The U.S. Navy in Haiti, 1915–1916*. Madison: University of Wisconsin Press, 1976.

Henderson, Paul V. N. "The Military and the Madero Regime: The Case of General Félix Díaz." *Social Science Journal* 12–13 (1975–76): 139–48.

Herbert, Paul. "Watch on the Rhine: The 1st Division in the Occupation of Germany, 1918–1919." *On Point* 15, no. 2 (Fall 2009): 34–41.

Hill, Larry D. *Emissaries to a Revolution: Woodrow Wilson's Executive Agents in Mexico*. Baton Rouge: Louisiana State University Press, 1974.

———. "The Progressive Politician as a Diplomat: The Case of John Lind in Mexico." *The Americas* 27, no. 4 (April 1971): 355–73.

Hobsbawn, Eric J. *Bandits*. New York: Dell, 1969.

Howenstine, E. Jay, Jr. "Demobilization after World War I." *Quarterly Journal of Economics* 58, no. 1 (November 1943): 91–105.

Hudson, Peter James. *Bankers and Empire: How Wall Street Colonized the Caribbean*. Chicago: University of Chicago Press, 2017.

Huntington, Samuel P. *The Soldier and the State: The Theory and Practice of Civil-Military Relations*. Cambridge, MA: Belknap Press, 1957.

Jeffreys-Jones, Rhodri. *Cloak and Dollar: A History of American Secret Intelligence*. 2nd edition. New Haven, CT: Yale University Press, 2003.

Jervis, Robert, Richard Ned Lebow, and Janice Gross Stein. *Psychology and Deterrence*. Baltimore: Johns Hopkins University Press, 1985.

Johnson, James Turner. "Historical Roots and Sources of the Just War Tradition in Western Culture." In *Just War and Jihad: Historical and Theoretical Perspectives on War and Peace in Western and Islamic Traditions*, edited by John Kelsay and James Turner Johnson, 16–19. Westport, CT: Greenwood Press, 1991.

Justice, Glenn. *Revolution on the Rio Grande: Mexican Raids and Army Pursuits, 1916–1919*. El Paso: University of Texas Press, 1992.

Kahle, Louis G. "Robert Lansing and the Recognition of Venustiano Carranza." *Hispanic American Historical Review* 38, no. 3 (August 1958): 353–72.

Kaplan, Edward S. *U.S. Imperialism in Latin America: Bryan's Challenges and Contributions, 1900–1920*. Westport, CT: Greenwood Press, 1998.

Katz, Friedrich. *The Life and Times of Pancho Villa*. Redwood City, CA: Stanford University Press, 1998.

———. "Pancho Villa and the Attack on Columbus, New Mexico." *American Historical Review* 83, no. 1 (February 1978): 101–30.

———. *The Secret War in Mexico: Europe, the United States, and the Mexican Revolution*. Chicago: University of Chicago Press, 1981.

Kaufmann, Chaim. "Intervention in Ethnic and Ideological Civil Wars: Why One Can Be Done and the Other Can't." *Security Studies* 6, no. 1 (Autumn 1996): 62–103.

Kazin, Michael. *A Godly Hero: The Life of William Jennings Bryan*. New York: Knopf, 2006.

Kennan, George F. *The Decision to Intervene: Soviet-American Relations, 1917–1920*. Princeton, NJ: Princeton University Press, 1958.

———. *Russia Leaves the War: Soviet-American Relations, 1917–1920*. Princeton, NJ: Princeton University Press, 1956.

Kennedy, Ross A., ed. *A Companion to Woodrow Wilson*. Malden, MA: Wiley-Blackwell, 2013.

Knight, Alan. *The Mexican Revolution: Volume I, Porfirians, Liberals and Peasants*. Lincoln: University of Nebraska Press, 1986.

Knudson, Jerry W. "John Reed: A Reporter in Revolutionary Mexico." *Journalism History* 29, no. 2 (Summer 2003): 59–68.

LaFeber, Walter. *The Panama Canal: The Crisis in Historical Perspective.* Updated edition. New York: Oxford University Press, 1980.

Langley, Lester D. *The Banana Wars: United States Intervention in the Caribbean, 1898–1934.* Lexington: University Press of Kentucky, 1983.

Lasch, Christopher. *The American Liberals and the Russian Revolution.* New York: McGraw Hill, 1972.

Latham, Earl, ed. *The Philosophy and Policies of Woodrow Wilson.* Chicago: University of Chicago Press, 1958.

Lazo, Dimitri D. "Lansing, Wilson, and the Jenkins Incident." *Diplomatic History* 22, no. 2 (Spring 1999): 177–98.

Lebow, Richard Ned. *Between Peace and War: The Nature of International Crisis.* Baltimore: Johns Hopkins University Press, 1981.

Levin, N. Gordon. *Woodrow Wilson and World Politics: America's Response to War and Revolution.* New York: Oxford University Press, 1968.

Levite, Ariel. *Intelligence and Strategic Surprise.* New York: Columbia University Press, 1987.

Link, Arthur S., ed. *The Higher Realism of Woodrow Wilson and Other Essays.* Nashville, TN: Vanderbilt University Press, 1971.

———. *Wilson: Confusions and Crisis, 1915–16.* Princeton, NJ: Princeton University Press, 1964.

———. *Wilson: The New Freedom.* Princeton, NJ: Princeton University Press, 1956.

———. *Wilson: The Road to the White House.* Princeton, NJ: Princeton University Press, 1947.

———. *Wilson: The Struggle for Neutrality, 1914–15.* Princeton, NJ: Princeton University Press, 1960.

———. *Wilson's Diplomacy: An International Symposium.* Cambridge, MA: Schenkman, 1973.

———. *Wilson the Diplomatist: A Look at His Major Foreign Policies.* Chicago: Quadrangle Press, 1957.

———. *Woodrow Wilson: War, Revolution and Peace.* Arlington Heights, IL: Harlan Davidson, 1979.

———, ed. *Woodrow Wilson and a Revolutionary World, 1913–1921.* Chapel Hill: University of North Carolina Press, 1982.

Livermore, Seward W. " 'Deserving Democrats': The Foreign Service under Woodrow Wilson." *The South Atlantic Quarterly* 49, no. 1 (Winter 1970): 144–60.

————. *Woodrow Wilson and the War Congress, 1916–1918*. Seattle: University of Washington Press, 1966.

Long, John W. "American Intervention in Russia: The North Russian Expedition, 1918–19." *Diplomatic History* 6, no. 1 (Winter 1982): 45–67.

Lowry, Bullitt. *Armistice 1918*. Kent, OH: Kent State University Press, 1996.

Lowry, Philip H. "The Mexican Policy of Woodrow Wilson." PhD diss., Yale University, 1949.

MacMillian, Margaret. *Paris 1919*. New York: Random House, 2001.

Mahoney, Henry Thayer, and Marjorie Locke Mahoney. *Espionage in Mexico: The Twentieth Century*. San Francisco: Austin & Winfield, 1997.

Mango, Andrew. *From the Sultan to Atatürk: Turkey*. London: Haus Publishing, 2009.

Maurer, Noel. *The Empire Trap: The Rise and Fall of U.S. Intervention to Protect American Property Overseas, 1893–2013*. Princeton, NJ: Princeton University Press, 2013.

Mayer, Arno J. *Wilson vs. Lenin: Political Origins of the New Diplomacy, 1917–1918*. Cleveland, OH: Meridian Books, 1959.

McConnell, Michael W. *The President Who Would Not Be King: Executive Power under the Constitution*. Princeton, NJ: Princeton University Press, 2020.

McCrae, Meighen. *Coalition Strategy and the End of World War I: The Supreme War Council and War Planning, 1917–1918*. New York: Cambridge University Press, 2019.

McCrocklin, James H. *Garde D'Haiti: Twenty Years of Organization and Training by the United States Marines Corps, 1915–1934*. Annapolis, MD: Naval Institute Press, 1956.

McDougall, Walter A. *Promised Land, Crusader State: The American Encounter with the World since 1776*. Boston: Houghton Mifflin, 1997.

McGovern, Rory. *George W. Goethals and the Army: Change and Continuity in the Gilded Age and Progressive Era*. Lawrence: University of Kansas Press, 2019.

Meiser, Jeffrey W. *Power and Restraint: The Rise of the United States, 1898–1941*. Washington, DC: Georgetown University Press, 2015.

Meyer, Michael C. "The Arms of the *Ypiranga*." *Hispanic American Historical Review* 50, no. 3 (August 1970): 543–56.

Meyers, William K. "Pancho Villa and the Multinationals: United States Mining Interests in Villista Mexico, 1913–1915." *Journal of Latin American Studies* 23, no. 2 (1991): 339–63.

Mitchell, Nancy. *The Danger of Dreams: German and American Imperialism in Latin America*. Chapel Hill: University of North Carolina Press, 1999.

Montague, Ludwell Lee. *Haiti and the United States, 1714–1938*. Durham: University of North Carolina Press, 1940.

Morison, Elting E. *Admiral Sims and the Modern American Navy*. Boston: Houghton Mifflin, 1942.

Morton, Louis. "Army and Marines on the China Station: A Study in Military and Political Rivalry." *Pacific Historical Review* 29, no. 1 (February 1960): 51–73.

Munro, Dana G. *Intervention and Dollar Diplomacy in the Caribbean, 1900–1921*. Princeton, NJ: Princeton University Press, 1964.

Musicant, Ivan. *The Banana Wars: A History of the United States Military Intervention in Latin America from Spanish-American War to the Invasion of Panama*. New York: MacMillan, 1990.

Nelson, James Carl. *The Polar Bear Expedition: The Heroes of America's Forgotten Invasion of Russia, 1918–1919*. New York: William Morrow, 2019.

Nelson, Keith L. *Victors Divided: American and the Allies in Germany, 1918–1923*. Berkeley: University of California Press, 1975.

Neu, Charles E. *Colonel House: A Biography of Woodrow Wilson's Silent Partner*. New York: Oxford University Press, 2015.

Neumann, Brian. "A Question of Authority: Reassessing the March-Pershing 'Feud' in World War I." *Journal of Military History* 73, no. 4 (October 2009): 1117–1142.

Nield, Robert. *China's Foreign Places: The Foreign Presence in China in the Treaty Port Era, 1840–1943*. Hong Kong: Hong Kong University Press, 2015.

Noble, Dennis L. *The Eagle and the Dragon: The United States Military in China, 1901–1937*. New York: Greenwood Press, 1990.

O'Toole, G. J. A. *Honorable Treachery: A History of U.S. Intelligence, Espionage, and Covert Action from the American Revolution to the CIA*. New York: Atlantic Monthly Press, 1991.

Parra, Carlos Francisco. "Valientes Nogalenses: The 1918 Battle between the U.S. and Mexico That Transformed Ambos Nogales." *Journal of Arizona History* 51, no. 2 (Spring 2010): 1–32.

Perez, Louis A., Jr. *Cuba under the Platt Amendment, 1902–1934*. Pittsburgh: University of Pittsburgh Pres, 1986.

———. *Intervention, Revolution, and Politics in Cuba, 1913–1921*. Pittsburgh: University of Pittsburgh Press, 1978.

———. "The Military and Electoral Politics: The Cuban Election of 1920." *Military Affairs* 37, no. 1 (February 1973): 5–8.

Prieto, Julie Irene. *The Mexican Expedition, 1916–1917*. Washington, DC: U.S. Army Center for Military History, 2016.

Quirk, Robert. *An Affair of Honor: Woodrow Wilson and the Occupation of Veracruz*. New York: Norton, 1962.

Rakocy, Bill. *Villa Raids Columbus*. El Paso, TX: Bravo Press, 1991.

Ramsey, Paul. *The Just War: Force and Political Responsibility.* New York: Charles Scribner's Sons, 1968.

Rausch, George Jay. "The Exile and Death of Victoriano Huerta." *Hispanic American Historical Review* 42 (1962): 133–51.

———. "Victoriano Huerta: A Political Biography." PhD diss., University of Illinois, 1960.

Rhodes, Benjamin D. "The Anglo-American Intervention at Archangel, 1918–1919: The Role of the 339th Infantry." *International History Review* 8, no. 3 (August 1986): 367–88.

Riccards, Michael P., and Cheryl A. Flagg. *Woodrow Wilson as Commander in Chief: The Presidency and the Great War.* Jefferson, NC: McFarland, 2020.

Richard, Carl J. *When the United States Invaded Russia.* Lanham, MD: Rowman & Littlefield, 2013.

Richmond, Douglas W. "La Guerra de Texas se Renova: Mexican Insurrection and Carrancista Ambitions, 1900–1920." *Aztlán* 2, no. 1 (Spring 1980): 1–32.

Rinke, Stefan. *Latin American and World War I.* New York: Cambridge University Press, 2017.

Rippy, J. Fred. *Haiti and the United States, 1714–1938.* Durham, NC: Duke University Press, 1940.

Ross, Steven T. *American War Plans 1890–1939.* London: Frank Cass, 2002.

Rouqié, Alain. *The Military and the State in Latin America.* Translated by Paul E. Sigmund. Berkeley: University of California Press, 1987.

Ryan, Capt. Paul B., USN (Ret.). "Ten Days at Veracruz." *U.S. Naval Institute Proceedings* 98, no. 6 (June 1972): 64–73.

Sadler, Louis R. *The Secret War in El Paso: Mexican Revolutionary Intrigue, 1906–1920.* Albuquerque: University of New Mexico Press, 2009.

Sandos, James A. "German Involvement in Northern Mexico, 1915–1916: A New Look at the Columbus Raid." *The Hispanic American Historical Review* 50, no. 1 (February 1970): 70–88.

———. *Rebellion in the Borderlands: Anarchism and the Plan of San Diego, 1904–1923.* Norman: University of Oklahoma Press, 1992.

Saunders, Robert M. *In Search of Woodrow Wilson: Beliefs and Behavior.* Westport, CT: Greenwood Press, 1998.

Savory, A. C. S. "Vladivostok: 1919–1920." *Journal of the Society for Army Historical Research* 71, no. 285 (Spring 1993): 8–23.

Schilling, Warner R. "Civil-Naval Politics in World War I." *World Politics* 7, no. 4 (1955): 572–91.

Schmidt, Hans. *Maverick Marine: General Smedley D. Butler and the Contradictions of American Military History.* Lexington: University Press of Kentucky, 1987.

————. *The United States Occupation of Haiti, 1915–1934*. New Brunswick, NJ: Rutgers University Press, 1995.

Schmitt, John. F. "Peacetime Landing Operations: Lessons from Haiti, 1915." *Marine Corps Gazette* 78, no. 3 (March 1994): 70–74.

Scholes, Walter, and Marie Scholes. *The Foreign Policies of the Taft Administration*. Columbia: University of Missouri Press, 1967.

Schoultz, Lars. *In Their Own Best Interest: A History of the U.S. Effort to Improve Latin America*. Cambridge, MA: Harvard University Press, 2018.

Schroder, Hans-Jurgen, ed. *Confrontation and Cooperation: Germany and the United States in the Era of World War I, 1914–1924*. Providence, RI: Berg, 1993.

Schultz, Kenneth A. *Democracy and Coercive Diplomacy*. New York: Cambridge University Press, 2001.

Shannon, Magdaline W. *Jean Price-Mars, the Haitian Elite, and the American Occupation, 1915–35*. New York: St. Martin's Press, 1996.

Shellum, Brian. *Black Officer in a Buffalo Soldier Regiment: The Military Career of Charles Young*. Lincoln: University of Nebraska Press, 2010.

Slotkin, Richard. *Lost Battalions: The Great War and the Crisis of American Neutrality*. New York: Henry Holt, 2005.

Smith, Daniel M. "Bainbridge Colby and the Good Neighbor Policy, 1920–1921." *Mississippi Valley Historical Review* 50, no. 1 (June 1963): 56–78.

Snyder, Jack L. "Rationality at the Brink: The Role of Cognitive Processes in Failures of Deterrence." *World Politics* 30, no. 3 (April 1978): 345–65.

Spence, Richard B. "K. A. Jahnke and the German Sabotage Campaign in the United States and Mexico, 1914–1918." *The Historian* 59, no 1 (Fall 1996): 89–112.

Stephenson, George M. *John Lind of Minnesota*. Port Washington, NY: Kennikat Press, repr. 1971.

Startt, James D. *Woodrow Wilson and the Press*. New York: Palgrave-MacMillan, 2004.

Still, William N., Jr. *Crisis at Sea: The United States Navy in European Waters in World War I*. Gainesville: University Press of Florida, 2006.

Stout, Joseph Allen. *Border Conflict: Villistas, Carrancistas and the Punitive Expedition, 1915–1920*. Fort Worth: Texas Christian University Press, 1999.

Strakhovsky, Leonid I. *Intervention at Archangel: The Story of Allied Intervention and Russian Counter-Revolution in North Russia 1918–1920*. Princeton, NJ: Princeton University Press, 1944.

————. *The Origins of American Intervention in North Russia, 1918*. Princeton, NJ: Princeton University Press, 1937.

Streeter, Michael. *Central America and the Treaty of Versailles*. London: Haas Publishing, 2011.

Swanberg, W. A. *Citizen Hearst: A Biography of William Randolph Hearst*. New York: Charles Scribner's Sons, 1961.

Sweetman, Jack. *The Landing at Veracruz: 1914*. Annapolis, MD: Naval Institute Press, 1968.

Tate, James P. *The Army and Its Air Corps: Army Policy toward Aviation 1919–1941*. N.p.: Air University Press, 1998.

Teitelbaum, Louis M. *Woodrow Wilson and the Mexican Revolution, 1913–1916*. New York: Exposition Press, 1967.

Thomas, Hugh. *Cuba: The Pursuit of Freedom*. New York: Harper & Row, 1971.

Thorsen, Niels A. *The Political Thought of Woodrow Wilson, 1875–1910*. Princeton, NJ: Princeton University Press, 1988.

Tien-yi Li. *Woodrow Wilson's China Policy: 1913–1917*. New York: University of Kansas Press, 1952.

Tilchen, William N., and Charles E. Neu, eds. *Artists of Power: Theodore Roosevelt, Woodrow Wilson, and Their Enduring Impact on U.S. Foreign Policy*. Westport, CT: Praeger Security International, 2006.

Tolley, Kemp. *Yangtze Patrol: The U.S. Navy in China*. Annapolis, MD: Naval Institute Press, 1971.

Trask, David F. *The AEF & Coalition Warmaking, 1917–1918*. Lawrence: University Press of Kansas, 1993.

———. *The United States in the Supreme War Council: American War Aim and Inter-Allied Strategy, 1917–1918*. Middletown, CT: Wesleyan University Press, 1963.

Trow, Clifford W. "Woodrow Wilson and the Mexican Interventionist Movement of 1919." *Journal of American History* 58, no. 1 (June 1971): 46–72.

Tuchman, Barbara W. *The Zimmermann Telegram*. New York: Macmillan, 1966.

Turner, Frederick C. "Anti-Americanism in Mexico, 1910–1913." *Hispanic American Historical Review* 47, no. 4 (November 1967): 502–18.

Unterberger, Betty Miller. "President Wilson and the Decision to Send American Troops to Siberia." *Pacific Historical Review* 24, no. 1 (February 1955): 63–74.

———. "The Russian Revolution and Wilson's Far-Eastern Policy." *Russian Review* 16, no. 2 (April 1957): 35–46.

———. *The United States, Revolutionary Russia, and the Rise of Czechoslovakia*. Chapel Hill: University of North Carolina Press, 1989.

———. "Woodrow Wilson and the Bolsheviks: The 'Acid Test' of Soviet-American Relations." *Diplomatic History* 11, no. 2 (Spring 1987): 71–90.

Vandiver, Frank E. *Black Jack: The Life and Times of John J. Pershing*. 2 vols. College Station: Texas A&M University Press, 1977.

Von Feilitzsch, Heribert. *Felix A. Sommerfeld and the Mexican Front in the Great War.* Amissville, VA: Henselstone Verlag, 2014.

———. *The Secret War in the United States in 1915: A Tale of Sabotage, Labor Unrest and Border Troubles.* Amissville, VA: Henselstone Verlag, 2015.

Walker, R. Scott. "The U.S. Third Army and the Advance to Koblenz, 7 December–17 December 1918." *Army History* 32, no. 1 (Fall 1994): 28–33.

Walker, Stephen G. "Psychodynamic Processes and Framing Effects in Foreign Policy Decision-Making: Woodrow Wilson's Operational Code." *Political Psychology* 16, no. 4 (December 1995): 697–717.

Walt, Stephen M. *Revolution and War.* Ithaca, NY: Cornell University Press, 1996.

Walworth, Arthur C. *Woodrow Wilson*, Vol.1: *American Prophet.* New York: Norton, 1948.

———. *Woodrow Wilson*, Vol. 2: *World Prophet.* New York: Norton, 1948.

Weber, Ralph E. "State Department Cryptographic Security, Herbert O. Yardley, and President Woodrow Wilson's Secret Code." In *The Name of Intelligence: Essays in Honor of Walter Pforzheimer*, edited by Hayden B. Peake and Samuel Halpern, 543–96. Washington, DC: National Intelligence Book Center Press, 1994.

Weibe, Robert H. *The Search for Order: 1877–1920.* New York: Hill and Wang, 1967.

Weinstein, Edwin A. *Woodrow Wilson: A Medical and Psychological Biography.* Princeton, NJ: Princeton University Press, 1981.

Welsome, Eileen. *The General and the Jaguar: Pershing's Hunt for Pancho Villa.* New York: Little, Brown, 2006.

Werking, Richard Hume. *The Master Architects: Building the United States Foreign Service, 1890–1913.* Lexington: University Press of Kentucky, 1977.

Winkler, Jonathan Reed. *Nexus: Strategic Communications and American Security in World War I.* Cambridge, MA: Harvard University Press, 2008.

Wolff, Larry. *Woodrow Wilson and the Reimaging of Eastern Europe.* Redwood City, CA: Stanford University Press, 2020.

Woodward, David R. *The American Army and World War I.* New York: Cambridge University Press, 2014.

———. *Trial by Friendship: Anglo-American Relations, 1917–1918.* Lexington: University Press of Kentucky, 1993.

Yarhi-Milo, Keren. *Knowing the Adversary: Leaders, Intelligence, and Assessment of Intentions in International Relations.* Princeton, NJ: Princeton University Press, 2014.

———. *Who Fights for Reputation: The Psychology of Leaders in International Conflict.* Princeton, NJ: Princeton University Press, 2018.

Zabecki, David T. *The General's War: Operational Level Command on the Western Front in 1918.* Bloomington: University of Indiana Press, 2018.

Zeiger, Susan. *Entangling Alliances: Foreign War Brides and American Soldiers in the Twentieth Century.* New York: New York University Press, 2010.

INDEX

1812, War of, 14–15
1916, election of, 128, 236

Adams, Herbert Baxter, 34
Adams, John, 5, 14
Aguilar, Candido, 113
Albania, 52
Ambos Nogales, 221–22
American Expeditionary Forces
    (AEF), 139–43, 146, 148–64;
    1st Division, 148–49, 151; 2nd
    Division, 151; 26th Division, 151;
    42nd "Rainbow Division," 149,
    151; 93rd Division, 151; 339th
    Infantry Regiment, 179–80, 189;
    demobilization of, 198–99; First
    Army of, 157, 160; and German
    occupation, 195–97; and Russian
    intervention, 178–89; Second
    Army of, 160
anti-Bolshevik forces, 167, 170,
    180–81, 184–85, 187, 203
anti-German sentiment, U.S., 7
Archangel, U.S. intervention in, 165,
    166, 174–75, 179–84, 185, 189–90
Argentina, 69, 101, 102, 104, 145
Arias, Desidero, 89, 90–91, 92
Arizona, 203
Army, U.S.: and China, 226, 229–30;
    General Staff of, 27, 108, 136;

and German occupation, 195–97;
    and intelligence, 26–28, 37; and
    Mexican Border War, 109–14, 118–
    21, 123–24; Military Information
    Committee, 27; and Russian
    intervention, 178–89; Signal
    Corps, 28–29; War College, 27,
    66, 108, 122, 136; and World War I,
    139–43, 148–64. *See also* American
    Expeditionary Forces (AEF)
Auguste, Tancrède, 77
Austria-Hungary, Balkan Wars and,
    52

Babcock, John V., 144
Badger, Charles, 68
Balfour, Arthur James, 175, 178
Balkans, 51–53, 54, 199–201, 237
Baltic, 141
Baker, Newton, as Secretary of State,
    20–21, 202, 232, 233, 238; and
    Mexican Border War, 108, 109,
    112, 114–15, 121–22; and Russia,
    177, 179, 181, 185, 191, 197; and
    World War I, 129, 130, 133, 134–35,
    136–38, 150–56, 158, 159–60,
    162–64
Baker, Ray Stannard, 24, 120
Banque Nationale d'Haïti, 48
Barbary War, First. *See* Tripolitan War

ABOUT THE AUTHOR

Mark E. Benbow is associate professor of American history at Marymount University. He earned his PhD from Ohio University. Previously, he worked for the federal government and as historian at the Woodrow Wilson House Museum in Washington, D.C. Benbow also serves as the director of the Arlington Historical Museum in Arlington, Virginia.

The Naval Institute Press is the book-publishing arm of the U.S. Naval Institute, a private, nonprofit, membership society for sea service professionals and others who share an interest in naval and maritime affairs. Established in 1873 at the U.S. Naval Academy in Annapolis, Maryland, where its offices remain today, the Naval Institute has members worldwide.

Members of the Naval Institute support the education programs of the society and receive the influential monthly magazine *Proceedings* or the colorful bimonthly magazine *Naval History* and discounts on fine nautical prints and on ship and aircraft photos. They also have access to the transcripts of the Institute's Oral History Program and get discounted admission to any of the Institute-sponsored seminars offered around the country.

The Naval Institute's book-publishing program, begun in 1898 with basic guides to naval practices, has broadened its scope to include books of more general interest. Now the Naval Institute Press publishes about seventy titles each year, ranging from how-to books on boating and navigation to battle histories, biographies, ship and aircraft guides, and novels. Institute members receive significant discounts on the Press' more than eight hundred books in print.

Full-time students are eligible for special half-price membership rates. Life memberships are also available.

For more information about Naval Institute Press books that are currently available, visit www.usni.org/press/books. To learn about joining the U.S. Naval Institute, please write to:

Member Services
U.S. Naval Institute
291 Wood Road
Annapolis, MD 21402-5034
Telephone: (800) 233-8764
Fax: (410) 571-1703
Web address: www.usni.org